Girls and
Philosophy

Popular Culture and Philosophy® Series Editor: George A. Reisch

For full details of all Popular Culture and Philosophy® books, visit www.opencourtbooks.com.

Popular Culture and Philosophy®

Girls and Philosophy

This Book Isn't a Metaphor for Anything

Edited by
RICHARD GREENE AND
RACHEL ROBISON-GREENE

OPEN COURT
Chicago

Volume 86 in the series, Popular Culture and Philosophy®, edited by George A. Reisch

To order books from Open Court, call toll-free 1-800-815-2280, or visit our website at www.opencourtbooks.com.

Open Court Publishing Company is a division of Carus Publishing Company, dba Cricket Media.

ISBN: 978-0-8126-9859-6

Library of Congress Control Number 2014949560

For Brooke Michelle Robison

Contents

Acknowledgments

Working on this project has been a pleasure, in no small part because of the many fine folks who have assisted us along the way. In particular a debt of gratitude is owed to David Ramsay Steele and George Reisch at Open Court, Rob Arp, the contributors to this volume, and our respective academic departments at UMass Amherst and Weber State University. Finally, we'd like to thank those family members, students, friends, and colleagues with whom we've had fruitful and rewarding conversations on various aspects of all things *Girls* as it relates to philosophical themes.

Thinking about *Girls*

Say what you will about Hannah Horvath—that young woman is real. In some cases she might even be more real than many of us are comfortable with (Q-tip scene anyone?). Though in many ways she might be kind of a horrible person (recall her behavior at her editor's funeral when she raises the issue of alternative suggestions for publishing her book to the editor's grieving widow), she has a commitment to truth that it is hard not to admire. She tells it like it is even when doing so is awkward.

Hannah's concerned with the authenticity of her work to the degree that she feels she shouldn't just write a story about drug use. She needs to actually do some coke so that she can write a truthful authentic story about drug use. She may not match the noble, high-minded stereotype that you might have in mind when you picture a person living a philosophical life, but she lives one all the same, in her neurotic, self-absorbed way. Hannah follows Socrates's call to "know thyself"—millennial style.

Girls is virtually chockablock with philosophical content, because *Girls* is stark and raw, which makes it accurate. It's very much about the commonalities of human existence, and ultimately the meaning of life. *Girls* tells the story of four millennials struggling to find their identities and places in the world. While some of the particulars are different (for example, not everyone grew up in the world of Facebook, twitter, smartphones, and really good coffee, nor did everyone grow-up in today's uncertain economic climate, or in Brooklyn), much of what *Girls* is about is common to all of us. Everyone wonders who they are and who they will become. Everyone struggles at times with how to relate to his or her friends or co-workers, or even strangers, for that matter. Everyone has to figure out for themselves what is rightly expected of them and which of those expectations they will choose to try to meet.

In this volume, we take Hannah Horvath's attempts to know herself even further. We also want to know Marnie, Jessa, Shosh, Ray, Adam, Laird, and even Thomas-John. To know these characters is to know ourselves. To that end, Kimberly Blessing and Samantha Wezowicz discuss the meaning of life for millennials. Hayley Addis, Chelsi Barnard Archibald, Rachel Crossley, Amie Zimmer, and Marie van Loon each offer a different take on existentialist philosophers and themes. Richard Greene considers the question of whether it's possible to reveal spoilers in a show like *Girls*. Rachel Robison-Greene faces up to a variety of criticisms leveled at *Girls*. Trip McCrossin considers whether Adam Sackler is heroic. Christopher Ketcham addresses human rights by contrasting Hannah Horvath with a counterpart of hers living in Darfur. Roberto Sirvent and Joel Avery address topics in existentialist ethics. Andy Wible does the same with respect to business ethics. James Edwin Mahon and Nicole Kimes Walker provide a novel look at the Seven Deadly Sins. Bobby Carleo and Paul D'Ambrosio apply Daoism and Confucianism to the musings of Hannah and the gang. Anna Keszeg looks at the cast's clothing choices through a theoretical lens. Toni Adleberg gives an ontology of "the ladies." David LaRocca investigates the ancient Greek notion of *paideia*. Zorianna Zurba applies the theories of Julia Kristeva to *Girls*. And finally, Kenn Fisher provides a Freudian analysis. As you can see, there is much that is philosophical about *Girls*.

Ideally, this book will get you thinking about life in the early twenty-first century, as much as *Girls* gets us thinking about such things. We hope you enjoy the book, perhaps with a few friends over coffee at someplace like Grumpy's!

I

Everyone here
looks how I would
look with a
nose job.

1
How Not to Watch *Girls*

David J. Frost

In the pilot for *Girls*, Hannah steals the tip her parents left for the hotel housekeeper. This scene foreshadows the bad behavior of Hannah and her circle of friends in the coming episodes. These young women are "self-centered," "vapid," "narcissistic" and much worse, according to many critics who disapprove of the show.

The characters' "unlikeability," these critics say, makes the show unenjoyable and perhaps even a bad influence in the culture. So, these critics arrive at a negative aesthetic judgment as to the value of *Girls*. But these critics are wrong and they are watching TV in the wrong way.

The characters' unlikeability is just one of the many things about the show that some critics don't like but that actually makes *Girls* unique and revolutionary among TV shows. What are some of the other revolutionary aspects?

First, *Girls* is frank and non-judgmental in its depiction of female promiscuity, at least in Hannah's friend Jessa's case.

Second, awkward, disempowering, and one-sided, but realistic, sexual encounters abound in Hannah's storyline.

And, finally, *Girls* gives lots of screen time to Lena Dunham's "non-Hollywood" body. None of this has been seen before on mainstream TV where, in particular, sex is depicted in a timid way. The act is often not shown at all but only hinted at, or if it is shown it's portrayed in a stylized, unrealistic manner. It's cleaned up and smoothed out. Everyone is loving, communicative, and sexually satisfied. Plus, on mainstream TV female promiscuity is always a judgment. And, finally, we are all well aware that mainstream TV partakes in the general culture's denigration of the average female body type, elevating and idolizing something more akin to a condition of anorexia. To challenge these aspects of the mainstream is a virtue.

What theory of how to watch television would hold that the representation of unlikeable characters, awkward sex, female promiscuity, and unglamorous nudity are laudable virtues of a TV show?

Answer: It's the theory offered by German-born philosopher of American popular culture, Theodor Adorno. Adorno argues that "the culture industry"—that is, the commercial institutions in which pop cultural artifacts are produced—results in TV shows that create individuals susceptible to totalitarian and ideological control. "The repetitiveness, the selfsameness, and the ubiquity of modern mass culture tend to make for automatized reactions and to weaken the forces of individual resistance," Adorno says in "How to Look at Television." "Mass culture is the seed bed of political totalitarianism," he writes in *The Dialectic of Enlightenment* (p. 218), implying that pop culture prepares people's minds to accept fascist rule.

Adorno's accusation that cultural products create unthinking automatons might seem exaggerated. But there is more than a little truth to it. We know that some TV is mind-numbing and some TV makes you think. And we should admit that individuals do not so much create society as society creates individuals. So, according to Adorno, what's important is not whether a show is good or bad in terms of aesthetic pleasure. What's important are the psychological effects TV has on each individual's critical faculties which, when sharp, allow us to see the tragic truth about our socio-economic position in the culture. When these faculties are dulled, we are imprisoned unthinkingly in our positions. "The effort here required is of a moral nature itself: knowingly to face psychological mechanisms operating on various levels in order not to become blind and passive victims" ("How to Look at Television," p. 158). So, TV that does not numb your mind, but rather exercises it can provide a path to what Adorno calls, "emancipation."

Girls is a rarity that avoids the very serious and consequential pitfalls Adorno finds in most products of the culture industry.

Standardization

Mainstream TV shows—such as safe, laugh-track shows like *Gilligan's Island* and *The Brady Bunch*—are "standardized" in Adorno's terminology, in such a way that we can't practice our critical faculties in the way we respond to the show. But, in *Girls,* thinking is required of the viewer in order to digest the novel aspects of the show.

Adorno says that in the case of popular music—produced in the same standardized way by the same culture industry that produces cookie-cutter TV shows—the songs are "pre-digested" and do not require a thoughtful response. Indeed, they inhibit one. "Standardization of song hits keeps the customer in line by doing their listening for them, as it were" ("On Popular Music," p. 79).

Particular aspects of TV shows will come "pre-digested" and without anything novel to stimulate a viewer every time those aspects are copied from an earlier show. Some aspects of *That 70s Show*, *The Big Bang Theory*, and *How I Met Your Mother* are copies of formulas from the commercially successful show *Friends*, which is itself a formulaic show copied from previous popular shows. There is no new thinking required by these standardized shows.

The culture industry's standardized product is psychologically debilitating. But how does standardization come about? Adorno says it's caused by the competition inherent in capitalism. Economists usually say that competition tends to create variety in the marketplace. But that's the capitalist line. Adorno saw, in agreement with Marx, that competition encouraged imitation of what had already succeeded, with the aim of creating the most profits with the least investment:

> As one particular song scored a great success, hundreds of others sprang up imitating the successful one . . . and the process culminated in the crystallization of standards. Under centralized conditions such as exist today these standards have become frozen. (p. 77)

What Adorno says here about popular songs applies equally well to TV shows and movies.

Capitalism, according to Adorno, "institutionalized the standardization and made it imperative," guaranteeing that "nothing fundamentally novel will be introduced." This standardizing process explains why there is such a repetition of forms in TV shows, popular music, and movies as well as in "motor cars and breakfast foods," as Adorno puts it. Thus, an audience is fed a variation on the basic ensemble of character types, such as The Hero, The Anti-Hero, The Love Interest, and the Buddy. Jerry, Kramer, Elaine, George and Ed, Peg, Kelly, Bud and Richie, the Fonz, Joanie, Ralph, et cetera. Other aspects of TV shows are standardized if thought successful, such as plot lines, locales, themes, and even particular jokes. The less novelty, the less thoughtful engagement with the show is invited.

In order to acquire a psychological benefit from any work of art such as a TV show, you must experience and interpret it. But for this, engagement and effort are required. Standardization and the fact that people are alienated from their labor operate hand-in-hand to prevent genuine experience of an artwork. The working person wants relief from the boredom of his or her job as well as relief from *effort*:

> A fully concentrated and conscious experience of art is possible only to those whose lives do not put such a strain on them that in their spare time they want relief from both boredom and effort simultaneously . . . They seek novelty, but the strain and boredom associated with actual work lead to avoidance of effort in that leisure time which offers the only chance for really new experience . . . The whole sphere of cheap commercial entertainment reflects this dual desire. It induces relaxation because it is patterned and pre-digested. Its being patterned and pre-digested serves within the psychological household of the masses to spare them the effort of that participation without which there can be no receptivity to art. (p. 81)

Work at most jobs is both tiring and boring. So in their leisure time, working people want relief from boredom as well as from effort. Standardized popular culture can supply relief from both boredom and effort. But non-standardized shows, songs, and movies are challenging and require effort to watch and understand. Mainstream cultural products offer no opportunity to practice effortful critical thinking and thus diminish the viewer's capacity for it.

Challenging TV shows that are neither predictable nor the same old same old require thinking and, therefore, allow for the individual to achieve "autonomy," "maturity," "emancipation," and "genuine experience." These are Adorno's words for the "most desirable effect of television" ("How to Look at Television," p. 158) and for the most desirable result of culture's role in the psychological formation of an individual's subjectivity and self-understanding.

Adorno is drawing on Immanuel Kant's claim that autonomy is maturity, the capability of exercising your own discretionary judgment, and making up your mind for yourself. When culture obstructs the development of critical consciousness of social reality, a more insidious "integration" is produced. Adorno believes that the main effect of the standardization of culture is the promotion of critical immaturity in the citizenry. The exercise of any critical faculties with respect to social reality is frustrated and prohibited by standardized art forms. "The very capacity for life experience may be dulled" (p. 171). But, it stands to reason, if a TV show is not standardized, is not predictable, but is thought-provoking and upends previous forms, then the TV show may help an individual achieve maturity, autonomy, emancipation and genuine independence from the conceptual categories offered by society. Hannah's body, for example, generates at the very least a mental realization that all the other bodies you've seen on TV are not at all average. The non-judgmental depiction of Jessa's promiscuity might get you to think that the usual stigma is unjustified, and so on.

The Fake-realism of *Sex in the City*

The same aspects of *Girls* that demonstrate that it's different from most other shows (that it's not standardized), also demonstrate that *Girls* does not participate in the structural form which Adorno calls "fake-realism." Fake-realism offers a fantasy world as if it were really attainable. The representation of promiscuity, the nakedness of what Sheila Ruth would call a "non-serviceable" kind, and awkward or disempowered sexual encounters, mean that *Girls* deviates from the standard form and content of most TV shows. And those same features of *Girls* also keep the show from evincing fake-realism.

Sex and the City definitely exhibits fake-realism. That show is ostensibly "realistic" insofar as it does not incorporate any surrealism, magical realism, or supernatural plot points or devices. And yet the reality depicted in *Sex and the City* is an unrealistic fantasy world. As Adorno writes, "The culture industry presents the everyday world as a paradise" (*The Dialectic of Enlightenment*, p. 113). And so what is pure, unattainable fantasy (for everyone except perhaps the one percent) is presented as a real world to which you must merely aspire. For Adorno, this fits the role of "ideological representation" in a capitalist mass culture: the real material conditions of ninety-nine percent of society are obscured or obliterated from consciousness by an alternate reality which claims for itself its own false legitimacy via naturalistic representation in moving images.

Fake-realism, then, is a form of representation that standard TV shows adopt in which a false and unattainable reality is offered to the masses. The masses receive it both aspirationally—something to hope for—and in terms of escapism—somewhere to flee to. It's aspirational, and yet as Adorno maintains, the fantastical promise is never fulfilled. In the end, it is a trick. As Lena Dunham says in the DVD commentary for Season One Episode One, because of *Sex and the City* "people moved to New York City" and yet "it didn't work out."

Escapism goes hand-in-hand with aspirationalism because when you aspire to what isn't, you turn away from what is, which helps obscure social reality from view. Fake-realism is thus perniciously ideological, doing nothing to expose the status quo. Fake-realism passes off the socio-economic and material conditions of life for the masses as natural and inevitable, Adorno says.

Escapist and aspirational TV shows exhibit fake-realism and thereby undermine an individual's emancipation from societal strictures. In fact, it binds them all the more effectively:

> When the audience at a sentimental film or sentimental music become aware of the overwhelming possibility of happiness, they dare to confess to themselves what the whole order of contemporary life ordinarily forbids them to admit, namely, that they actually have no part in happiness. What is supposed to be wish fulfillment [think of *Sex and the City*'s aspirational aspects] is only the scant liberation that occurs with the realization that at last one need not deny oneself the happiness of knowing that one is unhappy and that one could be happy . . . The actual function of sentimental music [or TV] lies rather

in the temporary release given to the awareness that one has missed fulfillment. ("On Popular Music," p. 83–84)

Aspiring to a fantastical life, escapism, and wish fulfillment might possibly have a pleasant psychological outcome. "It is catharsis for the masses, but catharsis which keeps them all the more firmly in line. . . . Music that permits its listeners the confession of their unhappiness reconciles them, by means of this 'release', to their social dependence" (p. 84).

Girls avoids fake-realism precisely by not being aspirational and not being escapist. The purposeful unlikeability of the characters prevents the audience having any aspiration to be like the characters. Recall the episode in which Jessa mercilessly analyzes the others at rehab, but cannot see her own failures as a friend. Recall when Charlie and Ray find and read publically from Hannah's diary in which she has condemned Marnie and Charlie's relationship. Instead of apologizing to Marnie, Hannah selfishly asks, "If you had read the essay and it wasn't about you, do you think you would have liked it?" And recall when Hannah thoughtlessly asks Laird, the recovering addict, to risk relapse by procuring heroine for her. You can't aspire to this kind of behavior. It would amount to "the tyranny of pluck," Elaine Blair writes in *The New York Review of Books*, to want on TV only likeable characters whose main concern is always doing the right thing or being happy-go-lucky. These characters, which Blair describes as "raw and bruised," are not to be aspired to.

Even though the awkward sex and the "non-serviceable" nudity challenge the culture industry's usual images and representations of women in media, these aspects are not presented as something to aspire to but which is nevertheless impossible to obtain. They are all too easy to obtain. Furthermore, no fantasy is offered into which we may fruitlessly escape. The pernicious ideology of fake-realism is thus avoided.

Hidden Messages

In "How to Look at Television" Adorno says that mainstream TV comes in a "multilayered structure," including "hidden messages" below the surface-level plot. The idea from psychoanalysis that persons have multiple layers of personality is used by the culture industry perhaps not entirely intentionally "in order to ensnare the consumer as completely as possible and in order to engage him psycho-dynamically in the service of [certain] effects" (p. 166).

Adorno takes as an example an "extremely light comedy of pranks," in which there is:

> a young schoolteacher who is not only underpaid but is incessantly fined by the caricature of a pompous and authoritarian school principal. Thus, she has no money for her meals and is actually starving. The supposedly funny situations consist mostly of her trying to hustle a meal from various acquaintances, but regularly without success. . . . Overtly, the play is just slight amusement mainly provided by the painful situations into which the heroine and her arch-opponent constantly run. The script does not try to 'sell' any idea. The 'hidden message' emerges simply by the way the story looks at human beings; thus the audience is invited to look at the characters in the same way without being made aware that indoctrination is present. . . . The heroine shows such . . . high-spiritedness that identification with her is invited and compensation is offered for the inferiority of her position. (pp. 166–67)

So, the manifest content of the script does not come with an explicit "moral to the story." No one behaving in a certain way is then given or denied a prize or a reward. Nevertheless, there is a message hidden in the way we are invited to identify (as in what happens with fake-realism) with the main character.

> In terms of a set pattern of identification the script implies: 'If you are as humorous, good-natured, quick-witted, and charming as she is, do not worry about being paid a starvation wage. You can cope with your frustration in a humorous way' . . . In other words, the script is a shrewd method of promoting adjustment to humiliating conditions by presenting them as objectively comical and by giving a picture of a person who experiences even her own inadequate position as an object of fun apparently free of any resentment. (p. 167)

Because we identify with the plucky schoolteacher we are given to think that the way she handles her situation would be appropriate for us. We are encouraged to adjust to humiliating socio-economic conditions. "The 'message' of adjustment and unreflecting obedience seems to be dominant and all-pervasive today," Adorno says. These stories "teach their readers that one has to be 'realistic', that one has to give up romantic ideas, that one has to adjust oneself at any price, and that nothing more can be expected of any individual."

Girls would transmit a hidden message except for the fact that identification with the characters does not take place. If a viewer were somehow to identify with the characters in *Girls*, then he or she would receive the hidden message that funny one-liners, careless valley girl blathering, myopia about the plight of lower socio-economic classes and about other people's problems constitute an appropriate response to the vicissitudes of life.

All this happens at the level of the subconscious. A show with a plot like that of the plucky, put-upon schoolteacher "does not pretend to touch anything serious and expects to be regarded as featherweight. Nevertheless, even such amusements tend to set patterns for the members of the audience without their being aware of it" (p. 167). As a matter of fact, "the hidden message may be more important than the overt, since this hidden message will escape the controls of consciousness, will not be 'looked through', will not be warded off by sales resistance, but is likely to sink into the spectator's mind" (pp. 164–65).

Looking at the hidden message in this way is in accordance with the "assumption shared by numerous social scientists that certain political and social trends of our time, particularly those of a totalitarian nature, feed to a considerable extent on irrational and frequently unconscious motivations." The majority of television shows today "aim at producing, or at least reproducing, the very . . . intellectual passivity and gullibility that seem to fit with totalitarian creeds even if the explicit surface message of the shows may be anti-totalitarian" (p. 166).

However, if a TV show does not exhibit fake-realism and if, thereby or for some other reason, does not allow a member of the audience to identify with the characters, then a hidden message of the kind Adorno discusses is not possible. *Girls*, thus avoids hidden messages of such a kind because *Girls* does not participate in fake-realism, the characters are unlikeable and thus cannot be identified with, and the show is not aspirational nor escapist.

By "identify with" I only mean identify in the sense of perceive as a role model or someone to aspire to be like. An audience member would not identify in this sense with unlikeable or immoral characters. However, an audience member could still "identify" with the unlikeable characters in the sense that he or she sympathizes with their difficulties and challenges and maintains enough interest through this kind of identification to continue to want to watch them on screen.

Bad Criticism

The professional critics who trash *Girls* often have a bad theory or no theory at all about how mass media affect the audience psychologically. Or these critics will have a bad theory or no theory at all about how to have a deep engagement with the representation of the characters of a story that will lead to an insightful interpretation of that story. Requiring likeable characters or requiring the characters be role models is a bad critical engagement with a narrative.

For instance, any worthwhile version of feminist criticism will not require that characters in a TV show be role models. A show with main characters who are unlikeable but rather more like anti-heroes can still be a feminist show, even if those characters themselves do not act as feminist role models.

In an article titled, "*Girls* Is Not Diverse, Not Feminist, and Not Empowering," Catherine Scott writes:

> What's there to celebrate for feminism when a show depicts four entirely self-interested young women and a lead character having the most depressing, disempowered sexual relationships imaginable?

How would Scott have a show's characters and events be depicted? It looks as though she would require that a feminist show only represent characters who are models of what feminism rightly hopes for women. Feminism is correct to advocate for a future in which young women are not narcissistic and arrange for themselves only empowering sexual relationships. But in a fictional text it simply won't help to achieve the just ends of feminism by only ever representing women as feminist icons. Role-modelism of that sort invites identification with the characters.

As we've seen, identification with the characters inflicts all sorts of pernicious effects on the audience at the psychological level of the subconscious. Perhaps that won't be a problem if the identification on the part of the audience is always with a faultless feminist hero. But the problem will be that if we demand, as Scott and others seem to do, that the characters always be role models there will be very little or no chance for a dialectical engagement with the text that sharpens our critical faculties. Imagine a world in which TV shows and other cultural products only represent characters as role models. Doesn't that strike you as insufferably uninteresting, unengaging, and in fact horrifically dystopian? The role-modelism in *Girls* criticism doesn't seem well thought out.

Instead, what Adorno wants in terms of good art and the concomitant good criticism includes TV shows and other works that break from established genres, that challenge mainstream clichés and conventions of representation, that eschew fake-realism, that avoid pernicious hidden messages of adjustment to our situation, and that requires active and critical thinking on the part of the audience if the audience is to achieve "autonomy" and "emancipation" with respect to the prevailing ideology of our time.

Girls does all that.

2
Don't Get Mad at *Girls*

RACHEL ROBISON-GREENE

My first exposure to *Girls* criticism came in the form of a Facebook status. A distant friend from grad school said something like, "Oh, I see the statement that Lena Dunham is trying to make about girls. They are all neurotic, self-centered, and immature. That is just great for the feminist movement."

I had just watched the first season and I thought it was such a work of art that I almost felt that my friend was insulting me personally. I later learned that there are a whole host of critics of the show, all of whom tacitly must accept the proposition that Dunham's Hannah Horvath herself asserts, which is that Dunham is the voice of her generation.

Do You Think I Think This Is the Best Use of My Literary Voice and My Myriad of Talents?

The characters on *Girls* don't behave well. Many of the chapters in this book focus on the worst behavior in the series, so I'll mention some of the more obscure but equally hilarious examples of bad behavior.

One of the lines that cracked me up the most was when someone asked how Hannah's very old and sick grandmother, Flo, was doing and Hannah replied, "Oh the old Flo Job, you know her just sluttin' around." Or, remember when Hannah applied for that job and she insinuates that her interviewer is a date rapist? She says, "I read a statistic that said Syracuse has the highest rate of date rape of any other school. . . . Which, weirdly, went down after you graduated."

Hannah is not alone in her tendency to act in ways that she shouldn't. Though the *Girls* are quite different, one thing that unites them is their tendency to make bad choices. In fact, as viewers, we can understand the subject matter of the show (if there is any definable subject matter) as the bad choices that these young people make, and their ways of coping with those bad decisions as they progress to real womanhood. Watching this happen is like watching a train wreck. My husband has, more than once, had to beckon me out of my hiding place under the covers when the *Girls* do something particularly inappropriate.

But this is part of what makes the show fun, and it might be a reason we respond to it. We may not have made the kinds of mistakes that these millennials make, but each of us probably has one or two life experiences where we did something so embarrassing that we still cringe to think about it.

In this regard, it would be hard to forget Jessa, who is another poster girl for the making of bad choices. She does drugs, she dates men who are bad for her, and, arguably, she runs from the very idea of doing anything substantial with her life. Her commitment to living as some sort of free spirit is also a commitment to acting in ways that she really shouldn't. After all, being a free spirit isn't always a good thing.

One criticism of the show that frequently comes up is that the characters are bad people. They aren't good role models. In fact, if you Google this criticism of *Girls*, you'll find that some responses to the show are quite vitriolic. There is a *hatred* for it that is off the charts. People don't like the fact that Hannah allows Adam to degrade her during sex. They don't like how entitled Marnie is. They don't like the fact that Jessa's self-centered, erratic behavior and frequent drug use is "glorified" as "bohemian." And they don't like how vapid Shoshana is.

Piggybacking on the "bad role model" criticism, many, including my Facebook friend, think that the fact that the *Girls* are bad role models makes them bad faces of the feminist movement. There are so few shows that feature women as main characters, the thought is, maybe the shows that get picked up that do feature women as main characters should represent those women in a more dignified light. This seems to be at the root of Catherine Scott's criticism.

This line of thought is not all uncommon. Google it. You'll see. But the feminist issues are not even the most common point of criticism. The loudest criticism of *Girls* is that it is not ethnically diverse. It's a show about white women who are friends with other white women and date and interact with predominately white men. Since the ethnic makeup of New York City is actually much different, this scenario, to many, seems a little far-fetched. Here is what Phoebe Robinson had to say about it in the Huffington Post:

> I'm confident that even if you don't look like me or have the same background as me, my point of view is universal enough because I've experienced all kinds of situations and people, so I say to you, Ms. Dunham: go out and learn some more shit, so you will have more things to write about. It's lazy to stay so self-contained and beyond unacceptable to pass off such a myopic view of the world as THE 20-SOMETHING EXPERIENCE. That is how the show is being packaged after all. Well, *Girls* doesn't represent me nor the women I know who have matured in NYC.

This type of response to the show is so intense that the first line of this opinion piece is "FUCK. THIS. SHOW."

To see whether the criticisms are warranted, we need to do some philosophical analysis of a number of different concepts. I think that real discussion of these issues is properly philosophical. Before we do this, I just want to acknowledge that there *is* a problem with the representation of women as main characters in movies and television shows and there *is* a problem with the representation of people of color.

You an Underdog? You Look Like a Fucking Kennedy

What does it mean to say that a show contains "bad feminism" or that a show is "bad for feminism"? That claim relies on a few assumptions about feminism:

1. **That there is one "correct" conception of what feminism is.**

2. **That the person saying this has the "correct" conception.**

3. **That Lena Dunham does not have the correct conception.**

4. **That there is one unified goal of feminism.**

5. **That all art should strive to further the goal of the "correct " conception of feminism.**

I think each of these assumptions is as wrong as rain. Let's go through them one by one.

First, there are lots of different approaches to feminism. One feminist thinker, for example, might think that pornography is, by its very nature, exploitative, while another feminist thinker might argue that it is possible for women to freely choose to participate in the sex industry and that it is not inherently exploitative.

Feminist thinkers have a wide range of positions on particular social issues, but also have a range of attitudes regarding what feminism even is and what it means to be a woman. They disagree about whether feminism is purely a political movement or whether it is a definable system of thought. We can easily make a list of what feminism *is not.* I think we can safely say that if you think that women are inferior to men, you aren't a feminist. If you believe in the subjugation of women, you are not a feminist. If you don't believe in social and political equality, you are not a feminist. If you use the term "femiNazi," you are not a feminist. Ann Coulter is not a feminist. That leaves a lot of room for different positions.

Most of the feminist criticism of *Girls* takes place in opinion pieces, often those that likely have word caps, so the authors don't have the opportunity to articulate their particular conceptions of feminism. What they do seem to do is make observations about the content of the show and just assume that the behavior that the characters are engaging in is *clearly* not feminist in nature.

What's going on here? What does a piece of art have to look like in order for it to count as feminist in nature? Does it have to look something like *Buffy the Vampire Slayer*? Do we only allow art that portrays women as tough, smart, and independent with all of their shit worked out? This is a topic that requires debate. I am not going to assume any one position on feminism here. However, a situation in which women are only portrayed as these superhero-caricatures isn't doing the feminist movement any favors. There is room for that kind of portrayal. I love *Buffy*. But it's a fact about the world that most women can't take down three-hundred-pound monsters with roundhouse kicks. Some women aren't smart, some women aren't independent, and most people don't have their shit together. Why do we have to portray women as ideal versions of themselves in order to satisfy the demands of feminism? It is far from clear to me that these authors have feminism right and Dunham has it wrong.

The behavior that comes up again and again in these articles is the demeaning sex that Adam has with Hannah. I get that some people have a problem with demeaning sex. It doesn't follow, however, that portraying demeaning sex in a show is immoral or contrary to feminist ideology. We could have a conversation about whether demeaning sex itself is anti-feminist. Even if it were, making demeaning sex part of a storyline in a work of fiction is not clearly so. There is a tacit premise that isn't being articulated in the argument. Here is the argument without the implicit premise:

> *Premise One*: **Demeaning sex is contrary to a feminist ideology.**
>
> *Conclusion:* **Portraying demeaning sex on television is contrary to a feminist ideology.**

Stated in this way, the argument isn't valid. The conclusion doesn't follow from the premise. Let's be more charitable and add the implicit premise to improve the structure of the argument:

> *Premise One:* **Demeaning sex is contrary to a feminist ideology.**
>
> *Premise Two:* **If a behavior is contrary to a feminist ideology, then it is contrary to the feminist ideology to portray that behavior on television.**
>
> *Conclusion:* **Portraying demeaning sex on television is contrary to a feminist ideology.**

Put this way, the argument has a good structure, but it's not clear that the second premise is true. Accepting the second premise or something like it to be true leads us down a very dangerous path. Do we really want to say that we shouldn't include behavior that is contrary to a feminist ideology in art? Art is possibly the best medium we have for conveying ideas and allowing people to reflect in a profound way on the subject matter. If what we want is social change, the way to bring that about is not going to be to stifle artistic expression.

Consider a similarly structured argument:

Premise One: **Racism is immoral.**

Premise Two: **If Racism is immoral, portraying racism on television is immoral.**

Conclusion: **Portraying racism on television is immoral.**

Does this ring true to you? If you find this argument compelling, then say goodbye to *12 Years a Slave, The Color Purple, The Help, All in the Family* . . . you get the idea.

In response, someone might say, "But Dunham isn't trying to make a point about how bad demeaning sex is. These other films are pointing out the injustice of racism and slavery. Dunham, in Adam, is creating a character that it would appear that we are actually supposed to like."

First of all, it's not clear that Dunham *isn't* making any point about demeaning sex. But even if she isn't, she isn't *advocating* it. She isn't saying "Hey everyone, go out and have some demeaning sex right away!" Demeaning sex happens in life. There is a legitimate debate about whether demeaning sex is necessarily contrary to a feminist ideology (some feminist philosophers, like Catherine McKinnon, argue that sex acts are, by their very nature, demeaning and violent). By portraying this behavior in art, viewers are invited to arrive at their own conclusions about what they find acceptable.

We've looked at three of the main assumptions accepted by those who offer feminist critiques of the show. There is no one, unified conception of feminism. If we could land on one correct ideology, it isn't clear that it should be the conception hinted at by these authors rather than the one put forward by Dunham. It's also far from clear that Dunham's work is hurting the feminist cause, if there really is a single such thing, in any way.

Let's deal with the last assumption, that the proper role of art should be to advance a particular political cause, in this case, the feminist cause. Why in the world should we think that? Why should we think that art bears some necessary relationship to morality? Art is about creativity and self-expression. Perhaps we shouldn't put restrictions on the range of things art can be.

So what if *Girls* was explicitly sexist? I would hope that we would all stop watching it (though the fact that shows like *The Bachelor* are still are the air gives me little hope for that). Would it then, somehow, not count as art? Of course not. It would just be sexist art.

Whatever conception of feminism you have, whatever goals you think that feminism should have, stifling the range of female experiences that can be portrayed in media and telling a woman what her artistic voice needs to sound like doesn't seem to jibe with any of those goals.

I Wanted You to Tell Me What's Wrong with Me

What about the criticisms of the show regarding its pretty much exclusively white cast? We should analyze this criticism in a similar way. We have a problem. No doubt. But what are people who raise this criticism of *Girls* committed to? I think their position must be the following:

1. **The entertainment industry needs to feature people of color more prominently in movies and television, in roles and storylines that reflect a diversity of possible experiences.**

2. **The best way to accomplish that goal is to have each individual writer be more cognizant of the limited role of people of color in the entertainment industry, with the desired result of writing more storylines featuring people of color prominently.**

3. **A writer is remiss if they don't include people of color prominently in their art.**

Point 1, is simply categorically, true. I am raising no challenge to that one. I will, however, challenge points 2 and 3. Is

encouraging writers to include more people of color in their
work the best way of ensuring that people of color will be featured prominently in film and television?

I don't think that it is. When an artist creates a work of art,
they can best ensure the quality of that art if the work arises
authentically and organically. Lena Dunham is not a stock
writer being paid to write television that meets a certain set of
pre-agreed-upon standards. She is an artist creating art for a
cable television network. Here is what she had to say about the
criticism in an NPR interview:

> I wrote the first season primarily by myself, and I co-wrote a few
> episodes. But I am a half-Jew, half-WASP, and I wrote two Jews and
> two WASPs. Something I wanted to avoid was tokenism in casting. If
> I had one of the four girls, if, for example, she was African-American,
> I feel like—not that the experience of an African-American girl and a
> white girl are drastically different, but there has to be specificity to that
> experience [that] I wasn't able to speak to. I really wrote the show
> from a gut-level place, and each character was a piece of me or
> based on someone close to me. And only later did I realize that it was
> four white girls. As much as I can say it was an accident, it was only
> later as the criticism came out, I thought, 'I hear this and I want to
> respond to it'. And this is a hard issue to speak to because all I want
> to do is sound sensitive and not say anything that will horrify anyone
> or make them feel more isolated, but I did write something that was
> super-specific to my experience, and I always want to avoid render-
> ing an experience I can't speak to accurately.

So, if we take Dunham's response seriously, and I don't see why
we shouldn't, Dunham is most comfortable and at her best
when she writes what she knows. This is how she creates the
best art she can create. Her experience has been mostly with
white people. Is that unfortunate? Sure. Is it the experience of
some people? Yep. If we want the quality of art that gets produced to be high, we shouldn't force artists to be inauthentic.
So, perhaps fixing the problem with race in the entertainment
industry shouldn't be focused on the level of the individual
writer or creator.

What, then, should we do? How do we bring about the
needed social change and at what level should it happen? The
first, and most crucial respect is to create. If you can create

good art that features people of color prominently, do it. It takes only a small amount of effort to complain about ethnic diversity on television. The recognition that there is a problem carries with it an obligation to do something about the problem. It helps no one to ask writers to inauthentically write something that they don't know about—that only makes the problem worse. If we do that, we'll get a portrayal of minorities and people of color that doesn't reflect the true quality of that lived experience.

The second point is that networks have an obligation to pick up shows that feature prominently people of color. They need to recognize good art that is produced by people of color; they need to hire people of color. They need to see to it that authentically written art about people of color gets produced.

I've tried to make a case for the position that, in fixing this problem, we shouldn't focus our attention on individual writers or artists because that would diminish the quality of the product and it might make the problem worse. But a further question we should address is whether writers who don't write people of color are behaving immorally.

In the opinion piece I mentioned earlier, Phoebe Robinson says, "I say to you, Ms. Dunham: go out and learn some more shit, so you will have more things to write about. It's lazy to stay so self-contained and beyond unacceptable to pass off such a myopic view of the world as THE 20-SOMETHING EXPERIENCE."

I think we can all agree that it is a good thing to have many diverse experiences. When we expose ourselves to all sorts of different people and places and cultures, we really grow as people, and as we become more educated, we are less likely to retain ignorant or hateful views about other people. So, in a sense, I agree with Ms. Robinson. Ms. Dunham, who seems to me to be a delightful person, would likely find her life improved if she sought out experiences with a diverse range of people. This is not to say anything about Ms. Dunham personally. It is trivially true in the sense that I think it is likely that *everyone's* life would be better if they had a more diverse set of experiences. Conceding that point, I don't think Ms. Robinson has a *moral* claim to make against Ms. Dunham. Ms. Dunham has had the experiences she has had. That is true about all of us. So long as she is not hurting anyone, why does anyone have any sort of claim on what kind of experiences another person has? If another person hasn't had the experience you have had, why does that make them lazy?

Imagine that someone attempts to commission a portrait artist to paint a mountain scene. It seems perfectly appropriate to me for the artist to say, "I don't paint landscapes. I don't know how to effectively portray a landscape. It isn't that I am opposed to other kinds of art, but if you want a good depiction of the mountain scene, I am not the best person to do it." This seems like an honest answer, and not one that would likely to be met with moral disdain. What changes in the case of *Girls?*

Ms. Robinson may be making the same mistake that my Facebook friend made. The fact that the show is called *Girls,* does not in any way entail that it is supposed to accurately portray all girls and women. Though it may address challenges for young people that are, in some cases, universal experiences, the show is about *these particular girls* dealing with those experiences. It is not about all women. It is not about all ethnic groups. It is a character-driven show about these particular characters.

The Voice of Her Generation!

In addition to the two major criticisms that I mentioned, critics are also concerned that *Girls* is classist. It deals with rich or middle-class white girls with first-world problems. I have a similar response to that concern that I have to the concern about race. Yep. This show is, indeed, about rich or middle-class white girls with first world problems. That is what Lena Dunham knows and it is what she chose to make the subject matter of her art.

Why are people so passionate about the claims they make about the subject matter of Lena Dunham's work? Why aren't people angry about the subject matter of *Bones,* or 2 *Broke Girls,* or *How I Met Your Mother?* I've said it before, and I'll say it again on the record. Lena Dunham is a creative genius and most people, on some level recognize that fact. Her work is so damn good that everyone wants it to be consistent with his or her ideals. Her show is about four girls. The voice of a generation need not speak for everyone. Hell, it would be sufficient to just have amazing insight into one person. It's the insight into a group of individuals, however small, and the masterful way she is able to use words to convey that insight, that is truly impressive.

Hannah Horvath may or may not be the voice of her generation—we'll see. For me, the jury is in on Lena Dunham.

3
Adam, Like a Hero

TRIP MCCROSSIN

"I was always here," Adam says to Hannah, in the closing moments of Season Two. He's just broken down her door, having run across town to rescue her, having learned that she's in distress. "You're here," Hannah whispers, amazed that he's standing before her, and what he says, he says as if simply to remind her. What *we* are reminded of in the process, as Hannah may be as well, is something he says in the opening moments of Season One. "I like you so much," she admits, but "I don't know where you disappear to," to which he responds, apparently baffled, "I'm right here."

The similarity between these two bookend scenes underscores the dissimilarity between the respective portrayals of Adam. In the earlier scene, while Hannah is clearly smitten, he's at best aloof, at worst indifferent, most troublingly with regard to his sexual behavior. While we may already be suspicious of Marnie's standards, her description of him as an "animal" shortly afterward doesn't seem at this point all that far-fetched. In the later scene, though, Adam is portrayed in far more flattering, even *heroic* terms.

What the storyline connecting these scenes offers, in this light, is an unusual perspective on what it means to develop as a *hero*—an old question still very much alive today.

Just Another Rom-Com Ending?

Don't we first have to worry, though, that Lena Dunham, creator of the series, who wrote the earlier episode and co-wrote the later one, doesn't *herself* describe Adam's behavior in the rescue scene as heroic in her 2013 interview with Glenn Whipp?

"Adam running to Hannah via FaceTime," Dunham tells us, "speaks to the intensity of rom-com endings." So clearly we're supposed to be amused, thanks to a clever *You've Got Mail* plot device for the Millennial Generation. Even so, there seems also to be something deeper going on. Hannah suffers from obsessive-compulsive disorder, which, if untreated, can be devastating. She's off her meds. To make matters worse, her publisher is brutally unsympathetic, and her father only somewhat less so. And she feels ashamed to see, or feels abandoned by, her closest friends, and regrets losing Adam, as was revealed by their chance encounter in the previous episode. All of this Dunham portrays in heartbreaking detail. "I feel like I'm unraveling," Hannah finally admits to Adam, as "FaceTime" reveals to him her recurring disorder, "I'm really, really scared." "Stay right where you are," he responds, "I'm coming to you." Dramatic music is cued. Tears begin to form.

Adam's behavior wouldn't be properly heroic, we think, if Hannah's distress were more mundane—the earlier splinter in her behind, for example. As Dunham portrays it, it's anything but. In addition to needing the distress to be relatively extraordinary, though, we need the response to be so as well, relative to what those who witness it expect of others, and of themselves. If it were Cary Grant running across town, for example, coming to the rescue of a 1950s-era Hannah—the humorous plot device here being, perhaps, stopping frantically, each and every block along the way, to call her from a phone booth—we'd likely think, okay, it's *Cary Grant*, and so *of course*—isn't this just what we *expect* of *someone like him*. But for *Adam* to do what he does, it's rather *not* what we expect, for better or for worse, in *our* day and age. It's not, that is, the *Millennial* thing to do. As such, taken together with the extraordinary nature of Hannah's distress, how can we not think of Adam's behavior as heroic?

"Don't people just meet at the coffee shop rather than run to the airport to find somebody?," Dunham adds, but "we also all want someone to run to the airport to find us. So we wanted something that did both." Why *both*? Because heroes are extraordinary, but we wish they weren't. We want what Adam does to be *both* heroic *and* happening "at the coffee shop"—for Adam's behavior to be as common now as we imagine Cary Grant's was back in the day.

Moving Mattresses and Chairs

We may *want* Adam to be heroic, but what more precisely *qualifies* him as a hero? The natural place to begin is with the first and only explicit reference to heroism in the storyline in question, which is in the moving-out scene that opens Season One's finale.

Marnie's discontent with Hannah's self-centeredness, which has been simmering since the pilot, finally comes to a head in the previous episode, and now she's moving out. Adam's helping in the process, and in this particular bit of slapstick, Hannah and Marnie are struggling to move a large chair down a flight of stairs, while he's trailing just behind them with a mattress. Halfway down, frustrated by Hannah's whining about "being crushed" by the chair, he insists suddenly that he's "got it," the chair in addition to the mattress, that is, and that they simply move out of the way and let him finish this part of the move by himself. To this Hannah protests, "You don't need to be like a hero about this," but she and Marnie do get out of the way finally, and he proceeds to get the job done handily enough.

He didn't "need" to be "like" a hero, by moving the mattress and chair on his own, but he did, and so for this is he a hero after all? In light of our earlier discussion, not so much it seems. Hannah's distress is relatively mundane. She's in no real jeopardy, or serious discomfort even, it seems. Adam's response is also mundane, albeit less so. Getting a mattress *and* a chair down a flight of stairs alone is perhaps not the easiest thing to do, but if he'd bailed instead, Hannah and Marnie would presumably have managed easily enough.

So, while he may be acting *like* a hero, in Hannah's estimation at least, in that he's suffering at least to some degree for the sake of others, it seems he's not yet properly heroic. Still, to take this bit of the moving-out scene seriously is to see Adam as at least flirting with heroism, if not yet actually embodying it. The question is, does he eventually move farther along in this direction, and does he ultimately get there?

Between Moving Out and (Almost) Moving In

The moving-out scene also sets up a one-episode storyline that sheds additional light on the question.

It begins, shortly afterward, with the moving-*in* scene, which is Adam's sudden realization, "Maybe I'll move in," which surprises and thrills Hannah. It ends, later the same day, with their dispute over its meaning and motivation. Sandwiched in between is Jessa's surprise wedding, with the drama it produces, leading to the dispute scene.

Hannah's chatting with Elijah and his boyfriend after the ceremony, and learns that they're not living together, and that Elijah is unhappy with his resulting living arrangements, and she invites him to move in. It's clearly a spontaneous gesture, but one that's also made self-consciously enough, that it's her first news when next she and Adam speak, good news she thinks.

"So you don't have to worry about moving in cause I found someone," Hannah tells him, "so if you felt obligated, don't." Adam's clearly offended, much to her surprise. "I thought you were trying to help, and I appreciate it," she offers in turn, as she begins to explain herself, but he cuts her off. "I don't want to *help*," he objects, which has to surprise us. "No one does anything because they want to *help*," he adds, which is also surprising. "I was doing it because I *love* you," he concludes, and we're relieved.

But our relief is short-lived, as he's only that much more offended by the surprised look on her face, which leads her to dig herself in only deeper, and finally he moves to exit. "I don't want to freak out on you at a surprise wedding," he says, unclear as to whether this is for his sake or for hers—adding as he leaves, "if you want to fuck me from behind, at least pull my hair back," which can't help but remind us of the pilot's first scene, as in "at least wear a condom." We're set now to complete the arc of the first season, as their dispute spills out onto the sidewalk and into the street—over, more broadly now, and also more angrily and eloquently, the nature of love and commitment in relation to vanity and fear.

What we want to focus on particularly here, given present purposes, is the very first bit of their dispute. As we listen in, we hear in Hannah's choice of words, and in particular "if you felt obligated, don't," an echo of her earlier one, "You don't have to be like a hero about this." In each instance she's discouraging Adam from pursuing the exemplary act he's considering, as *she* takes it to be, even if *he* does not, making clear to him that he doesn't "have to," needn't feel "obligated" to do so. But he must know this already, we think. Why does this matter?

Anything Could Happen—and Does

In the earlier moving-out scene, Adam is irritated, but also apparently *generous*, and generous acts are generous in the first place because, in part, we don't *have* to do them. What if instead, for example, Ray had happened along, found himself similarly irritated, and, with his usual gruffness, taken over the business of moving the chair and mattress down the stairs? We would not think of him, however gruff, as obligated to help, certainly not to help in this way, but he'd be helping out of generosity. The same applies to Adam, even though, having presumably agreed to help with the move in the first place, we think of him as *generally* obligated to help.

Back now to the moving-in scene. We know more here than in the moving-out scene, about what's motivating Adam. Looking forward, we have Adam's "I was doing it because I *love* you" description of what he was thinking and feeling at the time. Looking backward, we remember what he and Hannah say, and don't say, just before his "Maybe I'll move in" revelation. She's feeling guilty that Marnie's "just like really hurt," and Adam takes exception. "Don't waste time on guilt," he urges, "holding on to toxic relationships is what keeps us from growing." "You're forming every time you shed a layer," he tells her, optimistically, "getting closer to yourself." And the additional upside is, he adds, that the apartment is "half empty now; full potential; anything could happen," Hannah adding, as if completing his thought, "and all of Marnie's fake grown-up stuff is gone." Hannah's not at all focused, it seems, on such mundane considerations as making rent, and Adam even less so.

It makes perfect sense, then, that he would deny later on that he'd been motivated by a desire to help, given that the *need* for help was not at all an issue. And their dispute occurs later the same day, and so while it's conceivable that the question of need might have arisen earlier, there's no evidence within the storyline that this is the case. So *why* the later dispute?

What reason can there be but the one Hannah divulges to Jessa a little while earlier. "How can you be so sure?," Hannah asks, worried about the brevity of Jessa's pre-marital courtship. "Adam wants to move in with me," she admits, "and I can't even tell if that's good or bad." She's gone from "I like you so much" in the pilot, to securing him as boyfriend six episodes later, to wondering now whether living together is "good or bad." It's romantic progress, but not at nearly the pace that she finds Adam's been traveling.

We drew a connection between the moving-out and moving-in scenes, and within them between Hannah's "You don't need to be like a hero" and "If you felt obligated, don't" turns of phrase. We thought that if, as it seemed, Adam is flirting with heroism in the former, perhaps he's also doing so in the latter. But now it seems that the latter may instead be a better guide to the former. Hannah's "You don't have to be like a hero" is preceded by Adam's assertion that he's "got it," and in response to her statement he responds by neither affirming her claim, nor denying it, but merely reiterating, "I got it." His gesture here may *seem* to be generous, but it also seems to be the same sort of sudden realization that he has in the later moving-in scene.

Perhaps what's *not* going in the moving-out scene is what's *not* going on in the moving-in scene? Adam *could have* just as easily said in the former what he *did* say in the moving-in scene, which is, "I don't want to *help*. I was doing it because I *love* you." But Hannah "appreciates" that he's "trying to help," and so we seem to hear a different emphasis—"I don't *want* to help," but help "because I *love* you." Love, we conclude, means there are certain things we *just do*.

In Adam's world, there are things that love allows, and others that it requires. In the former category, as Adam tells us in the first moments of Season Two, we "don't have to be nice all the time." In the latter category, judging from the moving-out and moving-in scenes, we move loved ones' furniture up and down stairways by ourselves, and live with them whenever the opportunity arises. These aren't heroic gestures because, as we've seen, the distress is too mundane, or the assistance is, or both. They're *also* not heroic, it seems, for the same reason they're not generous, because they're done not because he *wants*, but because he *has* to act.

So, Is Adam a Hero in the End?

Whether he is or isn't heroic finally in the rescue scene depends, then, on different sorts of considerations.

We've already looked at two of them. On the one hand, Hannah's distress is serious enough, certainly. She insists, "You really don't have to do this," and, "Honestly, please don't worry about me," in the spirit of her earlier, "You don't need to be like a hero," and, "If you felt obligated, don't," but now her insistence is simply incredible, to Adam and to us. Adam's response, on the other hand, given the circumstances, seems also serious enough—the running, the music, being almost hit by a cab, breaking down Hannah's door, and so on.

But the additional consideration now is whether, from *our* perspective, in running across town to rescue Hannah, Adam *wants to help* or is *doing so because he loves her*. However serious Hannah's distress, however serious his rescue, whether he's heroic in the end seems to depend finally on this.

"I was always here," Adam says. He picks Hannah up, and cradles her in his arms. They kiss, embrace, and speechlessly fade to black. Adam has behaved well, *very* well it seems, at least this once, and we are, as we imagine Hannah is, reassured. Even so, we are also bound to have a *say what?* moment, however muted.

It's easy enough to imagine, based on their earlier chance encounter, that Hannah has regretted losing Adam and wanted to rekindle their relationship, and that his arrival signals to her that he too has wanted this. But we also remember that, in spite of Adam's bad behavior toward Natalia in the previous episode, and his "fuck her" outburst toward her in this one, we find them still together not long before, still a couple, however dysfunctional. When Adam gets Hannah's call, we know that Natalia is still not "done with" him, but is *he* done with *her*? Is he *now*, as a result of the call? "Stay right where you are," he tells Hannah, "I'm coming to you," but at *that* moment, *who* is he attached to, and *how*, and *how strongly*?

These are questions we can't easily answer, but then perhaps Adam couldn't either. He's attached to Natalia romantically, but perhaps not lovingly. He's attached to Hannah, not romantically, but perhaps still lovingly, though perhaps also not in the way he was before. "I was always here," Adam says, but *how* was he? And if the answer is that he "was always" there as still her boyfriend in some sense, is this a realization made in hindsight, and so not necessarily the way he's thinking and feeling when he sets off to rescue her in the first place? These questions aren't any easier.

A lesson from the moving-out and moving-in scenes seems to be that even if the circumstances *had* been more dramatic, Adam *still* wouldn't have been acting heroically. He was acting not out of a desire to help, that is, but out of love, which for him makes the act either instinctual or compulsory, and so not appropriately heroic. If a Good Samaritan is someone who acts to promote another's welfare, *on purpose*, but *not out of obligation*, then we can think of a hero in the same spirit, but not as just a *Good* Samaritan, but an *Extraordinary* Samaritan.

Isn't there a simpler story, though, in which heroism requires only heroic acts, without the additional worry over motivation? What if Batman, for example, regularly engages in acts of heroism (capturing criminals, saving lives, and so on, in generally extraordinary ways), but it turns out that he's simply *compelled* to do so out of love for his parents or the citizens of Gotham more generally, or his sense that *as Batman* it's *just what he does*? Would having such motivations make Batman less of a hero? The advocate of the simpler story would say no. Adam's behavior, however, suggests the different, more complicated story outlined above.

We can also contrast two less fictional examples from the real-life Gotham, New York City. First, let's think about Chesley "Sully" Sullenberger. On the 15th of January in 2009, Captain Sullenberger managed a successful emergency landing of US Airways flight 1549, disabled shortly after take-off, onto the Hudson, saving not only all aboard, but all those who would have been injured or killed if the plane had gone down in the city or nearby New Jersey instead. For this, the *New York Daily News* dubbed him the "Hero of the Hudson." While then Mayor Bloomberg was surely right, though, to praise him for having done "a masterful job of landing the plane in the river and then making sure everybody got out," why, in the midst of the "Great Recession," when he might well be on the lookout for available heroes, did he choose not to take advantage of the occasion? Presumably for the same reason that Sullenberger himself appraised his actions as simply "what we're trained to do." If everyone who does masterfully what they're trained to do is a hero as a result, that is, we've simply too many heroes for the title to be particularly meaningful any longer.

Contrast this with the case of Wesley Autrey, which Susan Neiman has drawn our attention to recently. On the 2nd of January in 2007, Mr. Autrey jumped into the subway tracks at the 137th Street station in Harlem to save Cameron Hollopeter, who had fallen in as a result of a seizure, laying over him in between the tracks as the oncoming subway rolled over them. For this, he was dubbed, among other things, the "Hero of Harlem." When asked to account for what motivated him to act as he did, however, he also avoided the language of heroism, as Sullenberger would two years later, saying simply, "I don't feel like I did something spectacular; I just saw someone who needed help. I did what I felt was right."

Autrey was "trained in the ideal of public service in the Navy," Neiman reminds us, as Sullenberger was in the Air Force, but "more important, he led a quiet life of unusual responsibility, caring for the indigent and a large extended family." Which is not to say that Sullenberger hadn't led such a life, only that such a life is less relevant to understanding Sullenberger's actions on his fateful day in January of 2009, than to understanding Autrey's two years earlier. It's hard to imagine the former, that is, turning to his co-pilot, Jeff Skiles, and saying, "I'm sitting this one out, so it's your call what to do," and not being judged unjust in the process. The latter, on the other hand, if he'd turned to someone on the subway platform and spoken similarly, we might well be sorry for the sentiment, but we would not similarly condemn him. To sit in a captain's chair is to accept certain obligations toward one's passengers, but simply to stand on a subway platform is to accept few, if any such obligations toward one's fellow commuters. Autrey was not obligated to act, as Sullenberger was, but acts rather as a Samaritan, and not just a good one, but surely an *extraordinary* one. It's not for nothing that he's more widely known as the "Subway Samaritan," and for precisely this reason he's also the Hero of Harlem. Is Adam heroic in this sense?

Perhaps tweaking the dialogue just a bit will help to answer this. Remember the ending of the dispute scene? That he's a "beautiful fucking mystery" to Hannah hits Adam like a truck, ultimately, figuratively *and* literally. As he's taken away by ambulance, he refuses to allow Hannah to come along, because, as he says, "she's a monster." Now, fast-forward a season. In keeping with the intended "intensity of rom-com endings," let's keep everything after "I was always here" as is. But when Hannah calls in distress, instead of saying what he actually says, let's imagine Adam saying instead, "Look, I still think you're a monster, and we're not getting back together, but you're in trouble, and I want to help, so stay right where you are, I'm coming to you." Bringing him more in line with an Extraordinary Samaritan, the additional language would seem more clearly indicative then of Adam's heroism. He *didn't* say this, but *might* he not have been thinking it, or thinking something like it?

Unfortunately not if we also remember what's sandwiched in between "I don't want to *help*" and "I was doing it because I *love* you." There we find Adam's *reason*, it seems, for why he *can't* be doing the former and *must* be doing the latter, which is, "No one does *anything* because they want to *help*." But if *this* were true, all that we'd be left with would be acts motivated by self-interest or instinct or compelled by love, which seems to leave us without heroes. If only he'd said, "We *rarely* do *anything*. . . ." Maybe it's what he *meant*? Maybe what he *says*, he says as a bit of Millennial overstatement? I for one am rooting for overstatement.[1]

---

[1] I'm grateful to Cait Callahan, my stalwart guide to all things Millennial, for the observation about Adam's behavior illustrated by the Cary Grant example, and to Deborah Greenwood for patiently helping me to understand the series as more than just a disheartening depiction of the generation. I'm grateful to the volume editors for the question about Batman's motives and for their patience and assistance throughout the writing of this chapter. Finally, I'm grateful to Erin Carlston and Carisa Showden for the Sully Sullenberger example and the helpful contrast it provides to Neiman's Autrey example, and for their patience and assistance in the late stages of the process. None of them is responsible, though, for what I've done with their insights and encouragement.

4
Why *Girls* Can't Be Spoiled

RICHARD GREENE

SPOILER ALERT: you may not want to read this chapter if you haven't watched *Star Wars, Episode V: The Empire Strikes Back*, or the original *Planet of the Apes*, or *Psycho*, or *Murder on the Orient Express*, or *Fight Club*, or read the Harry Potter books. But what about *Girls*? Is it okay to read on, if you're not caught up on *Girls*? Well, . . . that remains to be determined. Continue at your own peril!

Spoilers have existed for as long as there have been things to spoil. We can easily imagine some citizen of Athens in 429 B.C.E. leaving the Theater of Dionysus on the opening night of Sophocles's *Oedipus the King* shouting "OMG, Oedipus slept with his own mother!" (or something along those lines).

The ethics of spoilers, however, has changed over time. When I grew up in the 1960s my friends and I would race to be the one to reveal a spoiler to the entire group (though we didn't think of them as spoilers). It was a kind of competition: "Did you see *The Lone Ranger* this week? Tonto almost got shot!" No one would have dreamed of objecting upon hearing this news. Nowadays, of course, we're expected to be sensitive to whether we're revealing a spoiler. If you reveal a spoiler, the response might range anywhere from mild shock at the *faux pas* to downright outrage or anger. The revealing of spoilers is typically met with a cry of "Spoiler alert!" which is intended to suggest that you should not have done so.

And does anyone know why they now design trailers so that you can determine most or all of the major plot twists in a movie just by watching the trailer? When at the cinema watching trailers, I'm occasionally overcome with an impulse to scream "Spoiler alert!" for the duration of the trailer, just to save my fellow movie-goers from having movies spoiled for them.

A cry of "Spoiler alert!" can also be used humorously or ironically, in cases where it's clear that the "spoiler" in question is not a true spoiler. Suppose that just prior to watching Adam's Broadway debut in George Bernard Shaw's *Major Barbara*, Hannah were to say to Shoshanna that in the play "Cusins is going to marry Barbara," it would hardly count as a legitimate spoiler as the plot of the play is very well known, and it is well over a hundred years old.

My son at age six loved to yell "spoiler alert" on airplanes as the flight attendants were giving their flight safety spiel (usually around the time they were discussing emergency evacuations in water). This would always elicit a good laugh from the other passengers (except the very nervous ones who wondered whether he knew something).

So just what constitutes a spoiler?

Something's Rotten in Brooklyn

What we need is a list of conditions for a legitimate spoiler to occur. I'm using the term "legitimate spoiler" to distinguish those cases in which a spoiler was revealed and should not have been—the kind of spoiler that would yield the sort of moral disapproval described above—from a spoiler that rightly ought to be met with a "So what?" For example, if my wife and I were discussing an episode of *Girls* that she hadn't yet seen, and I were to report to her that Hannah wore a silly outfit, that would, I suppose, technically be a spoiler, but not one worthy of moral outrage. Why? Because, 1. Hannah almost always wears silly clothing, and 2. I'm not revealing something interesting about the story that was designed to arouse any sort of feeling of shock or surprise, or any of a number of similar responses in the viewing audience. It would be as if I reported that Marnie spoke, and in doing so used some vowels.

The fact that Hannah *always* wears silly clothing is relevant to whether or not my reporting it is a legitimate spoiler, but the timing of my reporting is also relevant. Were I to tell my wife before she had seen *any* episodes of *Girls* things about the show, such as that Hannah always wears silly outfits, or that Adam is a bit of a sexual deviant, or that Shoshanna is obsessed with *Sex and the City*, or that Ray is really blunt, then I at least run the risk of revealing a spoiler.

The term "spoiler" isn't just limited to plot twists. Potentially anything important in a show can be spoiled. One of my favorite moments from *Girls* occurs in the episode "Truth or Dare." Hannah, Adam, and Shoshanna are on a road trip. Hannah in a moment of frustration blurts out "I'm just realizing that this road trip is not a metaphor. It just isn't." At the time it seemed like the most hilarious thing ever. Had I known this line was coming, it might not have seemed so funny. The moment would have been spoiled.

Learning facts about the actors who play in movies and shows, can also, under certain circumstances, count as spoilers. Suppose that you learn that Adam Driver, who plays Adam on *Girls* is filming in Europe all summer, and that the entire fifth season of *Girls* is being filmed entirely in New York City at the same time. You could then conclude that Adam will not be featured in the fifth season. This, I should think, would count as a major spoiler.

You might think that you can avoid revealing legitimate spoilers by not being too specific. This's not true. Sometimes it's enough to say something like "There's a twist at the end" to be guilty of revealing a spoiler. Had I been thinking this all through *Fight Club*, the surprise ending would have been ruined for me (as will be now for you, if you haven't already seen it).

Finally, not every kind of entertainment can be legitimately spoiled. For example, it seems okay to report that such and such a team won the World Series (hopefully it will be the San Francisco Giants again this year) immediately after it happens, or to report something that you saw on the news (for example, that *Girls* has been picked up for another season, or that Lena Dunham won a bunch of awards again). Spoilers are pretty much limited to fiction. That said, if your friend tells you that she recorded the seventh game of the world series, and won't be watching it until later, it would be pretty rude to tell her the result before she watches it. Use your best discretion here.

Hey, I Think This Cheese Is Old!

So let's start compiling our list of things that need to occur for something to be a legitimate spoiler. You might think that you can't spoil something too old. The fact that Shaw's play *Major Barbara* is over one hundred years old is sufficient to rule it out as a candidate for being the source of legitimate spoilers. This seems right. The idea is that folks have some responsibility to see things in a timely manner, during which they should not be subjected to spoilers, but after enough time has passed, then it's okay to discuss things. Suppose that Shosh and Jessa are having a conversation about an episode of *The Mary Tyler Moore Show* (perhaps the one in which Mary dates Chuckles the Clown), which aired in the 1970s. Certainly, Shosh could not be criticized for bringing the show up, or mentioning details about the show, even if Jessa had never seen the episode under consideration. To deny this would be to maintain that you can never discuss anything that your audience has never seen (unless it were a matter of emergency, or were essential that you do so for some reason). This, of course, would be absurd. Things that are old enough are fair game.

What constitutes old enough? This is a tricky issue. Currently, in the United States, if you miss a television program when it first airs, or a movie when it is first in the Theaters, there are opportunities to see the show or the movie right away. Movies are often available for download or are released on Blu-ray within weeks of their theatrical release date. Television programs, such as *Girls*, are available on HBO GO and Amazon Instant Video, often within hours of being aired. Both movies and television programs end up on Netflix within months of being released or first aired. On the other hand, you might have to wait months or even years to catch a new Broadway show.

So, we're not going to be able to cash out what "old enough" means in terms of a specific amount of time, as that will vary from medium to medium, as well as place to place (most US-made movies are released in Europe after their US release date, and are released in Africa, Asia, and South America even later). So we'll have to adopt a standard of what seems reasonable given the medium, and the type of program it is (we should also keep in mind that some folks prefer to watch an entire series at once and may wait until the series had had its run, and the entirety is available in digital format). Here it's best to err on the side of caution. At the time of this writing it's probably still too soon to discuss the details of the final episode of *Breaking Bad* with someone who hasn't seen it. By contrast, certainly there can be no prohibition on discussing the final episode of *Seinfeld*, even though it contains many things that would have been considered spoilers at the time (for example, the fact that the four main friends—Jerry, George, Elaine, and Kramer—all ended up in jail together).

So the reasonable time standard sounds good, but there is a worry. It's been nearly forty years since *Star Wars* first appeared on screen. Suppose that Ray (I choose Ray for this example because he's the character on the show most likely to do such a thing) went in to a kindergarten classroom at PS 235 in Brooklyn and announced that Darth Vader is Luke Skywalker's father. This, I think, would be unacceptable. There are two ways of capturing this intuition. The first is to hold that the children are too young to be expected to have already seen *Star Wars Episode V*, and hence the reasonable amount of time standard still applies. This is not an entirely happy response, because I also have the strong intuition that Ray would be remiss were he to tell Adam or Marnie or anyone else who had never seen *Star Wars Episode V* that Darth Vader is Luke's father.

The other (and preferable) way of capturing the intuition that it's unacceptable for Ray to reveal that Darth is Luke's father is to hold that some spoilers never expire. Some plot twists rise to the level being so significant (or the shows, movies, plays, and books to which they belong are so significant), that they should never be revealed. Alongside Darth is Luke's Father on the Mount Olympus of spoilers we also find:

- **Snape killed Dumbledore! (And Dumbledore wanted Snape to kill him!)**

- **Norman Bates is "Mother"!**

- **Dorothy's trip to Oz was all a dream!**

- **All the passengers on the Orient Express conspired together to commit the murder!**

- **Soylent Green is people! (related: *To Serve Man* is a cookbook!)**

And finally, what many consider to be the greatest spoiler of them all,

- **The Planet of the Apes is really Earth!**

Perhaps the best way to put it is that even if someone has not seen these programs or movies, and even if they might never see them, they ought to. That is sufficient to require that they never be spoiled. Moreover, people who have not seen these shows or movies or read these books do not deserve to know these spoilers. So these few *bona fide* counterexamples to our reasonable time requirement don't cause enough worry for the requirement to be jettisoned.

Didn't We Already Have This Soup Last Week?

So what shall we next add to our list of requirements for something to be a legitimate spoiler? One thing that stands to reason is that you can't spoil something if people are already aware of it. So a legitimate spoiler must be something that is not common knowledge. Suppose, for example, that on our way to see the film *Pompeii* (that's right, I was one of the thirty or so people who actually saw this movie in the theater), I tell my wife that there will be a volcanic eruption in the film. Certainly this would not count as a spoiler, as it is virtually certain that my wife knows that the movie *Pompeii* will be about the eruption of Vesuvius. Historical events have a propensity to be commonly known is sufficient to rule it out as a legitimate spoiler. Even if my wife didn't happen to know that there would be a volcano in *Pompeii*, the fact that it is commonly known is sufficient to rule it out as a legitimate spoiler.

Again, we may employ a "reasonability" standard—this time a "reasonable person" standard. If it's reasonable to suppose that a reasonable person might know something, that's enough to conclude that telling them that thing can't count as revealing a legitimate spoiler. You can't reveal a spoiler about *The Tudors* by blurting out that Anne Boleyn gets beheaded, nor can you spoil *Apollo 13* by stating that they will say "Houston, we have a problem," nor the *Titanic* movie by saying "The ship hits an iceberg and sinks!"

It's not only historical events that count as common knowledge for our purposes. Suppose that Adam feels romantic and takes Hannah to a new film version of *Romeo and Juliet*. Since it's common knowledge that both titular characters die in the end, Adam could comment on this without revealing a spoiler. So both historical fiction, such as *Pompeii*, and well-known works of fiction, such as *Romeo and Juliet*, are essentially spoiler-proof (or at least the parts of them that count as common knowledge are).

Historical fiction poses an interesting case. It seems clear that revealing historical events, such as Anne Boleyn gets beheaded in *The Tudors*, does not count as a spoiler. But what about less well-known events? *Boardwalk Empire*, for instance, is based loosely on real historical characters that were in and around Atlantic City during prohibition. The show's main character, Nucky Thompson, is based on real-life Atlantic City politician and mobster, Nucky Johnson. Facts about the life of Nucky Johnson, in contrast to Anne Boleyn, are not so well known. It seems that if someone were to assert that Nucky Johnson went to prison in 1941, and did so just before the show was to portray events as occurring in 1941, then a spoiler would have been revealed. The relevant criterion, again, is whether something counts as common knowledge. In turn, whether something counts as common knowledge, can vary from group to group. Folks my age tend to know more things about the cold war than do millennials, so my mentioning something about the cold war to one of my peers when discussing, say, *Apollo 13*, may not constitute a spoiler, but Jessa making the same statement to Hannah, might. We can easily imagine similar examples, not based on age, but based on geographic factors, political affiliation, the kind of work we do, and so forth. The bottom line here is that you probably ought to use your discretion, and err on the side of caution. It's the polite thing to do.

Sparing the Rod

We now have two necessary conditions for something to be considered a legitimate spoiler: 1. the thing being spoiled cannot be too old (with a few exceptions, as we've seen), and 2. the thing being spoiled can't be considered common knowledge. Are these conditions enough? Suppose that I report, to someone who had not yet seen the episode, that in the Season Three finale of *Girls* Marnie casually mentions to Ray that she left her phone at her apartment. Since the episode aired just a few weeks prior to this being written, and it's not common knowledge, both of our necessary conditions for something being a legitimate spoiler are met, and yet still it doesn't have the feel of being a legitimate spoiler. Nothing was spoiled. It's akin to finding out that your birthday present was wrapped (assuming you knew you weren't getting something non-wrappable, such as a trip, or eleven favors on demand, or a divorce); knowing that the present was wrapped does not ruin the surprise.

This presents a natural third condition—one that we've already hinted at. In order for you to reveal a legitimate spoiler you must be revealing something significant, and not merely mundane. Some surprise must be ruined, or a plot twist exposed, or a moment diminished (as in the example from above where a funny line from *Girls* might not have seemed so funny had I heard it in advance). Darth saying "Luke, I am your father" is a moment in a movie that can easily be spoiled. Shoshanna saying "I think it's time to unchoose some of those choices" is not.

I Make the Good *Girls* Go Bad

We now have enough to go on to answer our titular question: can *Girls* be spoiled? The answer is a heavily qualified "yes," but not in the traditional ways. *Girls*, at least at the time of this writing, meets our first two conditions for legitimate spoiling. The show is somewhere in the middle of its run, so it's fairly recent, and, for the most part, there is nothing in the show that is common knowledge (aside from a few mundane facts, such as Brooklyn is in New York, and brownstones are nice). So the critical condition for our purposes is the third one: the requirement that the thing being spoiled is significant.

Girls is a drama with the customary story arcs, plot twists and turns, and events in the lives of the main characters that are critical and, at times, even transformative. So it would appear to be ripe for spoiling, and yet, arguably, it isn't. *Girls* is a show about its characters, and their various predicaments, existential crises, and myriad struggles. The plot twists are merely incidental; they are a backdrop for the brilliant conversations, emotional meltdowns, and (intentionally) stupid observations of the main characters (Hannah, in particular).

Consider the main plot line of the show: Hannah and Adam's relationship. While we never know what will happen next with Hannah and Adam (they break up and get back together with great frequency), there's never any suspense about it. Whatever happens next is just whatever happens next. Knowing in advance that Hannah and Adam break up in a particular episode doesn't diminish the experience of watching the show.

We can contrast the presentation of the Hannah-Adam relationship with any number of television relationships that are played very differently. Consider, for example, Ross and Rachel, or Sam and Diane, or Buffy and Angel, or Buffy and Spike, or Ted and Robin. This list goes on and on. In each case people tuned in weekly to find out whether they would finally get together, or break up, or get back together, and so forth. People "ship" these characters. Alternatively, no one "ships" Hannah and Adam. The same holds true for Ray and Marnie, Ray and Shoshanna, Charlie and Marnie, and Jessa and Thomas-John. It is to the credit of *Girls* that relationships on this show are more than manipulative plot devices designed to coerce us into tuning in one more time.

The same applies to plot turns on *Girls* that don't involve relationships. For example, it's a major development for Adam's character that he goes from kinda likeable, yet still pervy, loser in Season One, to a Broadway actor who constitutes the closest thing the show has to a moral center by the end of Season Three, and yet if we knew in advance that these sorts of changes were going to occur, our viewing experience wouldn't be diminished. Again, the plot twists and turns of *Girls* are nothing more than opportunities for what the show's writers and producers really want to express: what it's like to be a millennial in New York City.

So, in the conventional sense, it's not possible to legitimately spoil *Girls*. There is one sense, however, in which it possible to spoil *Girls*, and that's by revealing the delightfully hilarious lines from the show. I'm tempted to reveal my very favorite line from the show, but I don't want to spoil it for you, so instead I'll just say this:

Yes Hannah, I do want you to eat all the foods!

II

Am I seriously the only one of us who prides herself on being a truly authentic person?

5

What *Girls* Teaches Us about Millennials and the Meaning of Life

Kimberly Blessing (GenXer) and
Samantha Wezowicz (Millennial)

Imagine a group of girls. They are white, privileged, narcissistic, slackers living in Brooklyn. They're facing cliché-ridden problems: sex, STDs, abortions, smothering boyfriends, gay boyfriends, drugs, being broke, careers, body image, and friendship. They include: an aspiring writer; a Bohemian nomad; a perky innocent; and a pretty-girl. What could these flawed anti-heroines tell us about life's meaning?

There are some things, such as graduating from Oberlin, that are more meaningful than others, like winning a game of pool. Meaningfulness, which varies and comes in degrees, is something that only applies to human life, ordinary or extraordinary. When we do consider human lives we might consider the whole life: Is Mother Teresa's life more or less meaningful than Hannah's? Or some part of that life, including an individual action or set of actions, project, or endeavor: Did the casual sex Jessa had with her former boyfriend (which poor Shoshanna was forced to witness) make Jessa's life more or less meaningful?

Being Stuck in My Own Head Is So Exhausting that It Makes Me Want to Cry

Socrates famously proclaimed that "The unexamined life is not worth living." In *Girls* there is a lot of self-analysis and navel-gazing. Not so much self-examination. Self-examination as Socrates meant it requires that you ask yourself whether or not your life is good or noble—one that's worthy of esteem or admiration. If you can answer "Yes," this might be one indication that your life is meaningful.

Religious folks, along with others who believe that human life is sacred or intrinsically valuable, would agree to disagree with Socrates. For even if your life is lacking meaning, it doesn't necessarily follow that you should end it now. Henry David Thoreau (1817–1862) reminds us that masses of people "lead lives of quiet desperation." But just because these desperate people might not end up doing something admirable and meaningful with their lives, doesn't mean their lives are not still worth living.

Lots of folks believe that being goal-driven, or purposeful, is necessary for meaningfulness. Evangelical pastor Rick Warren's self-help book, *The Purpose-Driven Life* (2002), which argues that meaning can be found by knowing God's plan for us here on Earth, is the second most translated book after the Bible. As of 2012 its English edition had sold over thirty million copies, which is a little less than the population of Canada. If we took God out of the picture, would any other plan suffice? Hitler realized a plan that was morally evil. Moreover lots of people have plans for their lives that are *non*-moral, like achieving greatness in the arts, intellect, or athletics.

It's All Hannah, All the Time

Of all the characters on the show Hannah is the most purposeful or goal-driven. She very clearly wants to become a writer: "I think I may be the voice of my generation. Or at least, *a* voice of *a* generation." Moreover Hannah wants to become a *successful* writer. Simply writing in her journal or starting a blog won't be enough to satisfy Hannah. Something like getting her e-book released would be a step in the right direction.

Throughout the first two seasons we see that Hannah is willing to do anything to be a successful writer. Even her mother, a professor living up in East Lansing, Michigan said "I cut her off so she'd have something to write about." To provide material for her writing, Hannah deliberately seeks outrageous experiences—snorting coke or joyfully letting it all hang out in a fishnet tee "It's Wednesday night baby, and I'm alive." At times she even manufactures events in order to have something to write about.

It's often the case, however, that Hannah ends up disappointing herself and others. This is because she can't find real value or meaning in what she's doing, real or manufactured. What's worse is that she harms others, mostly her friends and family, for "the sake of art." In Season One, Adam expresses the pain Hannah has caused him: "You don't want to know me. You want to come over in the night and have me fuck the dog shit out of you and then leave and write about it in your diary" ("Hard Being Easy"). Two seasons later, Hannah appears to be experiencing growth. Hannah and Adam are in the tub talking about Hannah's fear of Adam leaving her because of his new-found happiness.

ADAM: Are you upset I'm doing the play?

HANNAH: No. No. I'm so happy you're doing what makes you happy because I love you and you're the only person I've ever loved and you're the only person I wanna love, so . . .

ADAM: Well, ditto. ("Incidentals")

Still, there are shocking displays of Hannah's emotional callousness and indifference, such as when she learns of the death of her publisher. All she cares about is whether or not her e-book will still get published. "It's just crazy that you don't know the depth of someone's power until their funeral. It's so sad."

From Greek mythology, Narcissus was the one who looked into a pool of water and fell in love with his own image. Hannah's biggest character flaw, as with many other characters in *Girls*, is her selfishness and narcissism. Both are evidenced in her relentless pursuit of her noble, non-moral goal of being a writer. Hannah's neighbor Laird, a recovering heroin addict, gets it. "You are the most self-involved, presumptuous person I've ever met." Her gay ex-lover Elijah, who gave Hannah an STD and slept with Hannah's best friend Marnie, agrees, "We're just all living in Hannah's world! And it's all Hannah Hannah Hannah, all the time." Even sweet Shoshana has a breaking point.

SHOSHANNA: I'm talking about the fact that you're a fucking narcissist. Seriously, I have never met anyone else who thinks their own life is so fucking fascinating. I wanted to fall asleep in my own vomit all day listening to talk about how you bruise more easily than other people.

HANNAH: Are you serious?

SHOSHANNA: Mm-hmm.

HANNAH: Okay, well, people have been calling me a narcissist since I was three, so it doesn't really upset me. You've gotta choose something more creative.

Is That All There Is?

By Season Three, Hannah is closer to realizing her goal of being a successful writer. But even if achieving our goals improves our welfare, this is only one aspect of human welfare. Other things bring meaning to our lives, such as having healthy interpersonal relationships with family and friends. Moreover, if meaningfulness is to be found in terms of achievement, what happens once this is accomplished?

In an ancient myth, Sisyphus is condemned by the gods to roll a boulder up a mountain only to have it come back down every time he gets to the top of the mountain. How could such a pointless existence be considered meaningful? Let's imagine that Sisyphus was permitted to roll many rocks up the mountain, with the goal of creating a beautiful temple. Once he has completed his task, he sits back to admire his temple. But then there would be nothing left. Only infinite boredom (Taylor, *Good and Evil*, Chapter 18).

So, it can't be achievement alone that will make a life meaningful. This is because achievements are temporary. Once a goal has been realized, such as graduating from college, we set new goals like getting a job. Then getting married. Then having children. And so on. Leo Tolstoy (1828–1910) was a more accomplished writer than Hannah could ever hope to be. Yet he didn't find meaning in his accomplishments. This is the guy who wrote *War and Peace*! Instead Tolstoy worried that if it all comes to nothing in the end—if nothing is permanent or lasts forever—then how could anything, including a very significant accomplishment, be meaningful? (Tolstoy, "My Confession").

I'm an Individual and I Feel How I Feel when I Feel It

Unlike Hannah, Jessa seems indifferent to success or accomplishment. "All that matters are that your rising signs are compatible, the sex is decent, and he supports you creatively." Jessa is a free spirit, a Bohemian world-traveler who acts spontaneously, often recklessly, in her quest to "suck the marrow out of life." Marnie asks, "Since when is Jessa even a drug addict?" Hannah responds, "She's really just a life addict."

This life addict is motivated by getting high, be it life, cocaine, or self-destructive behavior. "I am going to look fifty when I'm thirty. I'm going to be so fucking fat, like Nico, and you know why? It's because I am going to be full of experience" ("It's A Shame about Ray")! Just like Hannah, there is not a line that Jessa won't cross in her unapologetic search for the next hit. Jessa's pursuit of pleasure prevents her from holding down a job. "You know what the weirdest part about having a job is? You have to be there every day, even on the days you don't feel like it." She is also easily bored. "I'm attracted to everyone when I first meet them. And then it wears off. It always wears off."

As Jessa's ex-babysitter employer Katherine is watching Jessa self-destruct, she assumes a motherly role, which Jessa is desperately lacking. "You're doing it [sleeping with unavailable men] to distract yourself from the person you are meant to be." Katherine has the courage to tell Jessa what she does not want to hear: eventually Jessa is going to have to emotionally connect with someone. In response to this advice Jessa did the most adult-thing she could come up with. Get hitched. She marries a virtual stranger, the unbelievably smarmy venture-capitalist Thomas-John, which comes as a huge surprise to her friends. Jessa explains she admires Thomas-John for everything he doesn't know about. Of course the marriage is doomed, and Jessa eventually walks out. But not until she swindles her husband out of thousands of dollars just to get her to leave. She also manipulates her grandmother into giving her money, but only if Jessa promises to go to rehab. Spoiler alert! Jessa eventually gets kicked out, this time for sleeping with another girl.

Free to Do What I Want

Unlike Hannah (and many of the other girls and boys on the show) Jessa thinks she has it all figured out. The pseudo-feminist who is in control of her own destiny, writing her own rules, making her own choices. "I'm offended by all of the supposed to's. I don't like women telling other women what to do or how to do it or when to do it." Perhaps Jessa read a little Friedrich Nietzsche (1844–1900) while she was attending Oberlin College. (Of course she dropped out.) Nietzsche thinks meaning arises from the creative, passionate *process* of an activity, not by achieving goals. Nietzsche also believes that to live meaningfully in a world of chaos, we have to accept that we are fragile beings and that everything is contingent. If you accept this line of thinking, and live in the moment with passion simply for what it is, as if you could repeat the same exact moment for eternity, then life can be meaningful (Belliotti, *What Is the Meaning of Human Life?*, pp. 36–45).

Just like Hannah, Jessa is a narcissist. Just like Hannah, this character flaw creates a distance between Jessa and people she cares about, whom Jessa mistreats and takes for granted. At the end of Season Two, there's a very poignant scene in which Hannah is suffering from a resurgence of her OCD, which, among other things, leads her to rupture her eardrums and cut off all of her hair. In desperation, Hannah calls her friend Jessa and gets her voicemail. "You've reached Jessa. I would never listen to a voicemail. But if you insist on trying . . ." We watch Hannah slowing falling apart as she leaves the following message for her deadbeat friend Jessa:

> You fucker. Are you kidding me? Where did you go?
> [*Begins Crying.*]
> And who am I supposed to talk to if you won't answer your fucking phone? That anorexic Marnie? I mean Shoshanna? Or my stalker ex-boyfriend? None of them want to talk to me [*screaming into the phone*] and I don't blame them. Because I cut off all my fucking hair!
> [*Voice is cracking*]
> And now you're out somewhere, living it up, wearing a crop top.
> [*Screaming*]

> You probably got your vagina pierced. You're not answering your
> phone and you're forgetting about *everyone* who's fucking it up
> here. So I hope you're having a GREAT time!
> [*Screams*]
> LOVE YOU!
> [*Hangs up*]

As the series unfolds we come to see that Jessa's reckless pursuit of freedom hardly ever results in her taking responsibility
for her actions, be it her various sexcapades with unavailable
men, or stealing money from her employer to buy cocaine. Like
any good hedonist, Jessa only cares about the next high.

Follow Your Bliss

Jessa's and Hannah's attitudes and actions illustrate a subjectivist viewpoint about meaning. Subjectivists believe that
meaningfulness depends on the subject. For Hannah, meaningfulness depends on realizing her goals, no matter the consequences. For Jessa, meaningfulness depends on the satisfaction
of her desires, consequences be damned. Returning to the Myth
of Sisyphus let's imagine that the gods took pity and injected
Sisyphus with a drug that gave him the desire to roll rocks up
a hill only to have them fall down again. The pointless nature
of his existence remains the same, but now Sisyphus *wants* to
do this. The fact that he is following through on what he wants
or desires makes this pointless task meaningful (Taylor, *Good
and Evil*, Chapter 18).

Advocates of meaningfulness in terms of desire-satisfaction,
which is a very popular theory about meaningfulness, argue
that we can find meaning in life or activities if we are passionately interested or invested in them. Accordingly it is up to you,
the individual subject, to discover what is in your nature to do,
which will be different for each life or subject. "Yeah, but you
know what, Adam? I don't *want* to do it. And it's really liberat-
ing to say no to shit you hate. So you can go ahead. [*Yells*] *You
live your truth. I'll be here living my truth*."

Once you find your passion, you will find meaning in your
life. In other words, you can find anything meaningful because
it is up to you, the subject, to invest your lives and actions with
meaning.

The Excrement-Eating Fool

What if we were to compare a world-class pianist to an excrement-eater? Imagine they are both grinning widely. No matter how great his passion, no matter how big his grin as he spoons it down, the excrement eater should be an object of pity rather than envy, argues Erik Wielenberg. Thus meaning-objectivists argue that there are some things—no matter how deep your investment or lively your passion—that would never be considered meaningful. Who wants to eat *shite*?

Eating excrement is an extreme example. It might be that none of the characters on *Girls* are passionate about something that is so, how shall we say, distasteful. But we do see that both Hannah and Jessa engage in behaviors that are reckless (such as casual sex and drug use) and just plain wrong (lying, stealing, using or abusing friends and family). If you don't have an overarching structure or theory of meaningfulness, a meaningful life reduces to nothing more than an engaged life in which you are committed to certain projects you make your own, regardless of the moral status of the projects (Cottingham, *On the Meaning of Life*). It wouldn't matter that Hannah-the-writer is a selfish friend and lover. Or that Jessa-the-free-spirit lies to get what she wants.

Some people who believe that meaningfulness is objective, not subjective, claim that religion can provide such an overarching structure or theory. From a religious point of view humans will find fulfillment in lives and projects that are morally good. It's not that religion provides life with purpose and fulfillment that matters, because this could be accomplished from a subjectivist or atheistic point of view. Instead religion does guarantee that you will find your purpose and fulfillment in something which is inherently good. Subjectivists (like Nietzsche or Taylor) can't guarantee that whatever choices you make will be morally good choices, however purposeful and passionate you may be.

Religious folks believe in the power of goodness, a kind of "cosmic optimism." It's not glass-half-full-turn-that-frown-upside-down kind of optimism. It's that you have trust and confidence that even in the darkest moments of suffering and sorrow it all means something in the end. People who believe that meaning is purely subjective have to bite the bullet and admit that against all your best efforts towards living meaningfully, you could end up being cosmically screwed!

Loving That Which Is Worthy of Being Loved

That may all be well and good, but some readers are not religious. In fact religion never comes up on *Girls*, which might reflect the fact that the majority of Millennials don't identify themselves as religious. Susan Wolf's theory, presented in her book *Meaning in Life and Why It Matters*, is compatible with a religious point of view, but she herself rejects that point of view as implausible.

Wolf argues that meaningfulness requires a subjective as well as an objective element: "Meaning arises when subjective attraction meets objective attractiveness" (p. 9). This hybrid view is expressed in a pithy slogan: meaningfulness amounts to "loving objects that are worthy of love" (8). Wolf thinks that meaningfulness requires an objective component because she believes that there are certain projects and not others that are "fitting for fulfillment," or worthy of love. No human being should be fulfilled eating excrement. Moreover being fulfilled or satisfied isn't all there is to meaningfulness. For it also matters what *kinds* of actions and projects you choose.

It may sound as if Wolf wants to have her cake and eat it too. But her hybrid theory of meaningfulness presents one way to examine our lives and actions. Love, which requires both subject and object, plays a central role in Wolf's theory. Does Jessa (subject) love Thomas-John? Is Thomas-John (object) lovable? Does Hannah (subject) love working at Café Grumpy? Is this job (object) worthy of her love, given her talents and abilities? If Jessa or Hannah would answer "no" to one or both of these questions, then it may help to explain why the relationship or job in question lacks meaning.

Examined Living

It seems safe to conclude that Hannah's and Jessa's lives are not as meaningful as they could be. The lack of meaning in their lives probably has a lot to do with the fact that neither of them is living an examined life. Because Hannah and Jessa are so self-absorbed, they spend a lot of time analyzing themselves and their actions. This is not the same thing as critical examination.

Examined living is not about mere desire-satisfaction or the pursuit of pleasure. Instead examined living is not always easy or pleasant. Among other things, it requires sacrifice, facing fears, acting with courage, being vulnerable, exercising restraint. And examined living isn't about trying to "become who you are," as if there will be one magical moment in time when you "arrive." Instead examined living is ongoing. It's a life-long process.

This kind of life isn't simply about accomplishments or achievements. But that doesn't mean that you can't have definite goals and live purposefully. It's okay to want to succeed. One of the tricks is to make sure that your goals reflect your desires, and that you approach them with passion. You have to be authentic.

Being Your True Self

Examined living makes it possible to live authentically. Authentic living requires that you choose actions that endorse your own goals. Your goals reflect your unique situation (desperate or otherwise). In *Justice for Hedgehogs*, Ronald Dworkin says that you need to accept a "special, personal responsibility for identifying what counts as success" in your own life. *You* are then responsible for creating that life "through a coherent narrative." An authentic life is not something that's given to you. You have to *create* it for yourself.

Crafting a life narrative—your story—will help to unify your various life projects and goals. It will also help you to achieve "conscious consistency" in your life and social interactions. "Conscious consistency" just means that you are always aware of and working on your narrative. Like any good story or narrative, events, plot, and characters don't just come together by chance or accident. The author has to thoughtfully put all these parts together in a way that makes sense, or has meaning.

The most important aspect of authenticity requires that you assume responsibility for yourself *and* for the consequences that your freely chosen actions have on others. To do otherwise is to be inauthentic, or as Jean-Paul Sartre puts it, to live in "bad faith." In *Existentialism Is a Humanism*, Sartre claims that "bad faith" is a form of "self-deception," or a lie that is fueled by a person's ego. This lie that you tell yourself involves ignoring the freedom you have to be authentic or to change.

Hannah and Jessa lack authenticity. Jessa presents herself to the world as a tough, independent, carefree emotional nomad. We come to realize that this is merely a persona that Jessa has created because of her inability to emotionally connect with other human beings. This purposeless persona is not her true self. Hannah thinks she is authentic. "Am I seriously the only one of us who prides herself on being a truly authentic person?" But hers is a phony narrative. While Jessa manufactures a persona as a shield against experiencing reality, Hannah manufactures events to provide her writing material. Both are recipes for disaster.

What This All Means for Millennials, Written by a Millennial

For as long as we can remember we were told that if we are going to amount to anything, we "need to go to college." During our four (or six or so) years in college we accumulate massive amounts of debt. Diplomas in hand, we're released into the "real world." In a depressed economy that offers us few jobs and opportunities we're expected to support ourselves financially.

Growing up, we were told "you are special" by our teachers and parents who grew up watching *Mr. Rogers*. We were encouraged to "follow our dreams." "Be yourself." Every step of the way we were celebrated—getting awards for simply showing up. However, despite all the praise from our teachers and parents who encouraged us to become confident and successful individuals, we became resentful of the whole system. We redefined "success." We crave new and different experiences.

We grew up watching *The Real World,* and listening to Snoop Dogg tell us to "Drop It Like It's Hot." (My co-author has no idea what this means.) Internet celebrities taught us that it doesn't take much to become famous, if not rich. We began tinkering with, in some cases exploiting, our identities through Facebook. We make ourselves feel good relative to the number of people who follow us on Twitter. Ubiquitous exposure to technology changed how we socialize and what we value. Friends are like family. Hooking-up is the norm. Drinking and drugs are considered "recreation." And we have nothing to regret. YOLO. (Again, she has no idea what I'm talking about.)

Unfortunately Hannah and Jessa represent a large segment of Millennials. Sad to say, I know some of these girls. Fortunately, however, Hannah is only *a* voice who doesn't speak for an entire generation.[1] Some of us are different. We are striving to live examined lives. We care about authenticity. We take responsibility for our actions, and care about how our words and actions affect others.

Look, I'm not saying I've got this all figured out. I'm far from perfect. But when I am on my deathbed I want to be able to look back and think my life was worthwhile. Hannah says, "I just hope when I die that I don't see it coming. I hope I'm already dead and then five minutes later I'm like what the fuck? What just happened?"

I doubt that death comes that quickly or easily. Instead most of us will have time to ask, "Was mine a good and noble life—worthy of esteem and admiration?" "Was my life meaningful?" I'm not sure that Hannah and Jessa would be able to answer "yes." Sadly, I don't think they even care.

---

[1] My co-author wants me to point out that she agrees that these characters in *Girls* don't seem to reflect most of the young women whom she gets to know through her teaching.

6
Jessa the Existentialist

CHELSI BARNARD ARCHIBALD

Jessa Johannson does not allow the mandates of society to guide her experience, but lives authentically in the moment, no matter the consequences. She embraces the absurd and continuously accepts the meaninglessness of life.

Jessa embodies the ideal preached by the existentialist writer Søren Kierkegaard. Kierkegaard believed that an individual is solely responsible for bringing meaning to their life and living it as authentically as possible. With passion, sincerity, and above all authenticity, the individual creates values through complete consciousness.

Where most women would be emotionally affected by the decision to get an abortion, Jessa doesn't seem to see the situation as inherently good or inherently bad. Her relationship to her parents is static, emotionless, and arbitrary. It is a systematic traditional connection only perpetuated by society. More significantly, Jessa is a perfect example of what existentialists call "facticity," in that she does not blame her past for her choices, even though it's often implied throughout the series that Jessa has had a rough background and many "experiences" as she often refers to them.

Jessa's ability to stay personally driven and integrally subjective, embracing as the existentialist Albert Camus puts it, the "devastating awareness" of the meaninglessness of life, and then living it honestly, is how Jessa is able to survive the seemingly difficult environment of her early twenties, amidst societal expectations and the pressures of personal fulfillment.

An Authentic Life

The decision to have an abortion is something that remains highly controversial for most individuals in society. But the cleverness of the show's writing provided viewers with their first introduction to Jessa's character through this very fitting act. Only Jessa could take on such a thing in a perfectly subjective way, something crucial within the existential philosophy. To remain subjective, an individual guides her own experience without any influence or pressure from society. This is what constitutes an authentic life. This attitude sets Jessa up as the quintessential existentialist of the show.

Viewers are introduced to her by way of her younger, more worry-driven and anxiety-ridden American cousin, Shoshanna. It's implied that Jessa has arrived from months of travel in Europe, something frequent in her life. Shoshanna is enamored with the idea that Jessa doesn't even have a Facebook account, a thought that seems nearly impossible by today's popular youth standards.

We get the sense that Jessa is a nomad and tends not to stay long in one area. This is so evident that when she is first introduced viewers are never sure whether she's a main character of the show or someone who might come and go throughout various episodes. Both of these assumptions hold true. Jessa is indeed a main character, but the very essence of her spirit is to remain in action, mobile, and unable to be placed within a specific construct. There are large blocks of time in the series where Jessa is nowhere to be found and characters like Hannah speak of her as though she were a ghost.

The biological father of the fetus is never identified, but this remains unimportant. What is important is the reaction Jessa has to getting a possible abortion. Hannah Horvath, her longtime friend from Oberlin College, is worried after Shoshanna quotes a dating book in front of the girls on the day of Jessa's scheduled procedure.

The book advises that allowing a man to have sex with you from behind is degrading. Jessa is appalled by this assumption saying, "What if I want to feel like I have udders?" The very thought of societal construct or expectation as to what a women should expect or feel sexually, bothers Jessa and she rejects it entirely. To Jessa, the action of sexual experience is to feel and to be ever conscious of those feelings, no matter how odd or different they may be seen by society.

Hannah assumes that this elicits guilt in Jessa for considering an abortion and that she needs to talk about her feelings. Jessa rejects this notion immediately.

"I'm offended by all the 'supposed to's'. I don't like women telling other women what to do or how to do it or when to do it. Every time I have sex it's my choice . . ." says Jessa.

"Are you scared?" asks Hannah. "No," says Jessa.

"Are you angry?" says Hannah. "Who would I be angry at?" Jessa says.

"Maybe you're a little angry at yourself," Hannah says. "No," says Jessa.

Authenticity is the degree to which any individual is true to her own personality, spirit, or character. Jessa is able to maintain her authenticity despite external pressures and influences throughout her life. Authenticity is not necessarily a set of rules or tenets to follow, but rather all that is not a rule or code. It is that which exists outside of any preconceived notion of expectation in regards to society as a whole. It is not attached to any particular political or aesthetic ideology and cannot be arrived at by simply repeating a ritual or set of actions or taking up a set of positions.

Jessa recognizes the world around her as being both meaningless and absurd. She projects a sense of disorientation and confusion upon hearing the so-called advice from the dating book concerning sexuality or even the suggestion by Hannah that she would have an emotional response to being pregnant and needing an abortion. Jessa goes to a bar in lieu of the procedure and has sex with a stranger. She finds out during the sex act that she no longer needs the procedure as she has just started her period.

The Ever-important Individual

According to existentialism, each person is an individual, an independently acting, responsible, conscious being, rather than a label, a statistic, or a preconceived category (such as student, woman, slut, virgin, or abortion patient). Jessa recognizes that traditional roles are too abstract and remote from her experience as a human being.

For Jessa, an abortion is neither inherently good nor inherently bad. Since human beings can choose to act either cruelly or benevolently, they are then neither of those things essentially, and therefore an action like abortion is in itself neither good nor bad. The idea that there is no meaning in the world beyond what meaning an individual gives it was advanced by Albert Camus. This encompasses amorality—the absence of, indifference towards, or disregard for morality itself. Briefly stated, life is only unfair as much as people assume it is, when in reality life just *is* and nothing more.

This idea goes against the notion that "bad things happen to good people." In the world according to an existentialist, there is no such thing as good people or bad people or good events or bad events. Events just happen, to both good and bad people alike, because life is inherently meaningless.

Individuals like Jessa live by a set of amoral observations, which allow them to create their own value system and to always be brutally honest with themselves. In the episode, "Role Play," Shoshanna finds her drug-relapsed cousin sitting near an alleyway smoking a cigarette and tells her that she "looks like a junkie"; Jessa makes sure to correct her by saying, "I am a junkie." It's essential that each individual human being, through their own consciousness, self-awareness, or the idea they have of themselves, creates their own values and determines meaning in their life, no matter what. This requires firm unwavering vigilance and truth with the self.

According to Sartre, all existentialists accept the premise that "Existence precedes essence." In other words, humans come into existence without having any predetermined function or purpose. Your life is what you make of it—this is not decided for you. The actual life of an individual is what denotes their "true essence" rather than any arbitrarily attributed "essence" others may use to define them.

Kierkegaard takes this further by stating, "The crowd is untruth," meaning that in living by the social mores of the crowd the voice of the individual is not heard and the individual is reduced to merely a fraction of a whole rather than an true individual. The actions of the crowd do not lay blame on any one individual, thus no individual feels the need to be personally responsible. Only the overt singularity of the individual's existence and a conscious resolute conflict with the will and belief of the crowd is the driving force in staying truly authentic.

To an existentialist like Jessa, a complete rejection of any and all philosophies of life jars her out of a false reality over and over again. It's Jessa's own personal recognition of nothingness that dictates her actions and no one else's, not even the society of which she is surrounded and bombarded by or the supposed standards which are ever perpetuated through conformity. Her diligent cognizance of the absurd is crucial to maintaining her own unique essence.

An Impetus to Action

Most importantly, according to Sartre, an impetus to action must arise from the individual in question and can never be externally imposed upon them. No one individual can be forced upon this journey, they must consciously choose to live it themselves. The very idea of action is something that defines Jessa's character. If she feels like traveling to Europe, she simply does it and usually at a moment's notice.

In the episode "Females Only," Jessa's friend Jasper hypothesizes about her while they are in a rehab treatment program. "You have the accent of a little girl who grew up somewhere between Heathrow and JFK . . . Wisdom comes from experience. And I suspect you've had many, many experiences. Too many, probably, for someone of your age."

Jessa replies, "I've had fun."

Jasper quips, "But it wasn't always fun, was it?"

"No," says Jessa.

It's essential that an individual focus intently on having an authentic life because it concerns that person's relation with the world. It is only through a unique discovery of the absurd from moment to moment that the individual can stay completely awake. For Jessa, even when engaging in the acts of taking drugs and having sex, experiencing the world is an act of staying conscious, questioning, and remaining perpetually aware. An individual must avoid slipping into meaningless behavior, which does not coordinate with their own prescribed value system.

The most important value for Jessa is action. She is defined so far as she is acting. And she is alone responsible for her own actions at all times. Unfortunately for Jessa, this can sometimes lead to brief moments of angst when coming up against the reactions of those around her. After being fired from a nannying job because her boss's husband attempts to initiate an affair with her, Jessa is confronted by her employer Katherine, who says, "I feel like I want to help you, like I want to be your mother."

"But I don't need your help," says Jessa.

"I bet you get into these dramas all the time . . . where you cause all this trouble and you've no idea why. In my opinion, you're doing it to distract yourself from the person you're meant to be," says Katherine.

"Which is who?" asks Jessa.

In Jessa's mind, she doesn't see these alleged causations of drama as part of her value system. They are merely events which have occurred along the perpetual journey in the acceptance of an absurd world. An explanation by Katherine of who Jessa can or should be means nothing to her because it does not align with the self she has consciously created. She's willing to deal with the consequences, such as being fired from the job, but not willing to accept the blame or responsibility someone else might attempt to place upon her.

However, this particular event seems to spark some type of "bad faith" in Jessa in which she hurriedly marries a man she recently met. Initially, Jessa finds Thomas-John boring and makes fun of his lifestyle and penchant for material things, but after Marnie initiates a sexual make out session, Jessa rises to the occasion and becomes intrigued with the entire experience. A few days later, and with the influence of Katherine's words in the back of her mind, she decides to act impulsively and marry Thomas-John.

Jean-Paul Sartre and Simone de Beauvoir were two philosophers who described an act of "bad faith" as pressure from societal forces to adopt false values and to disown your innate freedom and responsibility to act authentically. Angst is a form of anxiety, dread, or anguish with negative feelings arising from experiences of freedom and responsibility. Jessa's tryst with her former employer could be seen as a brief moment of angst. Thus, she is propelled into entering an inauthentic marriage in a moment of panic. What initially was an attempt to stay ceaselessly in action, in reality lacked the scrupulous thought required to maintain her authentic journey.

However, Jessa acknowledges her mistake within a few short weeks of the marriage ceremony. It's important that when experiencing angst, individuals rise to the occasion and correct their course lest they fall into "philosophical suicide" as Camus puts it, a fate far worse than actual death.

This perplexes her mother-in-law in the episode "It's a Shame About Ray." She wonders how Jessa has the means to travel without a job or source of income. She then infers that Jessa married her son Thomas-John, an affluent venture capitalist, solely for his money. Jessa then reveals that she left college after seven months so she could check into rehab for a heroin addiction. When the couple returns home, Thomas-John is upset about the exchange to which Jessa replies, "What was I supposed to do, lie?"

To Jessa, the very idea of lying is more unthinkable than heroin addiction. Jessa attempts to explain this value system to Thomas-John by stating, "You think you're such a free spirit because you shacked up with me for two months? I've been living this way for twenty-five fucking years. I'm going to look fifty when I'm thirty. I'm going to be so fucking fat like Nico. And you know why? That's because I'm going to be full of experiences."

At the end of the episode we infer that Jessa's marriage is over as Thomas-John offers to pay her a dividend and entice her to leave the relationship. It's more important for Jessa to live truthfully, even if it displeases her husband or his parents. Kierkegaard would agree that a societal construct like marriage might not align with your authentic values. Kierkegaard often rejected religious and societal virtues due to a lack of questioning by the individual when faced with the institutional pressure to fit in and do their duty.

When her father-in-law says he's grateful that the Lord was looking out for her during her heroin addiction Jessa replies, "I wish there was a Lord, but I know there isn't." Kierkegaard states that bourgeois religious organizations block true experiences and furthermore, block any potentiality for authentic thought. He also goes on to say that there is no comprehensible purpose in God, which makes the very act of faith in God absurd. However, Camus reminds us that although embracing the absurd does not lead to the belief in a God it does not necessarily lead to unbelief either. In *The Myth of Sisyphus* he states, "I did not say 'excludes God', which would still amount to asserting."

Facticity and the Past

Because of the world's absurdity at any given moment in time, anything can happen to anyone, and a horrific event can force someone to be in direct confrontation with the absurd. This creates a devastating awareness of the meaningless of life. Jessa's continual struggle with addiction is something that forces her to come into contact with the absurd, which she willingly meets head on.

In the episode "Females Only," she is participating in group work at her rehabilitation program when she points out inauthentic behavior in her peers. After laughing at one man for crying about a Fro-Yo opening up on his block and changing the predictability of his world, the councilor asks her to express her own feelings.

"What do you want? Do you want me to cry? Is that what you want? It's really exhausting and boring. I figured my shit out when I was five years old. Heroin is really fun. But it can also kill you," Jessa says.

Jessa rejects the act of "leveling" which Kierkegaard sees as the uniqueness of an individual being rendered non-existent by an assumption that individual behavior is equated to all human beings, a cohort group, or a peer group. In order to achieve authentic faith, you must face reality, making a conscious choice and then passionately sticking with it. To face reality is to form your own opinions of existence, no matter how often they're questioned or criticized.

In the episode "Video Games," Jessa admits to being possibly molested as a child at one point or another, but doesn't name the culprit or dwell on the subject and states this to Hannah in a matter-of-fact fashion. Later on, when she addresses her father and they speak of their relationship issues he says, "We're not like other people." Jessa does have similarities with her father in that he has been to multiple rehabs, often disappears without any notice, and has started many different relationships and families. Jessa seems to accept this truth and does not assign blame to him for what other people assume are problems in her life.

Thus when a fellow rehab patient named Laura says, "I am a victim of circumstances," Jessa scoffs at this and outs her as a lesbian. "I feel like you are using being molested as an excuse. We can't go around blaming other people for our shit behavior," Jessa says. Later on, she sneaks into Laura's room and initiates her first lesbian encounter saying it was a "charity" offered to make her feel more authentic. The rehab director kicks her out and asks her if she feels any remorse for hurting Laura's rehabilitation process to which Jessa replies, "You can't make things that mean nothing mean something."

It is clear at this point in the series that Jessa is displaying facticity, a term that for Sartre means the mode of not being. To him, the past is a temporal dimension of time and does not constitute the self. The present and the future are the large majority of a life any individual may live and are most important in keeping with authenticity, thereby any attempts to blame the past for your behavior is inauthentic. However, a complete denial of the past creates inauthentic life as well. Thus Jessa readily admits her past in a factual manner but at no point does she place blame on it.

Freedom in the Void

Camus warns that there will always be a conflict between the human tendency to seek inherent value and meaning in life and the human inability to find any meaning no matter how hard they may try. The efforts of humanity to continuously find meaning will ultimately fail due to an abundance of information available as well as the vastness of the universe and the unknown. It is therefore impossible to garner any certain answers to life's biggest questions.

The ultimate conundrum is the individual search for meaning versus the utter meaninglessness of the universe. This is the confrontation of an individual's desire for significance, meaning, and clarity while staring the silent, cold universe in the face. For Jessa, this always implies action. Action anchors her in consciousness and allows her to avoid complacency.

After leaving rehab, relapsing on cocaine with Jasper, and being fired from yet another job, Jessa forces herself into withdrawals and begins consciously living yet again. She meets

Beadie, a disabled artist-photographer who is showing her work at a new gallery where Marnie has recently become employed. Beadie needs someone to help archive the massive collection of photographs she has in her home. When she asks Jessa what she truly thinks of one of the photographs Marnie wasn't willing to give a straight answer about, Jessa tells her the brutal truth and Beadie is so impressed that she hires her on the spot.

The two women become close and Beadie admits that she hates her existence and wishes to die. Camus argues in *The Myth of Sisyphus* that "there is only one really serious philosophical question, and that is suicide." To Camus, this is a confession on the part of an individual that life is not worth living because of its absurdity. It is a choice that implicitly declares that life is too much to handle and that the most basic way out of absurdity is the termination of the self and its place in the universe.

After Beadie finds out that Jessa can get her the drugs required to die, she asks her to assist in her suicide. Jessa protests at first, but realizes that it isn't up to her because it is not her life or her value system. She understands Beadie's loss at having to face the absurd and wants to help her live authentically. "I hired you because I thought you were the only person who would see how necessary this was," Beadie says. Jessa goes through with helping Beadie take the drugs and they wait together for her to die. At the last minute, Beadie changes her mind and demands that Jessa call 911, which she does immediately and the Season Three finale comes to a close.

Camus offers a solution to individuals who choose to continue living life despite its apparent absurdity and meaninglessness. An individual can choose to embrace their own absurd condition by accepting their freedom and the opportunity to give life meaning. This lies in the incessant recognition of the absurd. The absurd experience is truly the realization that the universe is fundamentally devoid of absolutes. Only when individuals can acknowledge this will they truly be free.

"To live without appeal" is Camus's philosophical move to define absolutes and universals in subject terms. This is a move to create your own meaning and purpose and to decide to think for your self. If an individual like Jessa or Beadie, can effectively be free in embracing the absurd, then that individual becomes the most precious unit of existence. They become a unique set of ideals that can be characterized as an entire universe all their own. In acknowledging the absurdity of seeking any inherent meaning, but still continuing the search regardless of this knowledge, one can be happy by simply developing meaning from the very search itself.

Camus makes sure to separate hope from authentic living. When you hopes for nothing, you fear nothing, and only when you fear nothing, not even the absurdity of life, are you truly free. By not having hope you're motivated to live every moment to its fullest.

Jessa is now faced with another possible consequence of living authentically. While she may very well serve jail time for her assistance in Beadie's near-suicide, Jessa still remains virtuous in following her own value system, rigidly, consciously, ever embracing the meaninglessness of life and stubbornly deciding to carry on anyway.

7
Can Hannah Rewrite Her World?

HAYLEY ADDIS

I almost joined Hannah when she cried at her desk. You remember when she realizes that the other advertising writers in her new job have allowed their dreams of writing creatively to die in favor of a job that pays the bills? And then recognizes that she's about to do the very same thing because, really, we all need to eat? I genuinely shed a tear.

Why do we end up neglecting our dreams in favor of a creatively empty paycheck? It got me thinking (I can't help it, I'm a philosopher . . .) about whether we can write our way into a better life like Hannah wants to.

Hannah is a writer. She's a writer who actually writes, no less. Writing is her dream and when we start the show she's already pursuing a career in it, although she is getting nowhere. Hannah is tenacious, however, and even when her parents cut her off in the very first episode she declares herself to be the "voice of a generation. Or, at least, *a* voice of *a* generation." If she's the voice of a generation—and, as a twenty-something girl myself, I suspect Lena Dunham is hinting that Hannah is writing about the generation we both live in—then it's very telling that her writing is entirely self-obsessed biography. Is that really our generation?

My favorite philosopher, Heidegger, agrees with Lena on this one; our generation is a product of a culture which he describes as being badly in the habit of *"enframing,"* which means that we see everything only in terms of how it benefits us and we look at other things (and people) as what we can get out of them. Heidegger was worried that a technological culture was developing to make *enframing* even easier than it is already, and that we'd then completely forget how to relate to other beings in a way that was healthy. Sadly I think he was right and Hannah, bless her, shows us this so clearly! (Heidegger was originally writing in German and did strange things with language to show his readers a new way of thinking, which English translators have then had fun with, hence odd words like 'enframing'.)

Hannah's World

I've already called her writing self-obsessed, and it is that way because *Hannah* is. The amazing New York swirls around Hannah, and she doesn't even notice! She asks a recovering junkie to get her drugs so she can have an experience to write about—and then blames her best friend Marnie for ruining the experience because Marnie once slept with Hannah's very-*ex*-boyfriend. At a funeral Hannah interrupts the grieving widow to ask about publishers, she steals a story about someone else's "cousin" dying from cancer to prove she has compassion and to hide her lack of empathy, and she doesn't once appear to consider the impact these actions have on the other people involved. Even the book she is writing is all about her experiences, because this is the whole of her *world*.

Heidegger uses the term "world" in a technical way but he is talking about exactly what you'd expect if I said: "Hannah's in her own little world!" (She really is!) Her "*world*" includes all of the things she interacts with, experiences, *and* all the relationships she has with those things *and* all the relationships she has with other people *and* all the meanings which are wrapped up in all these things, people and relationships for her. Like Hannah, we each live in our own *world* and our worlds expand and change as our relationships change. This is an important idea because we humans have spent a long time trying to understand what makes us human and what kind of world we live in, and Heidegger takes us back to basics in a way that revolutionizes philosophy: our *world* is simply where we live and everything we interact with, including intangible things.

As far as Heidegger is concerned the *world* isn't something we can doubt, as the Skeptics say, and it isn't just "matter" or "extension" as some philosophers argue. Our *world* is, most importantly, where we live, and we live in our relationships. Hannah is as affected by the relationships she does have and the meanings she finds in them as she is by the physical flat she calls home, if not more. If she didn't invest a lot more meaning in the title "writer" than thinking of it only as a description of an activity she enjoys and wants to make money from, she wouldn't have brought herself, or me, to tears in that episode! Her *world* therefore includes the importance she places in having the identity "writer." Even with all these components her *world* is small, however, because she relates to everything purely in relation to how it reinforces her all-important identity as "writer" and even her friends are extensions of who she is.

I'm the Good Friend!

Hannah's insistence that she is the good friend when she argues catastrophically with best-friend Marnie comes from the *enframing* of her *world*. Hannah can't see Marnie as the person she is, as her entire *world* revolves around herself and she doesn't understand that her view of the relationships in that *world* is not the entire picture. Hannah's relationship to her boyfriend Adam is the same; she is surprised to discover that he is a recovering alcoholic. "You never asked." He tells her in response, and she really hasn't. Her *world* is tiny and does not connect well with the *worlds* of others, which is not how we normally exist at all! When our *worlds* meet they connect up and we live together with each other in a collective *world*. We share stories and experiences, we relate to things in similar ways and we relate to others as people with their own *worlds*.

Adam, Marnie, and others point out to Hannah that she is strange. They recognize her way of existing in the *world* as weird, and even more dysfunctional than their own. This is why Hannah is so fascinating to watch—aside from the fact that we desperately want her to reach her dreams, not least because it would give us hope that reaching our own dreams is possible—she shows us a world that is both alien and familiar to us. Our natural tendency towards *enframing* (because we need to use things to survive) is taken to an extreme in Hannah. If she doesn't monetize her experiences, for example, she won't be able to buy any more food (not that she needs to, with the free snack table . . .) but the extent she takes it to also gets in the way of her engaging in relationships and existing with other people in the way that we naturally do. We are social animals and so to be so self-absorbed cuts us off from others and leaves us hurting.

The stress of writing to a deadline and the fact that she is writing about herself encourages Hannah to cut herself off from the larger *world* even more than usual and she does serious damage to herself—ending up in a hospital with a punctured eardrum! I'm sure we all recognize the isolation and focus that comes with pursuing a project that we are passionate about all too well, but we also recognize that the inability to relate to others as people with their own lives is not normal!

New York, New York

We are creatures with our own worlds, which are part of the whole collective world, and because of this we are constantly living and acting in relationship to other entities—including other people, things, feelings and events. When we cut ourselves off like Hannah we end up damaged! *Enframing*, then, is a seriously bad thing.

Heidegger reckoned that enframing could be undone by art because art shows us other entities in the world as they are. Watching the show, *we* can't use the dress that Marnie wears to Booth's party to dress ourselves up, so to engage with the artwork that is *Girls* we have to look at the dress as something with its own life—it represents something to Marnie, it says something to the other party goers and it means beauty or ridiculousness to us, telling us something about Marnie's state of mind, and our own. We aren't sat on the pile of take-away boxes with her in Hannah's story, so we have to relate to them as something that has a meaning and a story to tell in themselves; that some humans are slobs and by ending up with one she has fallen into a bad place! By doing this the stories and paintings open windows into other people's (and object's) *worlds* and our *world* expands. Hannah, however, refuses to engage with art outside her own creation like this, so she can't get outside her own *world*. Her *world* stays tiny.

Hannah has the whole of New York to explore, we see glimpses of whole *worlds* of people with stories to tell, art to share, and lives Hannah could join in with. But she doesn't.

Marnie, on the other hand, does. Marnie goes to parties and mixes with others, she listens to another friend, Ray, when he suggests she should chase her stated dream of being a singer and she opens doors for herself with that singing. Another *world* became possible with that first performance at Charlie's party in order to bring him back into her life. Regardless of the fact she ended up moping when he then turns ex again and puts an embarrassing video of her singing online (and refuses to take it down), her *world* has changed.

Marnie listened to Ray as a person with opinions, he listened to her as a person with dreams. They engaged with each other as individuals with their own lives and *worlds* and those worlds changed. Especially later when Ray is delayed from his basketball match . . . but that's another tale. The important thing here is that creativity allowed Marnie to expand the horizons of her *world*, because she did something outside of her previous experiences (she sang in public) and she connected with another being (Ray). Hannah's horizons do not expand because she turns inwards and repeats those experiences through her writing (probably eight times) rather than looking beyond them.

New experiences and relationships aren't quite enough to defeat extreme enframing, though, probably because it's a useful thing to do, at least up to a point. Hannah moved to New York to gain experiences which she could then share with others through her writing, but experiences alone are not enough. It is all in the attitude. Or the shirt.

I Don't Think I've Ever Seen Adam with a Shirt on Before . . .

The first time we see Adam outside of his flat is the first time we see him with a shirt on, and by the sound of it it's also the first time Hannah sees him with a shirt on, interacting with other people or, well, outside of his flat. Heaven knows how they met! At this moment Hannah's *world* does expand slightly as Adam's existence as a person with his own life (and a wardrobe) becomes clear. Her relationship to him changes along with her understanding of him as not only existing for her pleasure (or displeasure). She fights against this but it's too late, she will always have seen him in relation with the girls he was dancing with and so it has become possible to recognize him as having a life outside of their encounters, and impossible to un-recognize it!

The lack of control we have over the facts of the world we find ourselves in is what Heidegger describes as *thrownness*, which implies that we've been tossed into a space and have to get our bearings. As we're always *thrown*—it's part of our nature—we are constantly responding to the *world* around us, which in turn shapes it further. So when Jessa invites everyone to the biggest party of their lives, they are *thrown* to discover it is her wedding, *thrown* into a situation where they can only respond as best they can. Shoshanna is terribly upset by this as, not knowing, she wore white to someone else's wedding! *World* as the sum of all *worlds* is outside of our control. Hannah couldn't control Adam's appearance, Shoshanna couldn't change the fact that she made a wardrobe blunder, Marnie couldn't stop Charlie leaving after he read Hannah's journal entries about him. Each of them may have chosen to go to the wedding, but they were already *thrown* into a *world* where the wedding was happening, and where the expectation was there for them to turn up as invited.

When Charlie leaves the flat he, Hannah, and Marnie share, he takes the coffee table he made with him. The appearance and disappearance of this table is only commented on as though it is just furniture and it isn't until she seeks him out in his own flat and sees just how good he is at woodworking that Marnie finally recognizes Charlie's skills. This recognition changes Marnie's relationship to him as it allows her to see him more as his own person. He too engages in creative acts—building furniture to his own design—in order to change his *world*. By bettering his space, he transforms the relationship he has with it and the rest of his life. Adam works with wood too, but his relationship to woodworking is different from Charlie's. Rather than building furniture to make his life better now, Adam is building a boat to escape off on adventures with. In both *worlds* woodworking is for improving their life, but in different ways. The larger *world* is made up of both Charlie's and Adam's relationships to woodworking, but each individual lives in a different *world* because they have different relationships to it. The meanings they each find in woodworking, as home-improvement, or as a route to adventure, shape their *world*. Because *world* is actually a singularity, however, this allows them to live in the same *world* even when their *worlds* are different.

Expanding your world through writing, singing, traveling, or seeing someone or something in a new way can only happen if you are able to accept that there is a *world* outside of the *horizons* of your *world* and we can do that because the individual *worlds* are interconnected and create one gigantic whole.

Maybe We Shouldn't Have Taken Her Out of Rehab . . .

Jessa, the Brit with the Bohemian attitude, has been everywhere! And yet everything she does is in service to her view of herself as wild and free so it just reinforces her *world* as she already knows it. Just as with art and creative acts, travel can only serve to expand our *world* and allow us to reach our dreams if we engage with it in a way that lets us connect to others and understand new possibilities.

World is not a geographical space; even though she has travelled extensively Jessa's *world* is small—her *horizons* are close—because she focuses on maintaining a particular image. Hannah's world consists solely of her writing career and Marnie often cannot see beyond her own potential successes or humiliations. Each girl has a different *world*, and each *world* has very narrow horizons even when they shift or expand a little to include a relationship to Charlie's woodworking or Adam's life as a recovering alcoholic. Are all *worlds* naturally small?

The *worlds* in *Girls* appear to be particularly narrow, and contrasted against a particularly broad potential in New York City. We see repeated gatherings of people with interests in the wider art and writing worlds and yet our girls rarely seem to step outside of themselves long enough to expand into these new horizons. Living in a small *world* is normal. It is natural and generally sensible for surviving—if you're comfortable, why risk anything more? The short answer: because we want to. Because, like Hannah choosing to be a writer, Marnie longing to sing and Jessa seeking happiness, we want more than the humdrum. Living in the *world* in which we've been *thrown* makes that tricky and *Girls* is a simultaneously exciting and depressing show as it shows the longing for more and the challenges we face every day in reaching our dreams!

There's hope for Hannah yet, though, as she is basically Lena Dunham at an earlier point in her life, and we know that Lena has gone on to become a well-known, successful, and popular writer. At some point Hannah must, then, realize that there is a much larger *world* which she can inhabit and she must find a way to step into it. Hopefully, wearing a fabulous dress.

So What *Do* You Want to Do?

When Shoshanna goes to college, or when Marnie begins to sing, or when Adam destroys his boat and starts again, we find the key to changing our *world* and making rewriting it into a story with the adventures of our choosing possible. In each case they make a choice. They see the life they are living, they recognize the limitations of their *world* and they choose to take responsibility for what they want to do. Adam lets go of trying to escape into a fantasy and commits to the life he has with more energy than we've seen before. Marnie writes her own piece of music and then springs it on a party in order to both win Charlie back and to become a "singer." Shoshanna makes a plan and hits the books. Making a commitment, a choice, is not enough on its own though.

For Marnie engaging in the creative activity of composing was made possible in the world by the words of Ray and her courage in acting on them; without action, the possibility would have remained a dream.

On the other hand, Hannah writes a book of her life's stories before she turns thirty and even gets a book deal (however unsuccessful . . .) to have it published, but her *world* remains small. The activity of writing, or pursuing what you want, is not enough either. The difference? Hannah writes only about what has happened to her, she reinforces the stories which keep her horizons narrow and revisits the world she already lives in. Marnie, however, attempts to step outside of her *world* and engages in a new activity which changes how she perceives the possibilities open to her. She then takes up running, begins working on accepting herself without a boyfriend, and gets a kitten. At the start of the show these things would have been impossible for her, by Season Three she has transformed her *world*. She is much the same as she has always been, there isn't a great difference in her behavior because she hasn't changed, but her *world* has and it was triggered by the engagement with another person: Marnie allowed Ray to show her something outside of her normal view, which opened the possibility of the action that widened her horizons further.

We can imagine that if Hannah would now write about things beyond what she already knows, if she sought out experiences to write about that were different from the image she had built for herself rather than reinforcing them (much like Jessa does), her *horizons* would widen, opening possibilities that she currently can't reach.

We can also see that if Ray hadn't questioned Marnie, she wouldn't have started singing, but if she hadn't started the conversation with him—and then opened to engaging with the responses—his words would have had no effect. Hannah has stayed within her *world* precisely *because* she is unable, or unwilling to open up to people outside of that *world* enough to let her *world* grow to encompass them. However, in order to see outside our own *world* we have to be able to accept the possibility that there is a larger *world* of interconnected *worlds* with other people and things that exist outside of our own *world*.

How can we see outside our world if we can't, actually, see outside our world already? This is where art comes in. Art, for Heidegger, is something that has been made by someone and which shows us things outside of our *enframed* perspective. The filmed dress cannot be worn, so we don't look at it as something we can use, we see it as something with its own life.

Hannah's New Dress

We've already seen commitment to writing in Hannah, but what she lacks is the ability to properly connect with others and see the *world* as it is. Until the episode that made me cry. Until that point, she's living in a fantasy, disconnected from others and the possibilities of the world. She quits jobs because they don't match her image of herself, but forgets that those jobs can give her the money to make creating that life possible. After sobbing at her desk, however, she has recognized the reality of her existence as *thrown* and she doesn't leave—for the time being. . . . She takes responsibility for where she is and chooses to move forward from here. In that moment Hannah recognized her colleagues as having creative lives, as being people in their own right.

Her *world* changed. Perhaps this is the moment in which it all changes? Perhaps this connection with what is and with other people will allow her to reframe her perspective and open the possibility of a route to her dreams which she hadn't seen before.

It certainly allowed her to buy a gorgeous new dress! Ultimately that emotional connection lacked the window-opening power of art; after acting briefly in the new *world* in which she can open doors and look after herself financially whilst allowing her writing to be something bigger than a means to an end, Hannah will leave, unable to shift her perspective of the world in a way that allows her to have opportunities she is after and returning to the aimless state she was in. That self-absorbed *enframed-ness* stops her from being able to apply the new realization in a way that lets her manifest her ideals—the facts of the world don't match up with her vision for herself and she is incapable of adapting the trappings of the vision to make it real and so she ends up back where she began. Until the world *throws* her another chance to change . . .

Lena Dunham may still be writing memoirs, but now she shares them with the world in a new way, in a way that we can relate to. In writing her stories Hannah reinforces her *world* and it isn't until she connects with someone else that she can step outside of those *horizons*. So to change your *world* you need to recognize that you are *thrown* and there are therefore certain things you cannot control (like needing money) then you need to connect with other people and allow them to show you what is possible and then you start writing again. Rather than writing only about the *world* you already inhabit, how-ever, you write (or sing, or paint, or study, or build) what is pos-sible and that creates more possibilities for you. If you only treat writing in an *enframed* way however, only as a means to an end, it can never be more than a reinforcement of the world you already have.

In showing us Hannah's *world* Lena has reflected back to us exactly what she said she would; her generation. Rather than feel depressed about how *thrown* into this world I am, I'd pre-fer to get excited about the fact that catching those creative dreams is possible even with a generation that has fallen prey to *enframing*! Art cannot do its job if it is *enframed* and reduced to a resource, so to survive Hannah must, as we all do, recognise her *thrownness* and accept that she needs to earn a living in another way first to allow her writing to develop into something that can change the *world* for her. Only when it is strong enough to inspire a new *world* for Hannah and others can her writing really take off as a career.

That there is art that shows us the *world* we live in is the first step towards knowing what is real and what is possible; by which I mean, maybe if Hannah could watch *Girls* she'd be able to see what she needs to do to change her *world* and make her dream possible!

8

Can Millennials Be Authentic?

RACHEL CROSSLEY

Girls: just another superficial show about young people living in New York; or a dramatization of the existential angst plaguing a generation of the Western World?

Hannah Horvath, the cynically dissatisfied yet naively ambitious, consistently eleven pounds overweight twenty-something 'girl' with obsessive-compulsive tendencies and a penchant for self-absorption, in many ways represents the group of awkward young people typically living in urban squalor and perpetual quarter-life-crises that contemporary culture likes to label as 'millennials'. And the popularity and controversy of *Girls* seems to have brought her closer to realizing her drug-induced declaration that she may be "The voice of my generation. Or at least, *a* voice of *a* generation."

Is Hannah's dream of writing simply a naive self-indulgent ambition for success? Or perhaps merely a creative hobby? Or is there a deeper ideal of expression and truth at work here?

Millennials

When interviewed on *Conan*, Lena Dunham was asked if she thought *Girls* was *Sex and the City* for the next generation, to which she replied that *Girls* was more like "a show for the girls who came to New York having watched *Sex and the City* and wanting the life that they saw depicted on the show . . ." and then getting there to find that the dreams and ambitions they'd been presented with and aspired to were not reflected by the reality they were thrown into.

From the first episode of *Girls*, the show sets up and explores the typical uncertainties of Millennial life, of recent college graduates trying to navigate through the world, relationships, sex, jobs, and identity. And maybe the most representative of how young people trying to adapt and survive in the jungle of society is the very opening scene, where Hannah's parents drop the bomb on her that they will no longer be paying for her "groovy lifestyle."

Working an unpaid internship, struggling to make rent, and chasing a guy who won't text her back, having her income pulled away from her is confirmation for Hannah that life isn't turning out the way Carrie and the girls promised it would. In "Inside the Episode" (a behind-the-scenes companion to the show), Lena Dunham says of Hannah that, "Her shock is a little bit generational, because the kids who are coming out of college into the recession feel like they deserve something that the world isn't giving to them." This sums up a huge theme of the show very well. After unsuccessfully pleading with her parents to support her in pursuing her dream as a writer, the episode then ends with a disheartened, lost-looking Hannah, after waking up to find her parents suddenly gone, walking through a crowded New York, and you can't help but feel a little bit of the alienation and anxiety that Hannah seems afflicted with.

The characters of *Girls* often struggle to come to terms with their own freedom and to find their place in the world, while feeling the pressure of both external forces (such as societal pressure) and their own desires to determine their own lives and values. Jean-Paul Sartre, the most famous existentialist thinker, may have had a few comments to make about this struggle.

Angst and Freedom

We might all think we're well acquainted with angst, with our lives far too full of deadlines and diets, trying to make rent, friends that we can't live with and can't live without, masochistic Facebook stalking, the horror that is networking, and, ohmygee, being faced with the question that sends dread into the heart of every college student and graduate: "So, what are you going to do with your life?" Often asked by seemingly well-meaning (though I strongly suspect otherwise) relatives, this simple, torturous question makes you doubt every decision that you've ever made, from your college major, to thinking that you could pull off that floral playsuit.

Sartre's existential angst is of a different character, although the aforementioned 'dreaded question' has probably prompted or deepened a few instances of it. It's often said that contemplating things like this can cause us to suffer an "existential crisis," but what exactly do we mean by this?

We can broadly describe the concept of existential angst as a negative feeling, close to anxiety in nature, and often arising from the experience of human freedom and responsibility. Angst is a reaction to the fact that (as Sartre puts it) we're "condemned to be free." Man is "responsible for the world and for himself" (*Being and Nothingness*, p. 574). We have freedom and responsibility for our own lives; even in the face of overwhelming circumstances, we have the freedom to make choices and engage in self-determination. Or, as Jose Ortega y Gasset put it, "I am free by compulsion, whether I wish to be or not." It is this inescapability of freedom, the fact that we can never give up our own freedom, which is responsible for the experience of existential angst.

External circumstances may limit individuals (Sartre calls this limitation from the outside 'facticity'), but they cannot force a person to follow one of the remaining courses over another. So we still always have some freedom of choice. This means that when we do make a choice, as we inevitably must, we choose in anguish: we know that we must make a choice, and that it will have consequences for which we will have only ourselves to hold accountable.

Sartre says that we have "full and profound responsibility" (*Existentialism Is a Humanism*, p. 25). The realization of the extent of this freedom and responsibility is not, however, always a positive experience. Actually, it's usually the opposite, and if we find ourselves faced with this freedom, we'll often try to deny it or run from it. When it comes to the problem of our own freedom, we'd much rather pick flight over fight.

The consequence of man being "condemned to be free" is often that he feels overwhelmed by this level of responsibility to determine the choices and purpose or goal of his own life, especially when also faced with conflicting external pressures. The fear of this responsibility and freedom can result in an alienating depression and feeling of loss, now that the comfort of unreflective action and meaning has been snatched away.

Angst is distinguished from ordinary fear because it is not a fear of external events or particular objects. Angst is the disturbing, mysterious mood which summons a person to reflect on her individual existence and its possibilities.

When it comes to 'life decisions', Marnie may be the most angst-ridden of the characters. As Shoshanna drunkenly exclaims, Marnie is "tortured by self-doubt and fear" ("Beach House"). Marnie is the group's average disillusioned post-college girl. Less artistic than Hannah, with a more conventional standard of success and ambition, Marnie is a girl who believed and invested herself in the story that society and the media offered to her; the typical middle-class route to success and happiness of going to college and getting a boyfriend, taking the path that so many do with the promise of a bright future. But Marnie, like so many recent college graduates, has discovered that this path to success has suddenly been wiped out half way through the journey, leaving her without a map and destination.

Marnie's journey into angst begins in Season One when she's fired and her relationship ends, and then we really see her take an unpleasant turn towards existential anxiety in "I Get Ideas" after she suffers a painful job interview which leaves her directionless and lost. After years of unquestioningly planning and training for a career as a curator, Marnie is confronted with an abrupt gallery owner (who happens to be played by Lena Dunham's mother) telling her that she just doesn't see Marnie in the art world, and even more crushingly, that she doesn't know *where* at all she sees her. With this sudden dismissal, Marnie's plan for her life is extinguished, and as she contemplates what she's going to do now, she finds herself faced with the harsh truth of her own freedom and responsibility for her life.

Until this point, Marnie was trying to live an image of herself that she thought she should be, rather than thinking about what she really wants. Being told that this 'image' isn't going to work for her forces her to rethink her life, and it is then that she finds herself beginning to realize the inevitability of her own freedom, and the angst that comes with it.

Bad Faith

Marnie's anxiety over what choice to make when it comes to her life leaves her wishing to give up her own freedom: "I don't even know what I want. Sometimes I just wish someone would tell me, 'This is how you should spend your days' and 'This is how the rest of your life should look'" ("It's a Shame About Ray"). Later, however, she makes a choice to follow her own goal to sing, and thus to live in a more "authentic" way. For Sartre, to live authentically is to be true to your own character and make your own choices, even in the face of external pressures. This happens when we face our own overwhelming freedom and embrace it.

More often, however, we tend to spend most of our lives trying to avoid or deny freedom and the angst that comes with it. Sartre points out that, angst, as the consciousness of our own freedom, is not something that human beings welcome; rather, we seek stability and identity. One of the ways we avoid the truth of our own freedom is through "bad faith."

Bad faith is the phenomenon where, under pressure from societal forces, we adopt false values and disown our innate freedom to act authentically. One way this happens is if I adopt a third-person perspective on myself. I can try to look upon myself as the "Other" does. In existentialism, the "Other" is that which I am not, but which plays a role in defining me. What we mean by the "Other" in this case is simply other people, society in general, or my social group. I can be "taken hold of by others," in the sense of coming to define myself as I am for others. To do this is to see my own identity "on the model of the Other," as if I were to myself as I am to others.

When I see myself only through the judgments of others, I have lost my freedom to them. It is this loss of myself to the determination of others that Sartre was referring to when, in his play *No Exit*, he famously said that "Hell is other people."

Bad faith is not one set mood that we are always in. We can switch between different types and instances of bad faith, and there may be times when we are free from it. It fluctuates with our context and mode of reflection. We can see Hannah engaging in bad faith when she's asked to attend a group reading by an old college professor ("Leave Me Alone"). She initially picks an old writing of hers about spending the night stuck in the room of a guy she met at college who turned out to be an unexpected hoarder—a typical Hannah-style piece of writing. She then replaces this at the last minute with a piece on the 'deeper' subject of death, after Marnie and Ray are unimpressed by her original piece, with Ray telling her that if she wants to write she should write about real issues. Hannah caves to the judgments and pressures of her friends, reading a piece which is not true to her own personality or instincts.

Bad faith can also take the form of the opposite sin of not contemplating at all how I am for others. This might happen when I reject entirely the judgments of others and the role I play for them. I am also in "bad faith" if I view myself as only my past self, giving up my freedom to make future decisions, and seeing them as determined by this past self, which is my identity. Jessa and her estranged father might be seen as engaging in this form of bad faith when he dismisses their inability to commit to relationships as "we're just not like that," that's just not what they do, because it's not what they've done ("Video Games").

Bad faith is at least partly about self-identity, in that it involves a person's reflection on who they are and what they are like. Bad faith can be seen to be at work when I identify too fully with one of these objects of reflection—my past self, my objectified body, the image of myself for others, or my self-image—instead of balancing these different styles of self-reflection. Sartre said that human reality is "a being which is what it is not and which is not what it is" (*Being and Nothingness*, p. 58). What Sartre meant with this paradoxical remark is that no one type of self-reflection can give us the full story. Human existence is necessarily ambiguous and many-sided. Bad faith comes into play when, instead of facing up to this inevitable ambiguity, we ignore parts of our existence and immerse ourselves too fully in other parts, or just one part. Bad faith involves a denial of the self.

And everyday life is lived, in most part, in bad faith. The nature of angst is such that we will endeavor to avoid it by escaping into the comforting embrace of bad faith and the stability of others. Yet angst is also the thing which can attest to my nature as an individual, and might lead to acceptance of my freedom, and living authentically.

Authenticity

To live authentically is to avoid the temptations and traps of bad faith. Authenticity is the extent to which I remain true to my own character and goals, despite external pressures. My existence is an issue for me, and in confronting it I must make decisions about what to give to my life. I must develop beliefs and values, and interpretations of my situation in the world. I must determine my own priorities, such as what role work, religion, culture, or my heritage will play in my life, and what significance I will give these things. To live authentically is to embrace our freedom to make choices and guide our lives toward our own chosen goal or project.

After being faced with the anguish and uncertainty of her own freedom, and attempting to retreat into bad faith, Marnie finally acts authentically after Ray forces her to answer his question of "What's your dream?" "What do you really want to do?" He confronts her, "Stop thinking and start doing that" ("It's Back"). Marnie then admits that what she really wants to do is sing, and then makes this her "chosen project" that she works toward.

Hannah also experiences conflicts in trying to live authentically, as she struggles to balance societal and parental pressures with her own goal of being a writer. Hannah's writing is her way of living authentically: choosing her own goals, and trying to overcome her anxiety and isolation by expressing her character and connecting with others. When Hannah asks why she should sleep with her boss, Jessa responds by saying "Do it for the story." Jessa is encouraging Hannah to do it for the sake of expressing and experiencing her own freedom, although perhaps in a questionable way.

On the surface, Jessa, with her wild antics and spontaneous marriage, is arguably one of the most authentic characters, at least in the sense of being unconstrained by societal pressures and expectations. Jessa seems to make all her decisions simply for the reason that she chooses to. Out of all of the girls, she is the least bound by ambition and what's socially acceptable. She says, "I'm offended by all the 'supposed to's. I don't like women telling other women what to do," protesting that she is not "the ladies," and will not be forced to be "the ladies" ("the ladies" are the target of a dating advice book). But Jessa's strict rejection of the views of others and commitment to rebellion is itself a form of bad faith. And perhaps the mother of the kids she babysits is right when she says to Jessa, referring to the trouble she often gets herself into, "You're doing it to distract yourself from becoming who you're meant to be" ("Leave Me Alone").

Is Authenticity Possible in the Twenty-First Century?

What exactly does it mean to be 'authentic' in the twenty-first century? Is it even possible? Are the characters of *Girls* trying to achieve authenticity? Let's go back to the very first episode again.

After drinking a tea of opium pods, Hannah finds herself situated between the conflicting views of Jessa and Marnie, as they discuss what she should say to try to appease her parents after their announcement that they are financially cutting her off. Jessa proclaims, "Just tell them that you're an artist!" After all, rappers on the street did it, Mick Jagger did it, and now Hannah should. Marnie, as expected, provides the more sensible, practical view of "Just tell them you're gonna get a job."

Jessa and Marnie are, to use a crude simile, like the angel of authenticity and the devil of bad faith sitting on Hannah's shoulders. But Marnie's realism can't be denied. Hannah is not completely free to live as an artist, her circumstances (not to mention her parents) won't permit it. Although she's still free to make a choice, Hannah is restricted by external factors, like the economy and not wanting to starve. In Season Three we see Hannah finally get a stable, paid, real writing job. Well, of sorts—the less soulful sort. Hannah finds herself writing advertisements, which Ray tells her is "morally and creatively bankrupt" ("Free Snacks"). Despite enjoying the safety of the paycheck, and the free food, Hannah is panicked and almost quits when she hears that her co-workers all also used to be "proper writers" but then gave up on their own writing and projects once they started working and fell into the comfortable stability of bad faith.

Hannah wants to live authentically, as perhaps a lot of us do, but the need to get a job and live in society very rarely allows for this. Being authentic in the twenty-first century western world is almost always going to have to be a compromise if you want to be sure that you're not going to live in poverty. But this doesn't mean that we should give ourselves up entirely to the bad faith of societal expectations. We should still be brave enough to face our own freedom and remain true to our character and values as much as our situation will allow. As for the "So what do you want to do with the rest of your life?" question, the only appropriate response is Jessa's: "Hasn't anyone ever told you that's a rude question?" ("All Adventurous Women Do").

9
The Q-Tipping Point of Anxiety

Marie van Loon

> **Hannah:** I'm coming back from the hospital because I shoved this q-tip down my earhole.
>
> **Adam:** Jesus Christ, kid, be careful.
>
> —"On All Fours"

If I were Adam, I would ask Hannah: "Why the f*** did you do that?" Because that would be my first question if I ran into one of my friends and she had shoved a q-tip down her ear. Who does that? At first it might seem that Hannah's situation is far removed from our ordinary lives. Hence my next question for Hannah would go something like, "Are you nuts?" Well, as it turns out, not so nuts. It does seem crazy that someone would do that. Sure Hannah has OCD and sees a shrink—but what for again? "My parents think that I seem anxious" ("It's Back").

That's where it gets interesting. What are we talking about when we refer to anxiety as Hannah does here? It's a psychological state. As such, we could talk about it from a psychological point of view: this would mean scientifically inquiring into the mechanisms that operate and condition anxiety. That's one way to go—we could also look at the phenomenon from a philosophical point of view.

Leaving aside the scientific aspect of anxiety, we look at how anxiety works in a person's relation to her own existence, her own being and to the world. This is taking the matter not only philosophically but also more precisely existentially. Søren Kierkegaard—a Danish thinker from the nineteenth century—

for example, is a philosopher who explored the concept of anxiety. He's often been considered the "father of existentialism," as his whole philosophy revolves precisely around the person's problematic relation to the world and to herself, and this is what existentialism is about. Later on other philosophers such as Jean-Paul Sartre, in the forties in France, took up Kierkegaard ideas in their own works.

Girls shows the same interest in the individual—watching the series, we learn about life, maybe even about our own lives, through the stories of these four girls (and a few boys by the way). Someone like Sartre, with existentialism, makes close-ups of particular examples of situations to show us the true struggles which are at the heart of existence; so does Lena Dunham with *Girls*, or rather so do the characters. Each of them is going through a phase of their lives which is particularly relevant to the struggle of existence: this weird moment of "in-between" when for the first time we truly have to face the fact that while all possibilities lie before us, we have to make choices.

It's a bit like facing your computer on film night, knowing that you can pretty much get any movie you want and still finding yourself completely unable to make a choice. It's a bit like Hannah, free to take whatever step she wants in life, free of her parents' idea of what she should do, and yet, not being able to undertake anything serious. Being in your twenties, facing the infinite possibilities that lie before you is enough reason to get anxious.

Free as a Bird

Hannah is thrown out of the nest "into the world," given her freedom by being pushed out by her family. Her newfound freedom lies in her becoming responsible for her own survival, to put it bluntly. Hannah loses the financial support from her parents; so in that sense she is given her freedom at the beginning of the series. As for the rest of the "gang," Hannah's friends also experience major changes in their lives: Jessa comes back from God-knows-where, Marnie breaks up with her boyfriend, and Shoshanna is introduced to the group by welcoming Jessa into her life.

In the first season there's this overall sense of "starting anew," of new found liberty and what all these young women are going to do with it. Quickly we realize that this freedom is a burden, because after all, we have to do something with this freedom we're given, whether it's by our parents, our ex-boyfriend or social status. Freedom is hard to handle: that's when anxiety kicks in. Anxiety is the means by which we handle freedom, whether we handle it badly or not. Then, there are the different ways of dealing with anxiety. They seem to come down to being courageous or being cowardly.

Shoshanna: Becoming Me, Becoming Samantha

Hannah, Jessa, Marnie and Shoshanna all seem to struggle with their bundle of infinite possibilities. Shoshanna's very much concerned with becoming herself and growing into "a fully formed human being" as she puts it. In Season Two most of her fights with Ray revolve around the need to change. But earlier, in Season One, Shoshanna's relation to freedom is less obvious and concrete than it becomes later. Shoshanna has it easier than the others, with an almost *Gossip Girl*-like lifestyle and social circle.

But what Shoshanna has, compared to the others, is innocence. She confides in her new friends and tells them that she's never had sex. She's a virgin and therefore "innocent," in the most conservative and traditional sense of the word. We could say that freedom for Shoshanna, because she's innocent, is almost irrelevant to her situation. Not to forget that she's a huge fan of *Sex and the City*, which makes her role as "ingénue" even more evident, and slightly ironic. She admires women, like Carrie Bradshaw, older and more experienced, living in the full of their sexual power and femininity. The most ironic point is her identification with Samantha! In that sense Shoshanna is the one who's in a dimension prior to freedom.

How to Joke Your Way through Anxiety

Jessa, on the other hand, can easily be seen as the "free" one. How does anxiety work for her? Jessa is bright, beautiful, almost goddess-like, and has all the cards in her hand. More than anyone else in *Girls*, Jessa is free—from parents, material burden, and self-consciousness. It almost looks as if there's no place for anxiety in her life. If Jessa must represent a certain aspect of freedom, she clearly is divine freedom, who overcomes both the anxiety of everything and nothing.

Existential anxiety is not merely the anxiety of "something"; it doesn't restrict itself to the fear of determinate objects, like a choice or an event. Anxiety emerges from facing the "big nothingness" as well, when anxiety has no precise reason to be. This is the anxiety which creeps out on you on Sundays afternoons: feels like it's the week coming up—but without being able to put the finger on it. Or blown up to extreme situations, the anxiety of nothing is the anxiety of death.

For Katherine (Jeff's wife), who hires Jessa in Season One as baby-sitter, this seemingly unbounded freedom is merely a game. In a conversation toward the end of the season, Katherine even gives her a chance to face her situation:

> KATHERINE: I bet you get into these dramas all the time, like with Jeff and me, where you cause all this trouble and you've no idea why. My opinion? You're doing it to distract yourself from becoming the person you're meant to be.
>
> JESSA: Which is who?
>
> KATHERINE: You tell me. She might not look like what you pictured when you were sixteen. Her job might not be cool. Her hair might not be flowing like a mermaid. And she might really be serious about something. Or someone. ("Leave Me Alone")

In other words, Jessa's fluttering about reflects her fear of becoming herself and a serious woman. Ironically, Jessa's next move following the conversation is to go and get married. While marriage can be seen as the most serious of all commitments, Jessa turns it into a joke. Nothing is serious for Jessa and nothing is worth being serious about. For existentialist philosophers like Kierkegaard, seriousness, and the anxiety it brings, go hand in hand with freedom; you couldn't have freedom without "paying the price" for it. Is Jessa telling us that Kierkegaard and all the existentialists have it wrong? After all, as she rightly reminds her father: "I'm a child!" Claiming her childhood allows her the kind of total freedom a serious woman could not afford. It seems that Jessa hopes to untangle freedom from seriousness.

Fooled Ya!

Unlike Jessa, Marnie is far from being free. Marnie's attitude toward life is quite typical of what some existentialists, like Sartre, call "bad faith." Bad faith results from one way of dealing with anxiety in the face of possibilities. It is denying the possibilities, by either falsely believing that you're in control or believing that there is no way to control anything, placing yourself in the position of the victim of fate. Bad faith can also be the refusal of your own freedom, denying that you're responsible for who you are.

Marnie's breakup with Charlie is a good example of her bad faith. The breakup doesn't come about by a choice of her own, but by accident. The decision doesn't come out of Marnie's struggle. Even so, Marnie believes she has control over her own freedom. In that sense, bad faith is basically fooling yourself. In this kind of situation, anxiety becomes invisible.

On the other hand, when her anxiety does manifest, Marnie makes pretty clear what it comes down to: "I don't know what's going to happen next week." Ironically, even though Marnie is mostly in bad faith, it turns out she couldn't put more clearly what anxiety is about. If anxiety is particularly relevant to these twenty-something persons in search of themselves and becoming who they are, it's simply because they tend to face the future with more intensity than usual. And the future is nothing other the infinite unknown, in other words, freedom.

Marnie, Jessa, and even Shoshanna in their will to embrace their freedom, attempt to flirt with the world of "grownups"—metaphorically and literally. Flirting yes, but committing? No, even for the least serious games. Take Jessa's and Marnie's adventure at the businessman's apartment. When they push it too far and giggle at his attempts of seduction, Thomas-John reproaches both of them for their lack of commitment and ask them whether they even know what it's like to work hard ("Weirdos Need Girlfriends Too"). Marnie apologizes by saying that she was just trying to be free.

Seriously Anxious

Season One ends with Hannah falling asleep in the metro and getting lost in some obscure place in the city. "Where am I?" she asks. Hannah keeps on walking and ends up alone on the beach, eating Jessa's wedding cake. At the end of the next season, we'll get the q-tip scene. By then, it's all downhill. Although she's given an opportunity to be what she wants to be, a writer, it's the precise event that causes the downfall of Hannah. She's given the task to write a book, with a deadline. No surprise, she throws up right after the announcement. Hannah's struggles are no worse than her friends' until that very confrontation with the opportunity to carry on her ambition of being a writer.

Why does her anxiety culminate now that the infinity of possibilities narrows down to one—writing a book? What was an objectless anxiety, an anxiety of nothingness, has transformed into an anxiety that is aimed at some precise object. Hannah is given an opportunity to do something potentially great. And that's scary as hell. The moment has come for Hannah to do her part and then leave it to the will of somebody else. Now she has to make an effort and write her book. What she doesn't know is whether her effort will pay off or not.

The scariest part in doing what you really want and putting effort into it is the risk that it might turn out not as great as you expected. The same thing happens when you decide to commit to someone you love. The risk that it might end someday is always present, but you have to accept it. That's what Kierkegaard, in his book *Fear and Trembling*, called the "leap of faith." When you undertake a project, you have to overcome the fact that you don't know what the future holds: maybe you'll break up in a month, maybe your publisher won't like the book you've written, or maybe the world will end tomorrow. The leap of faith is deciding to write that book anyway, in spite of all the possibilities of failing.

Making the leap of faith is accepting anxiety. And that requires tremendous amounts of courage—so much courage that Søren Kierkegaard called those able to do it "knights of faith." It's not a surprise, though: being courageous is difficult. There are easier ways, and they're very tempting, but in the end only unhappiness comes out of them. It's all about becoming who you are or being authentic. Hannah teaches us that, by refusing to lead an authentic life. We see her struggling very hard to, in a way, avoid writing her book. Hannah can of course blame her OCD for her inability to make her deadline, but that's only bad faith. We've already seen with Marnie that bad faith can come in the form of a complete denial of her anxiety. It's easier in the end to blame some element external to yourself for your failures than to take responsibility for being the person you are. Marnie's bad faith affords her temporary relief. From apprentice curator to muse and then singer, Marnie walks with certainty towards what turns out in fact to be nothingness. She's the captain of a sinking ship, her failing projects, but at least she's a captain, her confidence seems to scream. For Marnie, bad faith enables her to save appearances.

The Q-Tipping Point

Bad faith is one way of dealing with anxiety—avoiding it. Hannah goes through something different. She is the person at the edge of a cliff torn both by the idea that she could fall and the idea that she could throw herself into the void. This is a famous example used by Kierkegaard and later taken up by Sartre. Sartre compares anxiety to vertigo. Hannah, in her turn, brings vertigo into her bathroom, in "On All Fours." This episode, though not the last of the season, culminates with the tension accumulated throughout the series in a shocking scene. Hannah's fragile mental state at this point and her solitude combine and emerge in her compulsive behavior disorder, as she cannot do other than brutally stick a q-tip in her ear. The scene is quite horrifying and illustrates sickening anxiety. If anxiety is the confrontation of a finite being with the infinity of her possibilities, then shoving a q-tip down her ear is quite like jumping into the void by fear of it. It's embracing the possibilities all at once.

Not without irony, the particular event of the q-tip shoving coincides with the moment Hannah should be done with her e-book. As the deadline approaches, falling short of possibilities, her anxiety climaxes. We follow Hannah very closely, in an elevator, in her apartment and in front of her mirror, and those terrible moments of silence echo with anxiety. Sitting on the wooden floor in her underwear, Hannah is busy procrastinating in front of her computer. An olive here, a pillow there and "ouch"—a splinter gets under the skin of her buttocks. These little accidents make Hannah's whole day in her apartment seem even longer and darker, with this feeling of having achieved nothing. Every moment seems to multiply into other moments, bringing with them more possibilities for Hannah of doing something other then writing her e-book. In front of her mirror, while cleaning her ears she's suddenly sucked into one of her obsessive-compulsive disorder episodes and shoves the q-tip down her ear. It's disconcerting for any outsider to the scene, and it doesn't seem pleasant for Hannah either.

Here Hannah surrenders to the unbearable infinity of possibilities, but we cannot yet speak of a leap of faith, or anything like that. What has Hannah achieved here? She hasn't gotten closer to her true self. She isn't freer. All she's done is to narrow down the number of possibilities lying before her—but that means relapsing into bad faith.

Now it looks like there's no way Hannah will make her deadline. And she has also made it seem like there was no other possibility than jumping into the void. Ironically, in these moments of total despair freedom turns into an unbearable burden. Knowing that you're free and therefore taking responsibility for who you are is difficult: it brings anxiety with it. Hannah refuses to take on the burden of freedom and as a result acts as if she has no choice. While for some choosing anxiety might seem less painful than shoving a q-tip in your earhole, Hannah stubbornly chooses to become the victim of fatality.

The Bushwick Redemption

Fortunately there's hope! Anxiety doesn't end with decadent abandonment to fatality. On the contrary. In the finale of Season Two, Hannah and Adam show us how even people like us can be knights of faith and surrender to something bigger than ourselves, opening possibilities of redemption.

Surrender comes at the very last moment for Hannah. She calls Adam and gives herself a chance of redemption, by offering him the possibility of helping her. Redemption, or surrender, is the stage that we reach once we have accepted anxiety. But what does it mean exactly to "accept anxiety"?

All these characters, Shoshanna, Jessa, Marnie and Hannah, in spite of their difference in handling it, know that, in the end, life is hard. That's why they all find ways to avoid difficulty and pain. Some of them, like Hannah, discover that you can actually surrender to anxiety and take the responsibility to leave it to the outside world. But we can understand why this is hard. It's like sending a message in a bottle: there is no guarantee anything will come of it. We might end up alone on our desert island, but there's also the chance that someone will come and rescue us.

Surrendering doesn't mean giving up. Giving up, escaping, fooling one's self, doesn't require courage but only cowardice. It takes guts for Hannah to call Adam, because surrendering is making yourself vulnerable to the other.

Anxiety Loops and Life Circles

From being "freed" from her parents to committing to men and publishers, Hannah goes through bad faith, despair, gives up, and finally surrenders to love. But by Season Three and the knowledge that life simply doesn't end with French-kissing in the rain, but goes on, we can be pretty sure that anxiety will come back. Freedom doesn't get easier to bear and it doesn't become less of a struggle to keep it than face it for the first time. We vanquish it once, but it'll come back and we'll have to do it again.

In the Woody Allen movie, *Manhattan*, similar conclusions about freedom and life are drawn. The characters are not twenty-something's but forty-something's. This difference doesn't change that they too face existential struggles. Like we've just seen, these struggles repeat themselves and it doesn't get easier. In one of the first scenes, set in a Manhattan café, not so far from the world in which Hannah and her "girls" struggle to become themselves, another group of friends reminds us that "the important thing in life is courage." *Girls* completes this idea of courage with that of anxiety.

The courage to be yourself, or rather to become what you are, entails the courage to face anxiety. Movies like *Manhattan* or series like *Girls*, because they take their audience into the personal journeys of their characters are particularly fit to expose the struggles of existence. The reason is that these hardships become salient in moments that requires you to take action or to make a choice; and it is these moments that *Girls*, in the same vein as *Manhattan*, portrays so accurately.

Girls shows that anxiety brings struggle; not only in its hardships but also in the fact that our relation to it is ambiguous.

Kierkegaard talks about antipathetic-sympathetic relation to our own anxiety. It's not as simple as fighting anxiety and over-coming it. Anxiety is tempting; we want to give in to the void. Like vertigo, anxiety makes nothingness both repelling and attractive. Accepting anxiety is part of being serious and becom-ing oneself. It implies great awareness and balance.

Adam sums up in a few words the hardship of the pursuit of your true self: "This shit's really hard. When I broke up with my girlfriend from college, so sad. I lost thirty pounds, I couldn't move, or talk or get my dick hard. But! It also made me go 'Hey! Who am I and what do I want?' Then I was like 'Boom! I know who I am.' I wanted to switch majors and buy a circular saw. And I promised myself I'd follow my gut no matter what. And I'd do what makes me feel good" ("Weirdos Need Girlfriends Too"). Adam explains to us that life is hard but that through the hardest struggles we discover who we are. By discovering who we are, we take responsibility for what we can become. Maybe it isn't as easy as "Boom!", but this difficulty is exactly what *Girls* shows.

III

If you're here to tell me what a bad person I am, I don't want to hear it.

10
Listen, Ladies! Or Maybe You Shouldn't

ROBERTO SIRVENT AND JOEL AVERY

When it comes to romance, what exactly are the ground rules? It depends who we ask.

Hannah favors friends with benefits. But then she wants more. Marnie finds it okay to have sex with the ex. But that only gives her more headaches. Shoshanna is waiting until she's in love. But soon enough, any guy will do. And Jessa, well, she's fine as long as she can treat her body as a roller coaster. Oh, and as long as it makes for a good story.

Gentlemen, what do you think? Ray avoids women who are either under twenty-five or who have slept with a drummer. But, he cautions, "It's not like they're commandments." Okay, not commandments but more like *rules of thumb*? Thanks, Ray. And Adam, well even *he* has boundaries. In the episode "All Adventurous Women Do," Hannah asks if Adam still wants to have sex after she pissed him off one too many times. "When it's appropriate, sure," Adam says. Then, in an attempt to learn from her past mistakes with Adam, Hannah gives an exhaustive list of dating do's and don'ts to her new man Sandy. To which he replies, "Why do you have so many rules?"

It's Not Like They're Commandments

All of us might be wondering the same thing. When it comes to love, sex, and romance, why *do* we have so many rules? And is it possible that in a realm as messy (both literally and figuratively) as human sexuality that rules and principles may actually *get in the way* of a morally worthwhile life? Before we can understand why we have so many rules, we should think about what *kind* of rules, or ethics, we have.

Two of the most popular ways of 'doing ethics' are deontology and utilitarianism. Deontological ethics, made famous by the philosopher Immanuel Kant, judges the morality of our actions based on how well we adhere to certain rules or duties. What matters is not what consequences will arise from my action. The only thing that matters is that I follow the right rule, and that I perform this action out of a sense of duty. Because these rules are seen as universal, objective, and independent, everyone is morally obligated to follow them—*all the time*. There are no exceptions when it comes to commandments, at least from a deontological perspective. This is why Ray says his general rules are not 'commandments.' He wants to keep his options open.

Utilitarianism, commonly associated with the philosophers Jeremy Bentham and John Stuart Mill, has a different take on ethics. A good utilitarian takes into account all that can go wrong or right with a certain course of action. You can think of this as the engineer's approach to ethics: measure twice, cut once. The goal is to achieve maximum utility. So, you go into your ethics lab, lay all your ethical concerns on the table, sort them out, weigh and measure them, draft various configurations, and finally select the best model that brings about the greatest good. This 'good' might be happiness, pleasure, or even the general welfare of society. But however we define the 'greatest good' or 'utility' is beside the point.

Ethics here is about engaging in a cost-benefit analysis. It's the kind of analysis Jessa engages in when Shoshanna asks if she'd ever sleep with a virgin ("Hannah's Diary"). "Depends on the virgin," Jessa says. Yes, the guy's virginity matters. But it's one of *many* factors that matter. And it's up to Jessa to weigh them all together.

It's easy to see the appeal of using such universal rules, principles, and calculations to navigate our ethical lives. After all, life is hard and romantic relationships are complicated, right? If only there were a map, or a *book*, that used deontological and utilitarian ethics to show us the way. Well lucky for us, Shoshanna's got our back. In the episode "Vagina Panic", she's found the perfect book to un-complicate the love lives of her dear and dejected friends Hannah and Jessa. The

Bible? No. *Fifty Shades of Grey*? Closer, but no. What else but the soon-to-be classic, *Listen, Ladies! A Tough Love Approach to the Tough Game of Love*.

Who Are 'The Ladies'?

To Shoshanna's surprise, Hannah and Jessa do not share her excitement for the book. Let's begin with one of Hannah's objections. "Here's my question," Hannah tells Shoshanna, "Who are *the ladies*?" This was the question asked by Danish philosopher Søren Kierkegaard (1813–1855) and German philosopher Friedrich Nietzsche (1844–1900). (Okay, no, they never literally asked, "Who are 'the ladies'?" But you know what we mean).

Kierkegaard and Nietzsche were each critical of a universal, objective approach to ethics like the kind found in Shoshanna's book. This doesn't mean that these methods are always or necessarily bad. They may have some merit, but what's most vexing about them is that these high-flying appeals to universal, objective ethics may actually get in the way of us living a good life. That's right: our ethical theories may be the very thing that prevents us from being ethical! Why? Because these approaches are too impersonal.

First, for both thinkers, deontological and utilitarian ethics fail to sufficiently take into account the *individual*. The meaning of an action can't be divorced from the personal history of the individual, as well as the particular goals, desires, needs, and values of that individual. We also can't forget that each individual is examining, rethinking, and re-orienting their values in her own *particular* way. So, to appeal only to an abstract ideal like duty or utility is to fail to ask a very important question: What does this act mean to this particular person in this particular circumstance?

What frustrates Hannah and Jessa about Shoshanna's book is that it lumps every woman into the category of 'ladies' and expects its moral advice to apply to all of them all the time. But any ethical advice that reduces them to simply 'girls' or 'ladies' fails to do justice to their uniqueness and particularity as *individuals*. Hannah, Jessa, Marnie, and Shoshanna are distinct 'ladies' with personal histories and current concerns. It would make for a pretty boring TV show—and world—if this weren't the case.

So what else bothered Kierkegaard and Nietzsche about utility and rule-based ethics? According to them, not only do *people* get reduced with such impersonal approaches to morality. Our ethics get reduced, too. We end up living our lives as if our problems can be solved with a kind of moral calculus. Now, of course, there are plenty of people telling us how to lead our lives. This is why so many self-help authors are filthy rich. Their lists, codes, and formulas promise us a simple, clear, and fast way to find true happiness.

Why is Shoshanna so obsessed with her new book? Because she wishes love were a bit easier to figure out. Marnie wishes the same for life in general. In the episode "It's a Shame About Ray," she begs the cosmos for some clear direction. "Sometimes I just wish someone would tell me like 'This is how you should spend your days and this is how the rest of your life should look.'" Marnie doesn't just want someone to save her from life's difficult decisions. She wants someone to make those decisions for her. She doesn't want a moral savior. She wants a moral dictator.

But what exactly makes us ethical? Are we ethical just because we follow instructions? Are we ethical just because we know how to plug in the variables of our lives into an equation and calculate the right moral answer? Is *this* what makes us ethical human beings? Or are we just looking for an easy way out? What, if anything, do we miss when ethics is reduced to mere calculation? And are we so afraid of moral struggle that we, like Marnie, search desperately for an instruction manual to life?

Hard Being Easy

For Kierkegaard and Nietzsche, standard ethical approaches tend to minimize the complexity of both the individual and ethics itself. So why do these approaches still appeal to us? This leads to their third criticism. For both thinkers, our reliance on such ethical systems is merely an attempt to avoid responsibility. It's not that we don't have ethical responsibilities—we do!—it's that we use ethics as a cover. We make it look like we're ethical beings (following the rules and so on), but what we are actually doing is *avoiding* ethical action—in the name of ethics! We simply kick the problem 'upstairs' when we act 'on principle', which Kierkegaard describes as an attempt to escape ourselves and avoid personal responsibility. It's sort of like making an ethical excuse: The principle made me do it!

In *Genealogy of Morals*, Nietzsche makes a similar critique. An individual's approach to life must be driven by her own goals, interests, and personal passions. The abstract, impersonal, and so-called objective nature of duty and utility is actually, according to Nietzsche, incompatible with the freedom and responsibility of what he calls the 'sovereign individual.' We can imagine that Jessa has traveled through Europe with Nietzsche in her backpack, especially in light of her furious reaction to Shoshanna's book. "This woman doesn't care about what I want," she says. "Fuck that silly fucking book! I'm offended by all the 'supposed to's.' I don't like women telling other women what to do or how to do it or when to do it. Every time I have sex is *my* choice." Nietzsche would be so proud.

We can also imagine Jessa agreeing with Slovenian philosopher Slavoj Žižek, who picks up these threads from Kierkegaard and Nietzsche and weaves them in with the thought of psychoanalyst Jacques Lacan. Žižek uses Lacan's notion of the "Big Other" to explain how our beliefs and ethics shield us from confronting the trauma of actually living our lives. The "Big Other" is the one that holds our world, or sense of reality, together. The easiest example is an idea like God, the "Big Other" that made and ordered the world. A lot of deontological ethical systems invoke God when they talk about duty and universal laws. We do something because "Big Other" told us to. But God is just one of many "Big Others." For Stalin it was History, for patriots it's Country, for conservatives it's Capitalism, and for liberals it's Progress.

All of these ideas function as the ultimate grounds of one's reality. More importantly, *all of them tell us what to do*. Even if the "Big Other" is Utility or Duty, we are appealing to something beyond ourselves, and in doing so, we attempt to escape the trauma of taking responsibility for our own actions. "Really, I'm a good person," we tell ourselves, "but Capitalism demands I act selfishly!" "Really, I'm a good person, but my Country calls on me to drop bombs on civilians." The "Big Other," then, not only helps us make sense of our world. It also gives us someone to blame. "Big Other" made me do it.

Off Limits

So are Kierkegaard and Nietzsche saying we should just do
whatever the hell we want? It would be a mistake to think so.
Their moral outlooks are richer and far more complex than
this. To give one example, Kierkegaard would have a lot to say
to Jessa who, in the words of Thomas-John, destroys people's
lives "because she's bored." This is the same Jessa who advises
Hannah to have sex because it makes for a good story. Here,
Jessa is acting as what Kierkegaard called the "aesthete." The
aesthete suffers the illusion that she can escape her boredom,
or angst, and the emotional cycle of satisfaction and dissatisfaction. What the aesthete tries to escape are unhappy circumstances, when the problem is located in the individual herself.

This is the challenge of Kierkegaard's ethics. If it really is
up to us, and not abstract principles ruling our lives, then we're
not off the hook—the hook goes deeper! Jessa can't escape her
unhappiness, because to do so would be to escape herself. We
can't escape ourselves, Kierkegaard tells us. And because it is
impossible to escape ourselves, attempts at escape through aesthetic pleasures will fail to bring us the happiness we ultimately seek.

To give another brief example, Nietzsche would be quite
critical of Hannah's behavior in the episode "Hard Being Easy."
Here we see a confused Adam asking her why she tried having
sex with her boss. "For the story," Hannah replies, following
Jessa's cue. Then, after a short pause, Hannah says, "I don't
know, just to be an asshole." Hannah is just one more person
trying to escape herself. From another angle, we also see what
Nietzsche calls ressentiment, or hatred towards others and
towards oneself. Hannah's self-hatred perpetuates hateful acts
upon others. In her case, a reckless sexual act actually functions to deny what is deeply beautiful about her sexuality—she
becomes "just an asshole." We might also wonder what
Nietzsche might have to say to Marnie and Elijah about their
awkward sexual encounter in the episode "It's About Time." It's
not out of self-exploration but self-hatred that both are accused
of trying to be something they aren't. This hatred prevents an
experience of happiness and beauty, resulting instead in
destructive self-denial. Wishing to be better than they are, they
end up worse off together.

We're not saying that 'anything goes' in romance. We should not throw out all rules and principles. Nor should we stop calculating how our actions might affect ourselves and other people. In clarifying this point, we feel a lot like Hannah in the episode "It's a Shame About Ray." Here we find Marnie offering her answer to the question: What exactly is 'off limits' in the bedroom? "I mean I just don't think anyone should do anything they're not comfortable with," she says. "Especially when it comes to sex." Hannah, pointing out the obvious, responds, "Well yes, Marnie. That's the principle behind not raping people."

So yes, *of course* there are principles that can and should guide us in the romantic realm. These might include care, consent, freedom, responsibility, and mutuality (just to name a few). But there is no simple way to determine ahead of time what each of these looks like in a given situation. Principles or rules can't hold our hand. The act of loving *actual* people is a complicated one, especially if we want to consider the particularity of each individual. If true, sexual ethics might have to rely a lot less on rule following and a lot more on creativity and vulnerability.

All Adventurous Women Do . . . What Exactly?

No matter how bad they want it, the girls of *Girls* explore sex—and life—without a clear sense of what is useful or right. Rules and cost-benefit analysis can only take them so far. They are opening themselves up to life, not as they thought it would be, but as they discover it to be along the way. Participation is essential to that discovery. These are people making their lives happen. And the way they engage sex, ethics, and responsibility has a lot to say about how they engage *life*, ethics, and responsibility. In a certain way, taking responsibility for our lives entails taking responsibility for our bodies.

So instead of asking what we should do, perhaps we're better off asking what kind of people we want to be. Aristotle (384–322 B.C.E.) called this virtue ethics, the cultivation of virtuous character for an authentically flourishing life. *This* is the moral project that Hannah, Marnie, Jessa, and Shoshanna engage in. They're not wondering what rules they should follow and they're not trying to master the cost-benefit analysis. They're each trying to become a certain kind of person. Each 'lady' is confronting all sorts of "Big Other" claims in her life: parents, career, peer/class expectations, and so on. If they are to take responsibility in the face of these claims, if they are to take responsibility for themselves, then the first site is the self, the body. Establishing their identities as sexual, subjective, and vulnerable persons is the first step. Every other act of responsibility starts here.

This is what Kierkegaard, Nietzsche, and Žižek want us to embrace. Instead of fleeing ourselves, our bodies, and hiding under the covers of ethics, we need to take risks. In her book *Undoing Gender* feminist philosopher Judith Butler talks about what it means to be a true self exposed to others. "Let's face it," Butler writes:

> We're undone by each other. And if we're not, we're missing something. One does not always stay intact. It may be that one wants to, or does, but it may also be that despite one's best efforts, one is undone, in the face of the other, by the touch, by the scent, by the feel, by the prospect of the touch, by the memory of the feel. [Sexuality] is to be understood as a mode of being dispossessed, of being for another, or, indeed, by virtue of another. (p. 19)

Love and sex are not safe. But Charlie sure wants them to be. In the episode "Hard Being Easy," he tells Marnie what it'll take for him to accept her back as his girlfriend. "Don't abandon me," Charlie says. "Don't make me feel safe and then abandon me." Charlie's defense mechanisms might seem a bit naive, selfish, and controlling. But it's nothing compared to the emotional wall Hannah puts up with Adam. And in the episode "Welcome to Bushwick a.k.a. The Crackcident," Adam finally calls her out on it:

> You never ask me anything, besides 'does this feel okay?' or 'do you like my skirt?' or 'how much is your rent?' I'm not gonna fuckin' talk your ear off about shit you don't ask about. You don't wanna know me. You want to come over in the night and have me fuck the dog shit out of you. Then you wanna leave then write about it in your diary. You don't wanna *know* me.

Common approaches to ethics offer safety. But we cannot be truly ethical unless we are vulnerable. We can't be ethical unless we risk. And we can't be ethical unless we surrender. This means surrendering our need for safety, certainty, and clarity. But more importantly, it means surrendering our refusal to be "undone" by the one we claim to love.

Oddly enough, love allows us to be both undone *and* our true selves. Against most conceptions of the moral life, then, *Girls* shows us that in order to be truly moral, we must be truly naked.

Truth or Dare

The body has always been a tremendous source of anxiety and uncertainty. And like everything else we fear, we try to control it. So it's no wonder that philosophers have devised rules and formulas to guide us. But how much can rules and moral calculations *really* help us out here?

The way forward is not to control our fears but to face them, not to reject vulnerability but to embrace it. Only by confronting head-on the risk and messiness of romantic love can we ultimately experience a new kind of freedom in the midst of the sexual unknown.

Life, like sex, is difficult. It can even hurt. There are no easy answers. And even if there were, we shouldn't want them. It's the same lesson Hannah learns when examined by her doctor for an STD. "Is that painful?" her doctor asks. "Yeah," Hannah replies. "But only in the way it's supposed to be."

11
The Seven Deadly Sins of *Girls*

JAMES EDWIN MAHON AND
NICOLE KIMES WALKER

The characters in Lena Dunham's *Girls* are extremely flawed individuals. They sleep around, they neglect their responsibilities, and they are excessively casual about hurting other people's feelings. Some might even say that's the point of the series.

As Season One's tagline suggests—*Living the dream. One mistake at a time*—the characters' imperfections are the show's sum and substance. They create the drama and humor and make the characters relatable. We sympathize with their weaknesses, in part because their misdeeds do not go unpunished. Poor decisions damage the characters' relationships, lower their self-esteem, and even affect their health.

Since the characters' faults form the crux of the show, they are worth looking at more closely. When we do, we discover that these very modern characters are guilty of the traditional seven deadly sins:

- **Pride,**

- **Greed,**

- **Lust,**

- **Envy,**

- **Gluttony,**

- **Wrath,**

- **Sloth.**

These sins, however, are due for an upgrade—a re-branding for the current generation. The seven deadly sins of *Girls*, then, are:

- **Self-Absorption,**

- **Entitlement,**

- **Sleeping Around,**

- **Hatin',**

- **Excessive Drink and Drugs,**

- **Irritability,**

- **Flakiness.**

Self-Absorption (*Superbia*)

The sin of Self-Absorption (*Superbia*) is opposed to the virtue of Humility (*Humilitas*), and is similar to *hubris* (excessive pride). Self-Absorption is love directed towards an improper end, namely, oneself, as opposed to one's goodness or one's virtue. It is what St. Augustine (354–430 B.C.E.) calls "the love of one's own excellence," except that here one's 'excellence' consists in simply being oneself, and not in the (good) acts that one performs or the (good) qualities that one possesses. Self-Absorption is loving oneself just for oneself—regardless of how good or bad one might be.

The early Christians who came up with the original designations believed this to be the worst of the seven sins, the "gateway sin" that leads to all the others. Self-absorption is the most prevalent sin of the characters in *Girls* and, yes, it does seem to lead them to commit the other six transgressions. It's their self-absorption, their tendency to put themselves first, that does the most damage to their relationships.

Self-absorption is a problem for all the characters, but Hannah is the worst offender. Her self-absorption is, in fact, a running gag that supplies a great deal of the show's humor. Adam reveals he never thought she was interested in a relationship because she was too self-absorbed to ask him questions about his life. "You don't want to know me," he says, to which Hannah hilariously responds, "Do you even think about me when I'm not there?" Another incident occurs after Charlie's discovery of Hannah's diary. Charlie is so upset by what Hannah has written about his relationship with Marnie that he breaks up with Marnie on the spot. Moments later, Hannah asks her, "If you had read the essay and it wasn't about you, do you think you would have liked it? Just as, like, a piece of writing?"

The death of Hannah's editor provides the perfect comedic set up to explore the tension between Hannah's desire to behave appropriately in social situations and her self-absorbed desire to get a new book deal. When she succeeds in landing a new deal, she calls her father, so excited to tell him about it that she ignores his announcement that he is recovering from a medical procedure. She does not bother to ask how he's feeling or even what the procedure was for.

Certainly, Hannah is aware of her self-absorption, if only because people are constantly calling her on it. Adam, Marnie, Ray, Laird, and Shoshanna all complain about it, with Ray memorably asking if she could place "Just one crumb of human compassion" on "her fat-free muffin of sociopathic detachment." Laird tells her she's "the most self-involved, presumptuous person" he has ever met. When, towards the end of the third season, Shoshanna calls her a narcissist, Hannah tells her, "People have been calling me a narcissist since I was three."

Marnie is almost as self-absorbed as Hannah is. When Marnie complains to Hannah's ex-boyfriend, Elijah, about Hannah's selfishness, he tells her that she and Hannah are "cut from the same cloth," and he has a very good case for saying so. Marnie has just cornered Elijah to talk about her problems, and it is very much a one-sided conversation. As Elijah tells her, "Here I haven't seen you since college, and you're complaining about the same bullshit I've been hearing since 2006."

To be fair, Marnie has just received a shock—she's just learned that, only two weeks after their breakup, Charlie has a new girlfriend. However, she is so dismissive of Elijah's criticism that she goes from complaining to Elijah about her problems to complaining to a complete stranger. As if that is not bad enough, she tops it off by telling the guy he would have a hard time getting over her if they had dated, at which point he simply stands and walks away.

Marnie doesn't seem embarrassed by this incident. Her self-absorption in some way inoculates her against its effects. She does not seem to notice when she has made a fool of herself, and it takes her a long time to acknowledge that there is anything wrong with her behavior. Even when Marnie realizes that she never once went to Charlie's apartment over the course of their relationship, she fails to evaluate her conduct or find fault with it. At the end of the first season, with no sense of irony, she confronts Hannah about Hannah's self-absorption.

However, as Marnie's travails increase, as she is rejected by a second guy, loses her job, and is forced to reconsider her career, she finally begins to become more self-aware. She asks Ray to tell her what's wrong with her, because she wants to "take responsibility for what has happened" in her life. Ray gets right to the point, telling her "You act like you're better than everyone and want no part of their lives, and then when you're excluded from things, you're outrageously offended."

Entitlement (*Avaritia*)

Ray's summation of Marnie's character describes not only her self-absorption but also another sin. The sin of Entitlement (*Avaritia*) is opposed to the virtue of Charity (*Caritas*). It's more than simply having a desire for wealth, status, and power beyond any amount that one might need. That, one might think, is not even sinful. It is also more than love directed towards material goods. That kind of fetishizing would not seem to be worth the punishment reserved by Dante Alighieri (1265–1321) in the *Divina Commedia* for those guilty of the sin, namely, to be bound, facing the ground, for all eternity. Entitlement is the belief that one *deserves* such excessive wealth, status, and power, because one is *superior* to others. Entitlement is, then, closely related to Self-Absorption, and Hannah and Marnie both suffer from a sense of entitlement.

In the first episode of the show, Hannah is shocked and dismayed when her parents withdraw their financial support. We learn that they have been supporting her since she graduated from college two years ago. Jessa counsels Hannah to tell her parents once and for all that she is an artist and that they can't possibly expect her to pay her own way. That night, high on opium tea, Hannah tells her parents they need to support her because she is the "voice of her generation, or at least . . ."

Marnie also believes she is more deserving of success than other people are. She is appalled when Charlie sells an app and appears to be doing better than she is. "Charlie is living the dream," she says. "I thought he was going to be broken for at least six years. I mentally budgeted six years of brokenness. He's not broken at all. And it just proves to me, like, it doesn't matter how right you do things. Because you know who end up living their dreams are like sad messes like Charlie. And the people who end up flailing behind are people like me who have their shit together."

Sleeping Around (*Luxuria*)

The sin of Sleeping Around (*Luxuria*) is opposed to the virtue of Chastity (*Caritas*). Traditionally, this sin was simply a matter of having sexual relations outside of marriage. However, by today's standards, this is surely not enough to qualify as sinful. What is at issue in this sin is what Pope John Paul II (1920–2005) was talking about in his lecture *Mutual Attraction Differs from Lust*, when he said "For the man who looks in that way, the woman ceases to exist as an object of eternal attraction. She begins to be only an object of carnal concupiscence." It is the sin of thinking of another person as an object of sexual gratification, and no more. It is the sin of reducing the other person to the level of a thing—a sex toy, as it were—and turning sexual relations with another person into mere masturbation. When you commit the sin of Sleeping Around, you're only concerned with yourself.

Dubious sexual mores create some of the most poignant or tragic scenes in *Girls*. In Season One, the sex Adam has with Hannah is fantasy-based. He is not having sex with her—he is imagining that she is someone else. As Hannah tells her parents, he is treating her heart "like monkey meat." He also sleeps with other women, as we learn when he sends Hannah a dick pic and then a text that says, "SRY that wasn't for you."

Hannah becomes so used to this kind of objectification that when she has sex with a former high school friend, she starts talking dirty to him, as she would with Adam, and ends up freaking him out. We're not sure who we feel sorrier for—Hannah who thinks that is an appropriate way to behave, or the young pharmacist who appears to like Hannah and to be trying to forge a genuine connection.

It's one of the show's sweeter twists that Adam ultimately falls for Hannah and offers to be her committed boyfriend. When she rejects him, he has a brief relationship with a girl named Natalia. The relationship ends when Adam subjects Natalia to degrading sex and then doesn't call her. When he finally runs into Natalia in a coffee shop, she tells Hannah that Adam is an "off the wagon Neanderthal sex addict sociopath who's gonna fuck you like he's never met you and like he doesn't love his own mother."

All the characters are promiscuous. Sexual encounters with total strangers are not uncommon. Hannah has sex with a man she just met after he complains that the café where she's been working has been leaving its trash in his trashcans—she goes to apologize, he invites her in, and they have sex ten minutes later. Shoshanna sleeps with a total stranger because she is having a fight with her boyfriend, Ray. This precipitates a tearful break-up with Ray and her bedding of a long line of boys. Jessa hooks up with a stranger at a bar. Marnie hooks up with a friend of a friend who is basically a stranger to her. She also has sex with Elijah almost as a matter of curiosity.

At least Hannah is willing to admit the problem with this sin. When, after she uses him for sex, Laird accuses her of being a terrible, self-absorbed person, she admits that he's right. "I don't have anything to say to that, Laird, except I'm sorry, and I didn't think about you as a person."

Hatin' (*Invidia*)

The sin of Hatin' (*Invidia*) is opposed to the virtue of Kindness (*Humanitas*). This sin is often thought of as desiring the same achievement or possession that another person has, such as a best-selling novel, or a brownstone in Brooklyn. However, it's better to think of it as desiring that someone else *not* have the achievement or possession that she or he does have. Or, even better, as desiring that the other person *not* have it, and that one *does* have it oneself. Hatin' is wanting to have the present uneven situation *reversed*. What lies behind this sin is not the desire that you do well, but the desire that others not do as well as you. As they say in Hollywood, in order to have a good day, it's not enough that your movie does well—your best friend's movie has to be a flop, too. Bertrand Russell (1872–1970) said that this was one of the most potent causes of misery in the world, since people who are jealous like this are not merely unhappy—they also wish for others to be unhappy, too.

In the episode that most clearly illustrates the sin of hatin', Hannah is so envious of the success of a former college classmate, Tally, who is now a published writer, that she even envies her the tragedy that serves as material for her novel. "She's so lucky," she says about the fact that Tally's boyfriend crashed his car on purpose. "Your boyfriend should kill himself," Jessa tells her. To this Hannah responds, "You're just saying that because you love me." Hannah then goes on to say about Tally, "She is passive aggressive, she's fake, she's not talented." She feels better when her former professor says, about Tally's book party, "Yeah, I know this probably seems like a big deal, but Tally is a shitty writer."

Jessa is also guilty of hatin'. When she discovers that a former friend of hers has recovered from her drug addiction and turned her life around, instead of being happy for her, she is mortified. She tells her, "Looks like you got it all figured out with your brownstone and your baby and your cool-looking husband. Don't call me when your life's in shambles . . . None of this is going to work out for you, by the way."

Not classy, girls. Not classy and not fun. Hatin' is bad for everyone.

Excessive Drink and Drugs (*Gula*)

The sin of Excessive Drink and Drugs (*Gula*) is opposed to the virtue of Temperance (*Temperantia*). In his *Summa Theologica* St. Thomas Aquinas (1225–1274) said that there were five ways to commit this sin—to consume what is too costly or exotic, to consume too much, to consume what is too elaborately prepared, to consume at an inappropriate time, and to consume too eagerly. However, none of this seems sinful considered by itself. Surely what is sinful about consuming things to excess is doing so while others go without, and doing so knowing the possible ill-effects that it will have, especially on others.

The characters in *Girls* are frequently spotted taking drugs or drinking to excess, and often the way they behave afterwards is harmful to others. Hannah sleeps with Laird after doing cocaine. She also sleeps with Frank, Jessa's teenage stepbrother, after getting high on whip-its. Frank later accuses her of using him—a clear sign that he feels harmed by her behavior.

Shoshanna accidentally does crack cocaine when she thinks she is smoking marijuana, and winds up hitting Ray with her handbag. Jessa, a former heroin addict, robs the store where she works after relapsing, and Elijah tells Hannah something that will hurt her after doing cocaine. Adam, a former alcoholic who is in AA, subjects Natalia to degrading sexual behavior after his own relapse.

Flakiness (*Socordia*)

The sin of Flakiness (*Socordia*) is opposed to the virtue of Diligence (*Industria*). It consists of outright refusing to acknowledge one's obligations, and in not taking them sufficiently seriously and being careless about them. The sin is not merely that of being lazy or failing to get things done, but of inconveniencing others and letting others down—others who are there for you. In the *Groundwork of the Metaphysics of Morals*, Immanuel Kant (1724–1804) imagines the indolent person as saying that it is okay to never help anyone, so long as one never asks for help oneself. The problem, as Kant points out, is that it is the indolent who regularly need the help of others. The truly lazy person is always asking others for help. The sin of being flaky, then, is actually the sin of not returning the favor—of regularly being in need of the assistance of others, but being completely unreliable about ever doing anything in return. Flakes can only be friends with non-flakes.

Jessa is definitely the show's flakiest character—unreliable and unable to commit to anything. In the first episode, when Marnie takes Jessa to task for her flakiness (Jessa has just showed up two hours late for a party her friends were throwing for her), Jessa interrupts to reveal her unwanted pregnancy. This effectively shuts Marnie up, but it also, to some degree, supports Marnie's claim. Jessa's friends go to the abortion clinic to offer her their moral support, but, much to

Marnie's disgust, Jessa fails to show up. As Marnie quips, "There is seriously nothing flakier in this world than not showing up to your own abortion."

The most obvious example of Jessa letting her friends down is when she vanishes for months without warning. She does this after Hannah has accompanied her on a trip to Jessa's father's house, outside of the city. Jessa abandons Hannah there, leaving her to find her own way back. She doesn't turn up again for months, and is unreachable during that time, saying on her outgoing voicemail message that it is pointless to leave a message for her, since she would never listen to it anyway. Hannah is furious, but when Jessa finally does turn up again, Hannah forgives her instantly, because Jessa is in rehab. Once again, Jessa escapes blame by trumping her friend's complaints with a disaster of her own making.

Jessa has limited employment options because she dropped out of college and never returned to finish her degree. More than that, however, she rarely attempts to find work. As Shoshanna points out, she does little aside from sit around and watch *Forensic Files*.

Whenever Jessa does secure employment, she inevitably manages to mess it up. While working as a babysitter, Jessa is so cavalier about her duties that she actually loses her charges. She soon loses the job as well—not because of how badly she cared for the children, but because of a situation she managed, through her carelessness, to create with Jeff, the children's father. Jeff has a crush on Jessa, and texts her one night to ask what she's doing. Jessa does not recognize the phone number, but texts back with the address of a party she is going to, just to see what will happen. Jeff takes her up on the invitation, and the night ends up being a disaster for him, as Jessa gets him into a physical altercation with some partiers, and later rejects his advances.

When Katherine, Jeff's wife, talks to Jessa about what happened, she says, "I bet you get into these dramas all the time, like with Jeff and me. Where you cause all this trouble and you've no idea why. In my opinion, you're doing it to distract yourself from becoming the person you're meant to be." Jessa asks Katherine who Katherine thinks she is meant to be, and Katherine suggests that "She might not be who you pictured when you were age sixteen . . . She might really be serious about something, or someone. And she might be a lot happier than you are right now."

Katherine is almost certainly right. Jessa would be happier if she were less careless.

Irritability (*Ira*)

The sin of Irritability (*Ira*) is opposed to the virtue of Patience (*Patientia*). Irritability is anger directed at someone who is innocent of any offense or harm, or whose offense or harm was trifling. According to Dante, it is the "love of justice perverted to revenge and spite." According to Seneca (A.D. 4–65), it is "worthless even for war." Unlike other sins, it does not have to concern oneself, and may be purely other-directed. This does not mean, however, that it does not stem from dissatisfaction with oneself.

All the characters are irritable, but Jessa, Ray, and Adam are especially so. Jessa is prone to fly off the handle at the slightest provocation. At a party in Bushwick, she drops a bottle from a height and then insults and spits on the men she nearly killed when they protest. Ultimately, Jessa's irritability ruins her marriage. When her new husband gets angry with her for sharing her spotted past with his parents, she not only verbally abuses him, she punches him as well. Later, in rehab, Jessa's irritability is such that she is incredibly cruel to the other patients, none of whom have done anything to harm her personally. Her behavior is so awful that it prompts a rehab official to say, "With most people, the more I get to know them, the more I understand them. But not you. Are you a sociopath? Are you a method actor researching a role?"

Ray is also very grumpy. As Shoshanna complains when they're breaking up, "You hate everything. Seriously, you hate everything. You hate the sound of children playing and you hate all of your living relatives, and you hate people who wear sunglasses even during the day. You hate going to dinner, which you know I love. You hate colors, you hate pillows, you hate everything. I can't be the only thing you like." Ray refuses to acknowledge the truth of this speech, telling her she is confusing negativity with critical thinking. It is clear, however, from Shoshanna's examples, that the subjects of Ray's hatred are trivial and that his negativity is most likely misdirected, possibly stemming from dissatisfaction with himself.

Ray flies off the handle a couple of times. When Joshua, a neighbor of the café where Ray works, comes over to inquire why café trash is ending up in his garbage cans, Ray escalates the conflict in a way that is unnecessary and even unreasonable. At Hannah's twenty-fifth birthday party, Ray becomes so incensed at the DJ's decision to change the music from the song he requested that he not only confronts her but manages to get into a physical altercation.

Adam is also frequently irritable. He is prone to little outbursts—walking off a play he is supposed to be performing in, turning off a song that Shoshanna is singing to—and big ones as well. At the end of the first season, he gets so enraged with Hannah that he unwittingly walks in front of a moving vehicle. Another time, he gets so annoyed at Ray that he abandons him on Staten Island, despite the fact that Ray is doing Adam a big favor at the time. And who can forget Adam's brawl with his unstable sister—one so emotionally violent that it ultimately gets physical. While the siblings do have problems with each other, the things that set them off are fairly trivial.

Marnie, Hannah, and Shoshanna also have their moments. At the end of Season One, Marnie and Hannah get so worked up that they throw their toothbrushes at each other. When the four girls go away for the weekend, Marnie gets so angry with the others for not following her agenda for the weekend that she ends up ruining it for all of them. The weekend's award for irritability, however, goes to Shoshanna, who, in a surprise outburst, gives them all a dressing-down, telling Marnie that her "self-doubt and fear" makes her unpleasant to be around, making fun of Jessa's stint in rehab, telling Hannah she is "mentally ill and miserable," and ultimately calling them all "a bunch of fucking whiny nothings." Very little triggered this outburst, making it a textbook example of irritability.

We Forgive Them

The characters of *Girls* all have their vices. However, that is not enough for us to completely abandon them, because in addition to being guilty of these sins, for which they are often roundly punished, they also demonstrate virtues, and in particular, the virtue of remaining friends with one another. They throw parties to celebrate each other's successes, bail each other out of various mishaps, and offer each other emotional support. The patience, vulnerability, and intimacy they show with one another is so sweet that we're willing to overlook their myriad faults or, if you'd prefer, their sins.

12
Vulnerable Young Workers

ANDY WIBLE

The girls in *Girls* are not girls. They are young adults who are trying to build a career and find meaning in their lives. The path to finding a career and an identity is not easy and it shouldn't be. A career takes years to hone and its meaning often comes from the hard work endured.

Yet, *Girls* shows how vulnerable these young adults are in the workplace. Hannah was an intern for two years with no pay; she was sexually harassed working at a law firm, and was encouraged to take cocaine to have an engaging story to write. Her friends have their own problems. Marnie has worked as a host at a gentlemen's club thanks to her good looks, and Jessa lost her job as a nannie after the father had sexual feelings for her. For the most part, the girls are objectified, harassed, and poorly paid. Even if they're not sexually harassed, should new younger employees be treated as other workers are?

The Case for Treating Young Employees Differently

There are some reasons to treat younger workers differently. After all they are young and inexperienced. They need experience to become more productive workers. One of the best ways to gain it is to learn from the ground up. Starting as a bartender at a restaurant and rising to become a manager, starting as a teller at a bank to become a loan officer, and starting on the factory floor as a means to becoming a supervisor are all legitimate ways of advancing your career.

A bartending job might not require a college degree, but experience being a bartender is helpful when overseeing bartenders as the manager or owner of a restaurant. Careers take years of labor and young employees are in the early stages of learning the various aspects of their fields. Young employees often expect to work hard in tough jobs to be rewarded later with appointments that fit their talents and education. Even doctors love to regale their listeners with stories of one-hundred-hour weeks during residency that trained them to be the venerable doctors that they are today.

Careers are how we identify ourselves. A career is not simply a job that you do. A career in large part makes you who you are. When meeting new people one of the first questions asked is: "So, what do you do?" Not having an answer is not having an identity as a person. Hannah is not identified by her law firm or coffee shop job, she is a writer. It is what she strives to be. Marnie strives for a career in the art collecting scene as she works a job as a host. A career is what a person wants to do, it is often what she's good at doing, and it serves as a kind of label. Careers are long-term processes that require long term sacrifices and these girls are not children who deserve special protections. They are adults and should be treated as adults who lack experience.

Working in the art world and being a writer are also coveted jobs. They are glamor jobs that millions of people would love to have. This may be a result of the perceived ease of the job or the fame that comes with it, but these are the jobs people covet. Thus, employers are in a position of strength. They know that there are others waiting patiently to get a chance at these jobs. Thus, they can make high demands while offering low compensation and still get quality work done. In a way, the market and people's desires, no matter how irrational they may be, dictate the difficult conditions that young employees face in these fields.

Such problems are exacerbated because young employees like the girls are often victims of the experience paradox. The types of job that their education qualifies them to do often require several years of experience that they don't have. But how do you get experience in the first place if it's necessary to have it to get the job? One answer is to take a job that does not require the education and experience. The young employee can then show that she deserves a promotion. A second path is to be a temporary or contract employee. Hannah gets contract writing jobs where companies do not have a commitment to her for the long term. A third way involves internships where young employees get experience in a short-term setting. The employee and employer can see if the engagement will work. Internships are seemingly good for both the employee and the employer.

As the argument goes, all of these reasons justify businesses treating young adult employees differently. Similarly, in the Armed Forces, we don't have to treat a private like a general. In fact if we want good generals, we need strenuous boot camps. The plethora of available talent, along with young employees' inexperience and desire for improvement, allows businesses to pay such employees little or nothing, justifies imposing special demands on them, and warrants embroiling them in seemingly degrading drudgery.

The Importance of Work

Tough working conditions like those that Marnie, Hannah, Jessa, and others face in *Girls* are often defended by supporters of the free market capitalist system. But against this, it can be maintained that young workers should be afforded greater protection and be treated with the same dignity as their fellow employees. One reason for this protection is the importance of work. Work takes up one third or more of a full time worker's day and the work often defines that person to the world. Work is important and deserves important workplace protections.

The old theory of work is that work is labor. It is a necessary evil. We work so that we can pay our bills and enjoy the time during which we do not work. Work is not meant to be fun. If it was fun, it wouldn't be work. Work should not define us any more than other despicable necessary evils such as bowel movements. Work is hard and degrading. If we didn't have to work, we wouldn't. So, work may be degrading, especially early in life, but it is necessary so we can achieve other important goals.

Another more convincing position is that work is necessary for us to live meaningful lives. Our work defines us and gives our lives meaning. It is important because work reflects who we are. Work is central to our essence as human beings. In the past many women lived through their husbands and their husbands' work. A woman was defined as the wife of the plumber or the doctor. But women today rightly want careers and meaningful lives of their own, tied to work. Hannah wants to work as a writer and to be known as a writer. We are beings who work. In fact the philosopher Al Gini writes that a more fitting dictum than Descartes's "I think, therefore I am," is "I work, therefore I am."

Also, given the importance of work to a flourishing life, we need to make sure that work is meaningful. Work must make us better and not worse. E.F. Schumacher says in his book *Good Work* that bad work is mechanical, artificial, affords no opportunities for self-development, and has no element of Beauty, Truth, or Goodness. Good work is challenging, inspiring, and honest. For example, a sales job that requires an employee to lie to customers grinds at that person's moral core. Or take Ray the coffee shop manager. Ray had little interest in the coffee shop assistant manager job he had and has little interest in anything more. Shoshanna, his girlfriend, threatens to break up with him for his lack of ambition and so he goes to the coffee shop to quit. But his boss then informs him that he is opening a new store and he wants Ray to manage it. The job now involves more challenges and greater opportunities and as a result of feeling respected, Ray is newly interested and inspired.

Another possible reason for Ray's excitement over his new job is that in some respects the new store will be "his" coffee shop. He will run it and be responsible for it. This ownership of our work is also likely part of the reason why Hannah likes to write. We all know Hannah is narcissistic, and when she writes, the finished product is hers. She is often paid for the work, but it still has her name on it. Pride in diligence and excellence can be seen in her work. Much of the work people do does not provide such pride. Workers are paid to work and the product or service that they provide is no longer theirs.

Karl Marx thought that this detachment and alienation from the products of our labor was a major pitfall of capitalism and as a result capitalism should be abandoned. Given the nature of many jobs, it seems that Marx was at least partly right. Perhaps Schumacher and others are right to reply that within capitalism there can be good work if workers are recognized and respected as moral beings.

The philosopher Immanuel Kant helps us understand why treating people with respect at work and in general is so important. Kant says we are moral creatures due to our rationality. Persons have the ability to make decisions based on intentional reasons. This intentional free action is what makes us intrinsically moral creatures. He says that ethics requires that we treat ourselves and others as ends and never as means only. In other words, we shouldn't use people.

Employees should be treated as subjects and not objects for making the business money. Businesses do use their employees to achieve the business's ends and the employee uses the business to earn the money needed to live. The relationship is unethical when respect is lost and people are treated as mere means only. There are many instances in *Girls* of people being treated as a mere means. The sexual harassment of Hannah and Jessa at work is a prime example. Another example is when Hannah receives a commission to write a book, with an unreasonable period of thirty days in which to write it. She's paid an advance but the unreasonable deadline is too much pressure for Hannah and it causes a debilitating reoccurrence of her OCD. For the editor of the company, what is important is the book and not the person writing it. Kant reminds us that ethically speaking it is people who matter.

I Can Do That

Kant's imperative that we treat people with respect is especially pressing when people are vulnerable. Greed is frequently elicited when it is easy to use someone to our advantage. Young employees as depicted in *Girls* are particularly vulnerable. By law they are adults and don't deserve the special attention children receive due to their undeveloped rationality. Nevertheless, the line between protected childhood and full adulthood is usually not as clear in real life as in law. Young employees have special characteristics that make them particularly vulnerable and ripe for mistreatment.

Young workers are vulnerable for many reasons. The first is that they lack experience. They don't know what to expect and so they often just take whatever is given to them. Poor treatment is accepted because such treatment might be all they know if it's their first job. Second, young workers have an extremely strong desire to succeed. They are laying the foundations for a career that could define them as persons and determine the course of their life. Young workers are taking a long view and are often willing to accept an early loss of dignity in exchange for possible future glory. Thirdly, young workers often do not have emergency funds to draw on should an employment crisis occur. Young employees simply have not had the time to save. Hannah has often had the financial support of her parents in times of need, but many, such as her friend Jessa, don't enjoy that cushion.

The changing nature of the workforce has also made young workers more vulnerable. There is much more turnover in young workers. The Bureau of Labor Statistics in 2013 reported that between the ages of eighteen and forty-four people will change jobs on average eleven times and change entire careers three to five times. Most of those changes happen early in a person's life. A job that will last for a lifetime if you show up on time and work hard is something that only the ancestors of Millennials like Hannah enjoyed. Younger workers are working scared, fearful the company will drop them when they are no longer found useful. Hannah has a series of contract labor writing jobs while her parents have secure tenure-track professorships at Michigan State.

Changing jobs does not necessarily make a person vulnerable. In fact it might be a sign of strength for young employees. "Treat me well or I will leave for somewhere that will" is a cocky pronouncement of some young employees. The problem is that often there are no jobs out there. The unemployment rate for 19–29-year-olds in 2014 hovered around twelve percent which is five points higher than the national average in the United States, and a 2013 Pew report shows that the unemployment rate for 25–32-year-olds is significantly higher than it was for previous generations. In recession-hit countries such as Greece and Spain the unemployment rate for young adults has been over fifty percent. A consequence of this high unemployment is that almost a quarter of Millennials in the United States (22.8 percent) are living with their parents. This is an unfortunate circumstance Hannah and her friends are currently avoiding, but the security, simplicity, and savings of living at home all tempted Hannah when she was visiting her parents in East Lansing.

Young employees are often treated immorally due to their vulnerability, but vulnerable employees also can treat the organizations for which they work unethically. One example is that an employee is usually wrong to leave a firm immediately after the employer has invested thousands training the employee. Secondly. employees have an obligation to inform their employer of unethical behavior. The National Business Ethics Survey found in 2003 that young employees between the ages of eighteen and thirty are much less likely to blow the whistle on internal wrongdoing than longer-term employees. The reasons for this disparity are partly due to developmental differences in moral cognition, but other factors that lead to an unwillingness to speak up are a lack of confidence and experience and a worry that repercussions could result. Whistle-blowing is a luxury of confident, stable, and secure employees, and few Millennials in the workplace fit that description.

On top of being the age that they are, the women in *Girls* are members of the "second sex." Women have historically been objectified and discriminated against in society and the workplace. Laws and awareness have improved the workplace from the *Mad Men* style of male domination of the 1950s and 1960s. But as *Girls* convincingly demonstrates, sex-based discrimination still exists, as does a reluctance of young women to blow the whistle. It's easier and believed best for long-term success to ignore wrongdoing.

There is a sense of hope in *Girls*. Charlie's internet business is full of young employees with open and diverse workspaces, which lessens the chance for such discrimination. Transparency, training, and strong labor laws have transformed the workplace for women. There is even a possibility that these changes are the main reason that the wage gap between men and women is narrowest for young workers. Young women earn ninety-four percent of what men make compared to seventy-seven percent overall according to the US Census Bureau.

The characters depicted in *Girls* are not the worst off of society. They are white, childless, and educated. Contrary to some people's opinion, a liberal arts degree from Oberlin College does give a person advantages in life. In fact the wage gap between those with and without a college degree has never been higher for full-time workers aged 25–32. In 2013 college graduates earned approximately sixty percent more than people with only a high school degree. A generation ago, the difference was only about twenty-five percent, according to a Pew Research Study.

Race matters even more. White women earn more than black and Hispanic men, and considerably more than black and Hispanic women. But this doesn't mean that Hannah and her friends are not vulnerable. Hannah works in a job at a coffee shop and Marnie works in a gentlemen's club. These are not jobs that generally require a bachelor's degree in English. Richard Vetter, an economist from Ohio University, points out that fifteen percent of taxicab drivers now have a college degree compared to one percent in 1970. So, college degrees are still beneficial, but they do not guarantee a meaningful and secure job with high pay.

How to Treat Young Workers

Does this vulnerability translate into a need for the protection of young workers? Age is a legally protected class, but the protections in question are generally thought to apply to older workers. The argument in general is that it should not matter how old you are, but whether you can do the work required of you. Airline flight attendants used to be aged out when they became too old. Now such restrictions are prohibited. We don't want to go too far the other way and say that if a four-year-old can do the job, then we should not prohibit her. Children do need special consideration and protection. Do young adult workers deserve special protection against discrimination? This is not quite as clear, for much of the difference in treatment is due to their lack of experience and knowledge, which are justified reasons for treating workers differently. Nonetheless, there are good reasons to be careful with young workers given their vulnerability. The process of creating a more welcoming environment for young workers may result in a more profitable workplace too.

Creating a better workplace is not as easy as just saying that all jobs should be challenging, treating people with respect, and allowing for advancement, as Schumacher suggests. Some people might like unchallenging jobs and some people might not want to advance. Marnie somewhat likes her job as a host at a gentleman's club and it would seem to be acceptable to her if she was told the job does not allow for advancement. Unless they start an art gallery, she does not want to become assistant manager. Also, it seems some jobs need to be done that cannot or should not be made challenging. A factory job putting a side mirror on a car shouldn't be made more challenging by making the employee jump through a ring of fire. A job should be made challenging only if does not harm the business and aids the employee.

There are actions, though, that can be taken to make sure younger vulnerable workers are not harmed in the workplace. The first step is for employers to realize that young workers are vulnerable. Awareness is often the first step when solving problems, and employers should know that young employees are likely both to carry out and to put up with immoral actions in order to fit in and to be wanted. Protection of young workers is then the second step.

Extra monitoring may be needed to make sure older employees are not abusing younger workers, and special attention should be paid to ensure that work requirements are not more onerous for younger employees than those that older employees would be reasonably be expected to meet. For example, I once worked at a paper factory and we would stack books as they came off a press. Our press churned out books the fastest because our supervisor thought that our team was young and could handle it. Every time my back hurts, I think of that miserable job.

A third thing that can be done is to be honest with young workers. Young workers should be informed of their rights, job requirements, and chances for advancement. A workplace should be transparent about its requirements and expectations, and backroom side deals should be eliminated.

Internships are a prime example where the need for change can be seen. Internships are intended to be educational experiences for students in the "real world." They do not guarantee employment as some apprenticeships provide, but are thought to be a vital part of getting the experience needed to start a young worker's career. The experience paradox can be overcome with an internship. Internships, though, have often resulted in these young workers being abused. Many interns are not paid. The employer is getting free work. The employee is supposed to be learning but is often just treated as another employee.

If an unpaid internship is the main path to entry to some career, then the result is that only those from privileged backgrounds like Hannah can afford to embark on such a career. Not many could afford to work for two years without pay as Hannah did. Thus, internships should be paid and they should offer training on how the business works. This training often justifies paying young employees less even when they are the most competent people in the business. Businesses that pay their interns are also more committed to them. Sixty-three percent of paid interns got job offers at graduation compared to only thirty-seven percent of interns who were not paid. Pay is a way of showing respect that has long term effects.

On this note, the medical community has seen internship and residency requirements change to protect young doctors and to create better outcomes for patients. Medical residents of the past often would work several days straight and over a hundred hours a week. They are now limited to eighty hours a week, they must have ten hours off between shifts, and they must not work more than thirty hours at one time. The justification for the long hours was that they have a lot to learn and that residency is a kind of boot camp for teaching young doctors the rigors of practicing medicine.

The problem was that it was not good for either patients or doctors. These residents were seeing patients, and their patients were being harmed by having sleepy, overworked doctors examine them. For the good of the patient, reform was needed. Second, those long hours and the associated lack of sleep often resulted in less learning rather than more. The trick of learning to sleep while standing up is not the medical education that should have occurred.

The reason that these unreasonable residency conditions persisted for so long, and that poor conditions prevail for young workers in general is that old workers essentially say, "I was abused and I became the competent person I am today, so the young workers of today should be abused." It is this attitude that makes even a thirty-hour work period seem reasonable. Most patients who are getting ready to see a physician on his thirtieth hour would likely disagree. More residency reform will likely proceed as young doctors and other stakeholders are treated with respect.

Two-Way Respect

Young workers like those depicted in *Girls* are hardworking, idealistic, and naive. They play a vital role in our economy and should be treated accordingly. Hannah, Marnie, Jessa, Ray and others deserve greater consideration at work than they get. They deserve respect, honesty, and guidance. There are many more laws to protect workers today than in the past. Yet employers don't feel the obligation to workers that they did in the past and so abuse, especially for legally unprotected workers such as young adults, is still endemic. Employers should realize the often debilitating effects discrimination or forced redundancy have on a young worker.

Young workers have obligations as well. They should treat their fellow workers, and the company as a whole, with respect. The fun young family atmosphere at Charlie's office where they work hard and play hard at work is due to respect and dedication flowing both ways between employee and employer.

Workplace relationships such as these will ensure that the *Girls* of today don't become the bitter *Golden Girls* of tomorrow.

13
A Tale of Two Hannahs

CHRISTOPHER KETCHAM

There are two women separated by thousands of miles and two continents who both have the same first name.

Hannah Horvath in Brooklyn (played by Lena Dunham) we know from the show *Girls*. We will call her Hannah B.

Meet Hannah from war-torn Darfur, in a remote village in western Sudan. We will call her Hannah D.

Both are the same age, intelligent, but otherwise average. Certainly their cultures are different, their living conditions are different, and even though both may aspire to be creative artists, do both have the same opportunity to do so? And what do their different cultures mean to the two Hannahs? Hannah B is white and Jewish, from a middle class background but lives near the margins in Brooklyn; Hannah D is a minority in her country, of Black African descent not Arab, and lives at the margins of her country. Hannah D is Muslim, and has always lived in poverty.

But the Hannahs have become women. They survived the ordeal called adolescence, they have been schooled, though for Hannah B her education was longer and more formal, and both have developed life and work skills that could be applied to different jobs or careers, even if it is to maintain a home or support a family. Some women will want partners, children and families, others won't. Some marry for love; for others marriages are arranged. As women enter adulthood are they not like the Hannahs, wondering, hoping—trying to understand who they will be and want to or can become? They ask, "I am Hannah. Who am I?"

While girls all over the world face some of the same challenges of becoming women and adults, there are differences.
First, countries vary in their support for human rights: not so
much in the Sudan; more in the US. Bribery and corruption may
be tolerated or not. Some cultures support equality for women;
others don't. Some cultures support education for women and
work outside the home; others don't. Economic, health and security conditions vary as well. So, everything's relative, right?

Is It All Relative?

According to some people, called relativists, we can't reasonably
criticize the practices in one society because the standards we
appeal to when we criticize are drawn from our own society. So,
the relativist says, it's perfectly normal that when we look at a
society with different standards from our own, we see things
that look wrong to us. But remember, when members of that
other society look at what goes on in our society, they see things
that look wrong to them. Since there's no absolute standard of
what's right and wrong, it's not reasonable to make judgments
about what goes on in a different culture.

So, for example, we tend to suppose that young people ought
to be free to choose their marriage partners and that marriage
partners selected by parents before the engaged couple have
even met, are obviously unfairly constricting on the lives of
young people. But someone who lives in a society where
arranged marriage is the norm might just point to the disturbing sexual behaviors we witness in any episode of *Girls*, and
say that these are the kinds of horrors which occur when inexperienced young people are left free to choose their mates.

People who reject relativism accept some version of what is
called natural law theory. They think that some beliefs and
practices are objectively wrong, by an absolute standard independent of any particular culture. For instance, many people
consider slavery or the Holocaust to be evil, regardless of how
southern slave-owners or Nazis viewed these practices. At first
glance it may look as if relativism is full of tolerance for people
who are different. But as C. Fred Alford and others have
argued, relativism can just as easily lead to intolerance, for if
all beliefs are equal, there can be no basis for thinking it wrong
to suppress any particular belief.

A modern way to look at this issue, seen in the work of John Rawls, is to ask whether there are some fundamental rights that all humans ought to be granted, regardless of whether they live in a democratic country like Hannah B or a hierarchical regime like Hannah D. Do human rights trump cultural practices and what does this mean for the transitional experience for girls to adulthood?

We know that in Brooklyn there are places where poverty is extreme and other places where the wealth of some is incredibly huge. In Darfur there are many poor villages and overcrowded refugee camps but there are also wealthy Sudanese, especially those who are members of the ruling and governing classes. Gangs and mafiosos roam Brooklyn, killing each other and others who get in their way. In Darfur, the Janjaweed militia, which many believe is supported by the Sudanese government, has been ethnically cleansing non-Arabs from the Darfur region since 2003. Rape and murder are common tactics of the Janjaweed. But what about our Hannahs, what is their story, how have they fared in their different worlds until now?

Hapless Hannah

Hannah B is searching for what she will become. In the first episode she tells her parents, "I have work, and then I have a dinner thing. And then I am busy, trying to become who I am." But at the end of the first season she's overcome by self-doubt when she says, "No one could ever hate me as much as I hate myself." Angst runs high for Hannah B.

She's left the Midwest for the big city but kept the financial lifeline to her parents. During the contentious dinner in the first episode where her parents cut off her financing, she says to them, "I could be a drug addict. Do you realize how lucky you are?" Hannah B is not the aggressive go-getter type. So her search for herself is at times listless. Nor did she date the quarterback in high school. She dresses plainly, even frumpily, in the fashion-conscious city. She doesn't live in either the affluent Brooklyn Heights or the trendy Park Slope district, but in the grittier working class Greenpoint neighborhood.

Hannah doesn't feel very special but as she says in the same episode, "I don't want to freak you out, but I think that I may be the voice of my generation . . ." She has aspirations to be a writer but on the driven meter, her dial is set very low. Then in Season Two an online editor offers her $200 an article but he wants stories about her doing a threesome with people she just met on Craigslist or snorting cocaine. She considers these suggestions seriously and then goes to Jessa for cocaine, "to snort for work because I'm planning on writing an article that exposes all my vulnerabilities to the entire internet" ("Bad Friend").

Otherwise, she spends most of her time just trying to get by in New York. She tends to sabotage herself in work situations and is ambivalent towards love and her sometimes boyfriend Adam. Her doubt boils over after she goes to Adam's apartment to break it off: "I really care about you and I don't want to anymore because it feels too shitty to me" ("Hannah's Diary"). But they still see each other.

Her world is small in a big city. Like others who come to New York, she's invisible to most beyond her small circle of friends and co-workers. But in her mind she has taken on the burdens of her group: "If anything, I think I'm just too smart and too sensitive and too, like, not crazy. So that I'm feeling all these big feelings and containing all of this stuff for everyone else" ("One Man's Trash"). Yes, Hannah B is just getting by. She says to Adam, "I'm really scared, okay? I'm really scared all the time" ("She Did").

Hopeful Hannah

Hannah D, like Hannah B, is just getting by . . . most of the time. In that part of the Sahara there are droughts and intermittent flash floods. Water is precious and not always clean. Her family's hut is made from bits of this or that and fabric. Planted crops produce marginal yields and sometimes fail and small herds of cattle suffer during the droughts. Firewood is a necessity which Hannah D must gather from a very long walk away, but firewood gathering requires protection from marauders and rapists, in armed gangs that mostly belong to the Janjaweed. But the women don't trust the civilian police who are supposed to guard the women on their firewood search.

Her father was killed by Janjaweed in the early fighting and her mother was raped two years ago by the Janjaweed but unlike most women who are taken by the Janjaweed she survived, unconscious, left for dead with a deep gash across her face which has now scarred over. Most of the men of the village were killed. Hannah D escaped this same fate because she was gathering firewood at the time and she and the other women waited for two days outside the village until the Janjaweed had gone. At the sight of the larger and better armed Janjaweed her male protectors fled. The Janjaweed took her five-year-old brother and he hasn't been seen since. Her mother under her scar looks like she's in her sixties not her real age of forty-three. There is a baby, who was hidden under blankets and not killed by the Janjaweed, and Hannah D, which is all that's left of her mother's children. There was only one poorly built and minimally staffed religious school in the village before the drive to eliminate non-Arabs and Hannah D learned how to read, write, and do sums but the school is gone now.

Darfur had a rich tradition of women singers, mostly praise and encouragement songs to the men to inspire them in their arduous tasks. With the troubles, much of this traditional singing is gone too (as Roxanne Connick tells us). But Hannah D learned many songs from the old women and has written these down in a journal where she also includes her own private thoughts. But she hides this journal from her mother who can't read and who would not approve of the writing down of things that are personal or intimate. Hannah D wears a head scarf as other Muslim women do in her village and she prays with the other women (women and men in Darfur don't eat together or pray together). Hannah D is old not to have been married but her father who would have arranged it is dead along with all his brothers and there are few eligible males left in the village.

In spite of her plight, Hannah D is hopeful, hopeful that a good man will find her and a male relative will agree to her marriage soon. Because if Hannah D does not marry she will be dubbed maiden, get less respect and will be excluded from many aspects of her community. And Hannah D is also hopeful that the talks in the country she keeps hearing about from the UN people will bring back the village she remembers from childhood. Beyond that horizon she can't see, for she doesn't know what the bigger world is.

Hannahs at the Margins

Both Hannahs are living at the margins of the world. The oppression of the big city with its outsized expense and ultra-competitive culture keeps Hannah B down because she cannot or will not push herself into its mainstream. Hannah D cannot see beyond her village because the country where she lives is in turmoil and the various forms of oppression from government, militias, and gang forces serve to keep Hannah D and her community from aspiring to anything beyond survival. The two women are in different places and circumstances but yet they are both near the bottom of what anyone might call personal fulfillment. For different reasons their life is filled with anxiety about the future and about what they could become.

What if both Hannahs were given the same rights and conditions of living; what would happen? Before we answer this question we must explore the idea of human rights to find what it is that would give both Hannahs the same opportunities for personal fulfillment. Then we must find a location where this could take place.

Human Rights

What if we put both Hannah B and Hannah D in the same place to see whether it is culture or individuality that brings people fulfillment? In order to do this we need to put them both in a place where the effects of culture is limited. What this means is a place where there are a limited number of rights and where the two Hannahs are not familiar with the local culture. So it can't be Brooklyn or Darfur.

What are most basic human rights the two Hannahs expect in this new country? John Rawls was a political philosopher, famous for his books about justice, which he defined as fairness. But when it came to basic and inalienable human rights Rawls considered the question, "In a world of different cultures what might the peoples of the Earth agree should be inalienable human rights?"

On the basis of this question, Rawls drafted *The Law of Peoples*. He reasoned that well-ordered societies whether governed by the people, such as in the US, or ruled hierarchically like in Darfur, would have to have certain basic human rights. However he steered away from rights that appeared to critique specific cultural or religious practices. Rawls thought that it would be hypocritical for any society to critique the culture of another society as long as the other society observes certain minimal human rights.

Rawls boiled down his Law of Peoples to five fundamental and inalienable rights:

1. Life including subsistence and security,

2. Liberty—no slavery or serfdom,

3. Formal Equality, meaning that if my issue, case, or situation is the same as yours we both are treated, judged, or regulated the same way,

4. Personal Property, and

5. Liberty of Conscience, meaning I can practice my religion and can think freely.[1]

However, equality of the sexes, and even guarantees for education for women or men are off the table. Different religions must be tolerated but there can be a state religion. Land ownership, healthcare beyond subsistence, prohibition of female circumcision, or the right of the individual to criticize the government are not required. Formal equality means that there is fairness in the courts and, "that the law is guided by a common good idea of justice" (*The Law of Peoples*, p. 66).

Rawls was not advocating that these five rights, by themselves, were ideal, far from it. His thought was that if a country had these minimal rights that other countries would not have the authority to interfere forcibly or militarily on the basis of human rights if the country was not otherwise aggressive. Rawls was being pragmatic: he was looking for the minimum we could possibly accept, even though we would desire much more. And he would want the world to use all its political and economic influence to help these minimally compliant countries improve their human rights record.

Liberty means a right to emigration but there can be bureaucratic red tape. But there is no such right for immigra-

---

[1] Rawls gave one version of these rights and then later updated and expanded them. Where the two versions differ, I go with the 1999 version.

tion so the tough immigration laws of the US would not violate the Law of Peoples. Also, given that all inalienable rights of the Law of Peoples are met, the people can be generally illiterate, live at bare subsistence levels, and be mostly out of work. What the government must also do is maintain reasonable measures to protect the people from gangs like the Janjaweed in Darfur or gangbangers in Brooklyn. Being in a state that adheres to the Law of Peoples may still produce the kind of life Thomas Hobbes called, "solitary, poor, nasty, brutish, and short."

The Law of Peoples has three roles.

First, it establishes a country's legitimacy both internationally and locally for its own people.

Second, it prevents invasion or other interventions by other countries as long as the country maintains the five basic rights.

Third, the Law of Peoples actually limits cultural diversity by requiring at least some rights for all regardless of cultural practices that may not have recognized these rights before ("The Law of Peoples," p. 71).

But where would we find a country for the Hannahs that just meets the minimum requirements for the Law of Peoples to help us answer this question: "If both Hannahs were in a place with at least these human rights what would change for either of them?"

Welcome to Blandland

This is a thought experiment and as such will require creating a fictional scenario that has everything to do with Hannah B's character but nothing to do with actual *Girls* show episodes. So, here goes.

Hannah B had nearly run out of money but refused to slink back to Michigan and her parents. But she gave up on Brooklyn and Adam and ditched her friends. She used the last of her funds to fly to Europe ostensibly to rediscover the Parisian literary scene of Ernest Hemmingway, Ezra Pound, F. Scott Fitzgerald, T.S. Eliot, and Gertrude Stein in the cafés of the 1920s, now at places like Shakespeare and Company. But to her everyone was just too into self-promotion, obsessing about their art. And her French wasn't too good which didn't help win her any friends. She left Paris and bummed around for a while in Spain, taking odd jobs here and there just to survive.

Hannah D and her entire village were evacuated to the Bredjing Refugee camp in Eastern Chad. Hannah D found conditions in the camp to be intolerable and sought a way out. Her mother refused to leave, wishing to stay with what remained of her villagers. Hannah D escaped the camp hidden in a UN vehicle. When the truck stopped she found a refugee support group in Chad that helped her emigrate to Europe.

Somehow both Hannahs ended up in Blandland, unmarried, and without job prospects and no local contacts.

Fictional Blandland is a small hierarchically governed country in Europe and it meets Rawls's criteria to be minimally compliant with the Law of Peoples. Many languages are spoken including English and Arabic. The state religion is Christian Catholicism but other religions are tolerated, though wearing veils or Yarmulkes is not. Not being a native born Blandlander is looked upon as second-class and natives are chosen over non-natives in many occupations.

It's a male dominated society and women are paid less and few work outside the home. Education for women generally ends about the eighth grade, though there is one college for women. Marriage is sometimes arranged and women marry young, generally in their late teens. The state controls the economy which is marginal and Blandland isn't part of the European Union. The army is large and defense-leaning, and it's the employer of choice for many young men.

Healthcare is state run and minimal; consumer goods are rationed. Aging public transit is the mode of transportation for most. Blandland is rural, with many villages and one major city. Most people are on some form of relief. Real property is owned by the state and apartments are overcrowded because of a chronic housing shortage. The ruling family is wealthy but tolerant and there is a small group of well-heeled industrialists, mostly connected with mining. The country has a long proud tradition of successful women and men poets, writers, singers and other performers as well as a rich agrarian and forest-based folk history, which has been the subject of much of the country's literary and musical output.

Living the Law of Peoples

What will happen to the two Hannahs in Blandland? The question is important because it aims at the heart of relativism. If both Hannahs are in a place where they each have the same basic rights of humanity as set out by Rawls, what determines whether their lives are fulfilling or not? Is it the individual that matters, or is it culture or both?

But you are protesting at the top of your lungs that women are not equal to men in Blandland so their opportunities for fulfillment are significantly less than for men. But not so much different if both aspire to become artists because the culture has its share of men and women writers and musicians who have done equally well in their professions in Blandland. But we know that there are gender differences whether biological or the social conditioning that begins from childbirth. How do these affect girls and their transition to womanhood and beyond?

Hannah B and Hannah D can get apartments with roommates in Blandland. Hannah B's will be about the same as what she had in Brooklyn, and like many others of her age she can live off the dole which will give her a lot of time to write. But will she write or will Blandland be like Brooklyn for Hannah B, a place where she can dream and be with others in a kind of holding pattern, not being any more than she was in Brooklyn, a hapless soul? And will she remain a pushover to others, following the crowd while searching for herself?

But, you say, Hannah B had every opportunity in Brooklyn, but she doesn't in Blandland. Yes, there was every opportunity in Brooklyn but was Hannah ready for these opportunities? So is Hannah B's character reflective of her existence, her living in Brooklyn, or is there a Hannah B that could become what she could become simply by changing her residence and culture to Blandland?

Hannah D, out from under her mother's watchful eye, might find more time to write, perhaps to chronicle or even sing the songs she has learned. Her circumstances are better than what she could have ever expected in Darfur and the camp in Chad where there were no opportunities. But like Hannah B this new freedom to be what she can be may be too much for Hannah D, and she too might drift along, maybe even with roommates and others from Sudan or other parts of Africa with whom she could commiserate, wishing for the village of her childhood. On the other hand, having tasted the opportunity she might want more, and expand her horizon of the world until she begins to feel fulfilled in her life.

How much influence does place and culture have over the personal fulfillment for either Hannah, or how much influence does the Hannah within have?

Is the Law of Peoples Enough?

Rawls asked, "What's the best I can get for every human in a world of well-ordered societies?" For the feminists, critical race theorists, liberal jurists and others The Law of Peoples will not be enough. Yet in many countries today we don't even have Rawls's minimum human rights.

For some the Law of Peoples might be acceptable as a good first step. But how far a step is that? Consider the US where there has been a long struggle to eliminate segregation and inequality, and where the seemingly intractable problems of poverty, opportunity, and personal fulfillment for minorities have never been resolved.

While it is up to Hannah B and Hannah D to find their own way to personal fulfillment in Blandland, they will face gender, religious, economic, class, and other pressures that will push back against them becoming who they eventually want to be or dream to become. Even with basic human rights in place and their own personal drive, other elements of society can get in their way of finding personal fulfillment.

So it isn't just my attitude alone but it's also the attitude of others in the society and my own circle of acquaintances and even my upbringing that will influence me, either to oppress me or to elevate me or simply leave me alone.

For some, personal fulfillment is the accumulation of wealth. For Hannah B it may be that all she wants is to be comfortable being Hannah B, nothing more. For Hannah D maybe it's having the opportunity to dream that fulfills her, knowing there can be more to her life than firewood-gathering and hiding from the Janjaweed. But for either, or both, it could be much more.

So, it's more complicated than human rights and opportunities. Sure, some are dealt lousy hands in refugee camps in

Chad where opportunities for personal fulfillment are minimal to nonexistent and you have to elbow your way to the UN supply truck just to get the meager staples you need to live. Then there are places of plenty like Brooklyn—but it's hard there too, for even with many opportunities you've got to elbow your way into its fast moving stream or drown. And even if you are in a place where everyone has minimal rights and some opportunities, the attitude of others towards you, your gender, your race or place of birth may be oppressive.

What's the solution for personal fulfillment for everyone—or is that a reach so far that we can't ever grasp for it? Suffice it to say that personal fulfillment is a thorny dilemma. It's a mixture of basic rights, personal drive, acumen, and societal attitudes. Is there one perfect place in the world where everyone could become personally fulfilled? Look around your world: who's had everything and become nothing; who came from nothing and has become fulfilled; who has simply become what they want to become which isn't much but is enough? What contributed to each and why? Perhaps if we can get answers to these questions we will gain a better understanding of humanity and personal fulfillment. So what do you think is the future for Hannah B and Hannah D?[2]

---

[2] I would like to thank a fellow student of philosophy at West Chester University, Majid Ali, originally from Sudan who provided helpful insight into the conditions in Darfur. I would also like to thank Niemat Ahmadi, President, Darfur Women Action Group in Washington DC for her careful reading of the text and critical comments on my understanding of the circumstances of Hannah D and other women in Darfur and the refugee camps.

IV

I thought this would be a nice opportunity for us to have fun together and prove to everyone via Instagram that we could still have fun as a group.

14
Forever Unsatisfied

KENN FISHER

Adam: Is this the game? You chase me like I'm the fucking Beatles for six months, and then I finally get comfortable and you shrug?

—"She Did"

Doesn't that just about sum it all up? Hannah Horvath spends the first season of *Girls* being all-but-obsessed with Adam so long as he continued one important trait: indifference towards her. As soon as he starts to show a little bit of interest in her, she loses her once thriving passion.

This is a recurring theme in *Girls*—the characters want something badly, so long as they are unable to get it. They get off on the rejection. Suddenly, when the tables turn, and they are being accepted (sexually, or otherwise), they fall into a sort of Alvie Singer (channeling Freud through Groucho Marx) state of *"I wouldn't belong to a club that would have a guy like me as a member."* In the end, desire is something that is ultimately incapable of being fulfilled. Is there not always something more that we may seek, hoping that maybe it's the thing that will finally make us complete—or happy? This tendency becomes the main obstacle for the characters of *Girls* to having any real happiness, or developing their dreams.

This lust for rejection is actually a part of human desire, specifically in a psychological sense of the word. Humans have long wanted exactly what they couldn't have, and modern psycho-analytical theory has had a fun time observing and dissecting this enigma of the human character.

Girls has a lot to say about this aspect of human condition. When we look at the history of desire as interpreted by modern psychology, we can see that psychologists have practically written the stories of the four main characters of *Girls*. What's more, *Girls*, as a commentary on contemporary twenty-somethings, criticizes the inability of its subject matter to commit to what they want.

Freud, and His Ability to Mother My Mother

Sigmund Freud (1856–1939), unquestionably the father of modern psychology, spoke very little about desire in the sense that we're examining. This is not to say that he did not discuss desires, but he looked at them mostly in the sense of their being repressed. Freud saw desires as forces we may be unaware of, springing from our subconscious minds. According to Freud, these desires originate in the Id, a dark, inaccessible part of our personality. These desires are overwhelmingly powerful but completely blind and thoughtless. We can become aware of them only indirectly, for example by analyzing dreams or by looking closely at people's strange and neurotic behavior.

These blind, chaotic urges from the Id represent the striving for instantaneous pleasure—they are kept in check by other parts of the mind: the Ego and the Superego, but these parts of the mind also disguise the desires coming from the Id, so that they we can't directly observe what it is that we really want.

The Id is basically thoughtless want. It is Hannah in the Season Two episode, "Bad Friend," on cocaine, dancing to the well-chosen song "I Don't Care (I Love It)," with her nipples out in public. She is yelling out the chorus, completely absent of societal pressure or norms. She lays out her wants, and has little regard for anything other than immediate pleasure fulfillment. There is no thought of long-term repercussion of her actions—just satisfaction and the now.

The Ego is where the Id hits reality. It is our personality rationalizing our primal (but not long-term) desires within the construct of our society (and all of its damned rules). It places desires in order, realistically compromising certain desires for the sake of others. In the Season One episode, "Weirdos Need

Girlfriends Too," Hannah wants to be fit and lose weight but does not actually want to do the exercise that is required to get that result. While running with Adam, she explains her root desires simultaneously with Adam's interpretation of higher order desires:

> **HANNAH:** I don't like this, Adam. I hate this. I hate this. I HATE THIS!
>
> **ADAM:** Yes, yes. Fuck, yes. I fucking love it. Hannah, you're doing awesome. That's great.

In the end, we're constantly living through this internal confrontation. *I want the cake, yet I don't want to be fat. I want to take the day off of work, yet I want to be able to pay rent. I want to go to the orgy, yet I don't want to get the STD.*

The Superego is the part of our mind that reflects internalized cultural rules. It's the part of the personality that interprets society's rules. It is the part of the mind made up of the long list of things that we're not supposed to do, so that we can live with others who have the same wants, and must follow the same rules. It can appear to us as God's omnipresence, or as the fear of other people's negative opinions of our reactions.

Perhaps the best example of the Superego in action in *Girls* is not one from within the show, but instead, from its very audience. Now, this could technically be said about the relationship between the characters of any program (or movie, or book)—however, I do feel that there's a special relationship between Hannah and Dunham's audience. Her critics have poked and prodded the heroine regarding her raw honesty (both literally, and the superficially honest way that she bares her body) to the point of bullying. In response, Hannah upped the ante in the second season with her forthright portrayal of an OCD downwards-spiral and, of course, more in-your-face nudity and rare ability to be blunt with the sexual exploits of modern New York twenty-somethings.

This reaction is clearly Hannah's Ego consciously (or otherwise) choosing her Id over her Superego. Dunham responds to this in the Season Two episode, "One Man's Trash." Hannah quickly becomes close with Joshua, and the two form their own version of a domestic relationship. It is not until Hannah becomes emotionally intimate that Joshua rejects her, representing the very fear that the Superego creates within all of us.

According to Freud, it is exactly the constant choice between these three categories of the mind that creates and prods at our psychological desires. Desires are usually those things that we repress, although our Id would prefer that we did otherwise. Usually the Superego wins out, which leads our frustrated Egos down a path of unhappiness (including any number of mental health issues).

Freud 2.0

Jacques Lacan (1901–1981) was a prominent psychologist and a theorist in the fields of: psychoanalysis and literary, feminist, and film studies. He ushered a return to Freud and prompted others to focus on Freud's original texts again. Like Freud, he was likely the most important psychoanalytical theorist of his time, and was equally as controversial.

Lacan focused on desire. According to Lacan, desire is the "untold." That is, literally, that which has not been spoken of. It is often lingering in the room, and in the setting of an analyst's office, it is perhaps either considered to be so obvious that it does not need to be spoken, or it is unrecognized by the patient. Either way, it is the aim of psychoanalysis to uncover it. An important part of the process, according to Lacan, is that the desire is not only uncovered, but articulated by the patient. Lacan said that, "it is only once it is formulated, named in the presence of the other, that desire appears in the full sense of the term." He described naming the desire not necessarily as just being able to put a title to something that already exists, but at times as bringing "a new presence in the world."

When Hannah goes to her parent's house in the Season One episode, "The Return," she becomes reacquainted with Eric, an old high school roommate. While having sex with him, Hannah starts asking him some kinky questions—*do you want me to keep my boots on? What's your favorite part of fucking me?*— and eventually, puts an unsolicited finger in his ass. This is Hannah's articulation to the audience (the audience here being Eric, as well as us) of her desire. This is the first time that we see that she is as kinky as Adam, and suddenly we understand her desire for him.

Often in fiction the audience knows something that the character does not. Usually, it is who the killer is, or something like that. In *Girls*, it is frequently something about the characters themselves that they do not know—or that they do not fully understand. Hannah seems to know (to some degree) that she is self-involved, but likely not as much as is actually true. In the case of desire, we know throughout Season Three that Shoshanna wants to have Ray back. It's not until she finds out that he has been sleeping with Marnie that she realizes it (although subconsciously, she knew all along). When it comes to desire, the characters of *Girls* are always the last to know.

Lacan agrees with Freud's distinction between the ideas of drive and instinct. A drive is not a biological need because it can never be satisfied and does not aim at an object but rather circles perpetually around it. He uses the term "jouissance," which is literally translated as enjoyment, but is usually left untranslated because Lacan has a specific definition of the word. Lacanian "jouissance" is a drive that goes beyond the Pleasure Principle (Freud's term to describe the force that drives the Id). "Jouissance" is what compels the subject to constantly attempt to transgress the prohibitions imposed on his enjoyment. It is the repetition of movement of the feeling of desire, around the object of desire, which itself is also in constant movement. In other words, desire is not a constant. You can't desire another, get them, and desire them for the rest of your happy lives together. Shoshanna and Ray both desired one another throughout the latter half of Season One and the first half of Season Two. But their desires changed. No one is immune from this.

In "The Signification of the Phallus," Lacan describes desire as something different than demand, or even need. Need, he says, is a biological urge, demand is the articulation of that urge. Desire, however, "begins to take shape in the margin in which demand becomes separated from need." This is the beginning of the idea that desire can never be satisfied. Think of desire not as the thing that the subject wants, but rather a place in the subconscious that exists regardless of what you have, or what previous wishes have been fulfilled. Hannah makes it clear from the pilot that she wants to become a professional writer. In the middle of Season Two, Hannah gets an e-book deal and is only temporarily satisfied. In fact, that satisfaction very quickly turns to a nightmarish climax where she has the worst case of OCD that we have had the chance to witness. Desire is not for a particular thing, and therefore will never go away, however it will drastically change form.

The Brain from Sloven; Ži Ži Top

> Desire's raison d'être is not to realize its goal, to find full satisfaction, but to reproduce itself as desire.
>
> —Slavoj Žižek

Slavoj Žižek is a contemporary Slovenian philosopher, psycho-analyst, and cultural critic. He has made a career of interpret-ing Lacanian theories through contemporary popular culture and world political events. He takes the idea of unfulfilled desire a step further:

> In what precise sense is object *a* the object-cause of desire? Object *a* is not what we desire, what we are after, but rather that which sets our desire in motion, the formal frame that confers consistency on our desire. Desire . . . a set of fantasmatic features which, when encoun-tered in a positive object, insures that we will come to desire this object. Object *a*, as the cause of desire, is nothing but this formal frame of consistency . . .

This model of object-cause of desire can be seen in any roman-tic relationship in *Girls*. All four of the girls spend their time absolutely longing for the men that they have crushes on, but respond with nothing less than fear when they actually get what they want. These aptly titled 'girls' do not desire the sup-posed end-goal, but rather the comfortable feeling of the chase. This is why they are constantly seeking exclusively that which rejects them.

Marnie's relationship with Charlie is an ideal example. As the series begins, Marnie is unsatisfied with her long-term boyfriend, who showers her with love and attention. She avoids sleeping next to him and constantly complains about his atti-tude towards her. This would hardly be a surprise to anyone who has been in such a relationship. There is almost nothing more unattractive than that much-expressed love.

In the middle of Season One, Charlie finds out about this and leaves her. Once Charlie has shown this ability to live without her, she goes to him and tries to mend things. Their relationship is healthiest for a few moments while they are not even together. Only once they repair the relationship does she lose the attraction again. While having make-up sex, Marnie breaks up with him. She then spends the next dozen episodes (taking her to the end of Season Two) regretting this decision more and more. This is because, of course, Charlie got over her. He went on with his life, and became happy without her. Because he no longer needed her love, her love for him grew.

In Season Three, Marnie continues her pattern without Charlie. In "Only Child," she goes to Ray's house explicitly looking for him to tell her what is wrong with her. He proceeds to give her a list of character flaws ("extremely judgmental, . . . unbearably uptight, . . . huge, fat fucking phony"). How does she respond to this list of rejections? She has sex with Ray for the first time, after years of showing nothing but disdain for him.

This is not the first (nor the last) time that we see a character from *Girls* react to rejection with the offering of sex. Hanna and her friends live in an almost surreal cycle of relationships that go (roughly) as follows:

Character A wants to be with character B only while character B shows little or no interest in character A.

Once Character B gives in, character A immediately rejects character B.

This applies to Hanna and Adam (several times), Jessica and Thomas-John, and Shoshanna and Ray. In non-sexual terms, this applies to the characters' relationships with their careers, and even with each other.

All Adventurous Women Do

Nowadays, you can do anything that you want—anal, oral, fisting— but you need to be wearing gloves, condoms, protection.

—Slavoj Žižek

Girls is an excellent commentary on a very specific demographic. I have heard it called the "Lost Generation," however, I believe that that name is already taken. There are, undoubtedly, millions of people born after 1980 that have seen a shift in the employment landscape that has led them to years of unpaid internships following their acquisition of useless arts degrees. The success of *Girls* is not only to show their plight, but also to poke fun at their inability to grow up. After all, the twenty-somethings in this show are not ready to be in a series called *Women*.

The behavior of the characters in seeking that which rejects them is part of this commentary. The generation that they are depicting is the first in Modern Western Society to have so much flexibility in careers and relationships. They have more choices, and can make more mistakes than those that came before them. Unable to reach the level of success that they were once promised, the characters have molded their lives in a fashion where they are comfortable. After all, the alternative is failure or rejection.

In 2008 the University of Michigan released a study concluding that while humans experience desire and fear as psychological opposites, desire and fear have the same brain circuitry. The characters of *Girls* deny the acceptance of a partner's love because they are afraid of what that would mean in terms of responsibility. Would they have to settle down? Would they have to get married? Have kids? How can they do this when they can't pay rent? Instead, it is easier to fall down, and borrow more money from their parents.

This is not to say that the series is labeling the aforementioned generation victims of outright regression. It's deeper than that. The characters (and the writers) are sexual pioneers. They're displaying human sexuality and twenty-first-century social media interactions in a way that is so layered, that the aptly-titled *Girls* need the breathing room to figure it out before they grow up. It is undeniable that the technological, economic, sexual, and social changes that set the stage for a series like *Girls* are happening at an alarmingly fast rate. Perhaps they need a little more time than normal to grow up.

15

What Their Clothes Tell Us about Those Girls

ANNA KESZEG

According to Dr. Michael Carter, noted historian of clothing, fashion theory begins with nineteenth-century Scottish philosopher Thomas Carlyle's novel about the philosophy of clothing, *Sartor Resartus* ('The Tailor Retailored'). In a fashion (pun intended) similar to Carlyle's, TV shows can use clothes as metaphors of individual personalities and their ways of thinking.

The Foursome of Romantic Sitcoms

Before there was *Girls*, there was *Sex and the City*, which utilized a similar format: offer four perspectives on fashion and dress to exemplify four distinct clothing philosophies of urban culture.

In the making of the first *Sex and the City* movie, stylist Patricia Field, explains the clothing culture of each character: the fashionable uptown chic of Carrie, the sexually explicit and dirty chic of Samantha, the sweet preppy style of Charlotte, and the androgynous career gal look of Miranda.

While the stylist sees all those fashion habits in terms of brands, designers, and accessories, let's accept the challenge to define them in terms of fashion theories. And I'll keep with simple associations: I'll use Roland Barthes for Carrie, Thomas Carlyle for Samantha, Herbert Spencer for Charlotte, Thorstein Veblen and Georg Simmel for Miranda.

Roland Barthes spoke about the fashion system as a set of signs and meanings connected to all clothing habits similar to a language capable of expressing facts and meanings about the whole world. Thomas Carlyle uses the clothing metaphor to describe the moral depravity of humanity. Herbert Spencer considers that there is an end to fashion evolution in the principle of equity and reason. Thorstein Veblen and Georg Simmel defend the classic sociological view that dress expresses achieved or idealized social status or belonging.

The fashion system of Barthes applies to Carrie because there is meaning in each of her outfits: they are like academic texts full of invisible footnotes referring to collections, fashion anecdotes, codified information and professional savoir-faire. For Samantha, Miranda, and Charlotte the classic sociological and contextual fashion theories are inter-connectively operative: the sexually explicit dress of Samantha is the other side of Charlotte's moderate womanhood in the protestant tradition of classic elegance. And in the case of Miranda the theorists of trickle-down clothing well express her professionalism.

In those three cases the biological and social functions of dress play a decisive role. In non-professional settings, people use clothing to identify with a particular group or subculture. Doing so legitimizes even shocking or freaky choices, while assuring an easiness of self-expression. There are only two problems with the appropriation of fashion in this way: its cost, and the difficulty of choosing a well-developed wardrobe. Even if it's expensive and difficult to organize and understand, fashion is a very reassuring factor in the life of *Sex and the City*'s protagonists and the well-being of characters is related to their success in managing to be always well-dressed. The fashion system is good as it is.

Same Sign of Four?

It's easy to see the four main characters of *Sex and the City* characters as two-dimensional stereotypes (or fashion archetypes), but doing so is not so easy with the four main characters of *Girls*. This is so, in part, because the characters bear problematic relations to the protagonists of the older sitcom. When Jessa moves to Shoshanna in the pilot of the series, there is a *Sex and the City* poster on the wall (Shosh is a huge *Sex and the City* fan: "seeing *Sex and the City* is a necessity like being on facebook.")

Jessa had never seen an episode of the series and Shosh— in her usual never-caring-about-the other's-answer-style—

gives her account of how the four "girls" relate to their *Sex and the City* counterparts. She states, "You're funny because you're definitely like a Carrie with some Samantha aspects and Charlotte's hair. It's like a very good combination. I think I'm definitely a Carrie at heart, but like sometimes . . . sometimes Samantha kind of comes out, and then when I'm at school I try to put on my Miranda-hat." Shoshanna is the least intellectual of the four girls, and as such is the only one who would define herself in terms of *Sex and the City*. The other "girls" have more complicated relations to the fashion system.

Unlike *Sex and the City*, *Girls* is not a series about gender roles and women's biographies, it's more about growing up and experiencing adulthood. And even with an emphasis on the female characters, the sitcom is working on the ethos of *the* or *a* generation and not on the symbolic values of big city womanhood. The clothing culture has to be rethought in the frame of adult self-definition and of new models of consumption: Jessa exemplifies desires from sensual pleasure and immediate gratification. Marnie exemplifies a struggle to grow up, and is often out of control. Shoshanna, by contrast, is largely in control—she's focused on her education, and is ambitious. Hannah exemplifies the radical otherness of her own life-experience. (She tells her parents while asking for their financial support: "I don't want to freak you out but I think I may be the voice of my generation." After seeing their underwhelmed faces, she changes it to "A voice of *a* generation.")

In *Sartor Resartus*, Thomas Carlyle tells us that the dress of the western culture makes visible the differences between the natural order of things and the non-natural human existence. These differences constitute a main feature of his pessimistic and morally condemning views on fashion. For some, this attitude fell into disfavor around the middle of the twentieth century. At that time, dress culture, in many ways, became about the adequate relation between the natural order of personality and non-natural order of society.

For the characters in *Sex and the City*, being a single woman in New York is uneasy; there are problems with the social roles of women. For the characters on *Girls*, the focus is on the difficulty of the complications associated with being an adult. Somehow grown-up roles become unnatural and it is difficult to become content. Let's say, then, that all the patterns of the relation to dress proposed by former clothing philosophies (fashion as social status, fashion as expression of sexual power, fashion as expression of individuality and fashion as symbolic system) have to be changed. Let's look to new models to illustrate the fashion statements of our four "girls."

The Girls' Fashions

In the *Seinfeld* episode, "The Jacket," Kramer says to Jerry upon seeing Jerry's new suede jacket: "That's more you than you've ever been."

Marnie has never made a wrong fashion choice: she has the perfect break-up-with-Charlie outfit (think of something along the lines of Carrie's post-wedding-break-up wardrobe here), she has perfect dinner outfits, she has perfect day-at-the-beach wear, and perfect doing-something-morally-dubious outfits. Marnie's clothes are in perfect harmony with her desired social status, and she believes that the perfect dresses will perfectly show one's status and personality ("Jessa, I put you in the lighthouse because it's bohemian.") It's a fashion world without failure. Her fashion territory is that of pure social representation.

And while Marnie (in her own mind) is the perfect "cool person" with whom other "cool people" can't wait to work, nothing in her life matches with that conception of coolness: no cool working place, no cool boyfriend, and she loses contact even with her best friends. We see the social system of clothes in complete freefall—at least for the time being, Marnie's fashion choices are out of sync with who she really is.

For Jessa, fashion is the art of self-expression. Specifically, she's expressing her life as a heroin addict. She adopts the very European style tradition of an Yves Saint-Laurent. She asserts, "Down with the Ritz—long live the street." Jessa's attitude smacks (pun intended) of the struggling of western civilization with its outcast others: non-western cultures, tribes, peasants, and the working class. (While traveling to Marnie's weekend house, Jessa insists on sitting in the back of the bus for "political reasons.") And, as in the case of the sixties-seventies trickle-up fashion revolutions, a bohemian-guilty feeling will always be part of her ensemble.

Jasper, Jessa's rehab-connection, uses the "people like us" term for describing themselves, and that strong conscience of undeniable otherness is the main feature of Jessa's fashion choices. Everything is classy because she is the one who wears it—Jessa has confidence. (Even when donning a geisha-dress with big floral print mixed up with UGGs.)

As for the bubbly Shoshanna, there is a Krameresque side of her fashion-comportment. What William Irwin said of Kramer— the "K man"—that he is par excellence the aesthetic stage of Kierkegaardian human existence," works for Shoshanna Shapiro too. What she finds interesting and pleasurable is constantly changing, and what's even more: without any consequence. Equivocation is always the answer! Even if it's always something tricky in her choices, she manages keeping them up by negating them. All dressing issues are like her famous equivocations, Shosh states, "I think it's time to unchoose some of those choices." And in that girly pink room there is space for very elaborate fashion decision, later asserting, "I feel like my bandana collection is like my most developed collection." Oh. Em. Effing. Gee. It's like bandana is the new shoe.

Negating Fashion in the Terrible Twos

Finally we arrive at Hannah. As one might expect, things are getting more complicated with her. Her narrative voice always keeps changing because Hannah is, in her own words, "busy with trying to become who she is." We might need a little help here. And we'll seek it again from Jerry Seinfeld. Again, quoting the episode "The Jacket," in his opening comedy routine monologue, Jerry says, "I hate clothes, okay? I hate buying them. I hate picking them out of my closet. I can't stand every day trying to come up with little outfits for myself. I think eventually fashion won't even exist. It won't. I think eventually we'll all be wearing the same thing. 'Cause anytime I see a movie or a TV show where there's people from the future or another planet, they're all wearing the same thing. Somehow they decided, 'This is going to be our outfit. One-piece silver jumpsuit, V-stripe, and boots. That's it." Jerry's attitudes on clothing fit Hannah to a tee (pun intended).

In the eighth episode of the first season of *Girls* ("Weirdos Need Girlfriends Too") we encounter an iconic pair of pyjamas: a cream one-piece sleeper with buttons on the front for boys and girls equally. Hannah seems pretty comfortable in it; she even leaves the house with them on (this appears to be a subtle allusion to the many pyjama-on-the-streets-scenes from *Sex and the City*). There's truly something symptomatic about those pyjamas: it's a form of dress beyond the standard consumption circle. It represents efforts to rethink the whole system of fashion. The procedure of inventing it is completely childish, anarchic and radical: clothing needs only one feature to be validated and this is its functionality. Those pyjamas are the complete negation of the fashion industry—as a child would negate its existence. Because it's too hard to pick clothes out of the closet, it's too hard to fill the closet, it's too hard even going shopping.

Adam invented what Jerry dreamed about—what I call a "sophomoric dress." It's a clothing piece which reinvents the whole set of attitudes toward clothing and fashion: the social status is unimportant, the age, the gender and the individuality equally, but there are so many benefits that come with it that those losses are worth it: you can get fat in it, you can sleep in it, it's colorless and it doesn't even require boots.

But inventing that uniform doesn't annihilate all clothing. They need to be reinvented in that sophomoric frame. For Hannah there's not even one piece of proper clothing, which is obvious. Somehow she decided that she has a whole range of dresses and accessories created by the fashion system that she uses as a fashion-illiterate; she hasn't a clue about the meaning of dress and the rules of using it. So she has to start from the beginning: she picks up every single piece of clothing and walks around in it like the first human who had worn it. And there's always something wrong with her appearance. As Jessa puts it to Marnie, "have you ever noticed when she gets dressed up and she puts on a good dress and nice shoes and she does her lipstick and then she leaves her forehead shiny? It's like you came so far, wash your forehead."

During the whole series Hannah never speaks about her fashion choices: it's as if her entire clothing system has an inner evaluation principle, which avoids critics (or attempts to do so). And here we see a connexion with Elaine Benes of *Seinfeld*, who is an excellent mate for the three boys of the *Seinfeld* series until her fashion choices come to light. In the episode "The Shoes," the Botticelli shoes of Elaine become the main source of drama. Elaine apparently doesn't like it when anyone talks about her shoes, nor does she like to think about them. But when she's forced to give them away, she decides to lose them instead. It's the same with Hannah: even totally neglecting the fashion system (she seems to work very hard on doing so), she still has a huge wardrobe and spends a lot of time preparing her manicure and inventing interesting patterns and combinations. The complete negation and the intense involvement are equally strong components of her attitude toward fashion. There is a kind of ambiguity in her attitude.

This ambiguity is the basis of the sophomoric attitude: smart and wise, and foolish and dull, all at the same time. And what that attitude has gained over time from its invention in the Judd Apatow movies and in *Seinfeld*, is the extraordinary self-confidence of the characters who adopt it. We can call this "the perseverance of the sophomoric." If in *Seinfeld* and in most of Apatow's movies it was explicit but presented only like an exception, in the *Girls* it's a whole bunch of folks who are alike, a whole sophomoric society. This is why they have to come up with a new fashion system, emotional theory, social hierarchy, and dating habits. The sophomoric logic is that of Shoshanna's failed argumentation. It's the logic of equivocation.

But how can we apply the rules of critical thinking—formal and informal logical fallacies—to a dress? Jenn Rogien, costume designer, provides the basis. Let's take the famous example of her favorite costume joke of the series: Hannah's *GQ* colleague Joe wears, during Hannah's first work day, the same shirt as Hannah wore during one of Season One's group portraits. This is what we could call a wardrobe equivocation. *Girls* logic is all about that transformational attitude: you heard a story and you heard it like many times with little differences and then you make it work for you—pick a sense that only works for you (or for an unrepresentative minority) and use it like it's a universal given. Like Jenni Konner, writer and producer on *Girls*, does it even on twitter, "I am in Tokyo and almost everyone is Shoshanna."

Twenty-Something Teenagers

Rousseau and nineteenth-century educational philosophy enjoyed a childish innocence. As for us, we decided to fall for teenagers. Because their seriousness about their innocence is

so much more interesting. With *Girls* we have the whole culture and the whole world reinvented by the teenage attitude of
those twenty-six-year-old adults.

It has been said that the conflicts of the second half of the
twentieth century were gender-based, and the first epoch of the
emerging twenty-first century are based on generational differences. In his 1923 essay *The Problem of Generations*, Karl
Mannheim defined the generations as "important agents of
social change." *Girls* nicely exemplifies that phenomenon. As
dresses have to be reinvented, filled with content and appro-
priated, so do adult life histories. It's always difficult to think
about *Girls*, because each affirmation is somehow part of an
uneasy adulthood that lies at the heart of each protagonist's
problems.

As radical feminists often hold, only a woman can speak in
the name of and about womanhood. Similarly, for the sophomoric generation only the sophomoric perspective works. And
this perspective is based on the main logical structure of the
show: the equivocation, a form of logical fallacy that involves
interchanging those definitions. It's the same in the case of
Kaspar Hauser, who was a cultural curiosity in the nineteenth
century because of his innate method of logical thinking. And if
his arguments were used to rethink the academic logic of his
epoch, Hannah Horvath is our Kaspar Hauser who keeps on
developing her equivocations.

Consider some exemplary moments from the series, which
bring to light this logic of equivocation. Shoshanna states,
"Basically it's been a very sexually adventurous time for me.
I'm alternating nights of freedom with nights of academic
focus. So at the end of my senior year I will have had both experiences while also still being super-well-prepared for the professional world."

Hannah seemingly goes through periods or phases in which
self-contained psychological episodes play out. She had her
period of mental illness, she had periods of crisis and depression, and she's experienced professional burnout, all while she's
in her first serious relationship and experiencing her first serious job.

And, finally, we have Adam who is wise and advises the others, "You might just need to face up to the fact that you're just
not meant for a job in the traditional sense." Later he states,

"Holding on to toxic relationships keeps us from growing." Hannah sums up Adam as follows, "I'd say in some ways he's the most mature person I've ever met and in other ways he's not yet been born." And if Adam's sentences make sense, we have all the necessary elements for the correct interpretation of his statements: we just have to laugh at his actions.

This is what *Girls* is putting clearly in front of us: there has to be a lot of equivocation behind social conventions, if it's so easy to misinterpret them. Their sophomoric attitude to life and culture is so comfortable to watch, because after all—like Jessa—we don't like women telling other women what to do, or how to do it, or when to do it. Nor do we like anybody to tell us these things. What about wardrobe and fashion issues? All of our clothes are finally back in business.

16
Who Are the Ladies?

TONI ADLEBERG

In Season One of *Girls*, Shoshanna shares a book of relationship advice with Hannah and Jessa. The book's called *Listen, Ladies!* and it includes advice like: "If a man doesn't take you on a date he's not interested, point blank," and "Sex from behind is degrading, point blank."

Jessa is unimpressed. She's so unimpressed that she doesn't even bother to argue that the book offers bad advice. Instead, she implies that the book's advice *does not even apply to her* when she sharply insists: "I'm not 'the ladies'."

When Jessa denies being "the ladies," she may mean that she does not identify strongly as a woman or that she does not possess many of the qualities that the stereotypical woman has. Whatever she means, Shoshanna clearly finds her statement absurd and immediately responds: "Yes, you are! You're 'the ladies'!"

Shoshanna seems to represent a common-sense view that philosophers call "biological determinism." This is the view that there is a real, unambiguous distinction between men and women and that there are biological features that all men share which make them men and biological features that all women share which make them women. If we asked her, Shoshanna might say, for example, that all women (and only women) have two X chromosomes and female reproductive organs. These shared features make roughly half of the population "the ladies," whether they like it or not. Shoshanna, of course, does not explain her reasoning. She just asserts what seems obvious to her: "I'm a lady. She's a lady. You're a lady. *We're the ladies.*"

Is "The Ladies" a Biological Category?

Despite its intuitive appeal for people like Shoshanna, biological determinism is actually quite controversial among philosophers who study gender. For one thing, some have argued that recognizing any clear-cut distinction between the genders can be politically problematic. As Judith Butler puts it, "identity categories are never merely descriptive, but always normative, and as such, exclusionary." In other words, the position that a group of individuals *does* share certain features seems to imply that they *should* share those features.

When Marnie tells Charlie that going about his business and "not giving a fuck" is "what men do," she's not merely offering him a description of men's behavior; her descriptive claim has a clear normative implication: Charlie *should* do what other men do. Any descriptive claim about a group of people will necessarily describe some members of the group better than others and carry the implication that the atypical members of the group should change.

Biological determinism is not as widely held today as it once was, but there are still many people who argue that there are some differences between men and women that are "hard-wired" or "innate." In 2005, the president of Harvard University caused a controversy when he suggested that men might perform better than women in science and math because of innate biological differences. It's also common to see popular science articles in the news citing neuroscientific evidence for gender differences. For example, the corpus callosum, which is the bundle of nerve fibers that connects the right and left brain hemispheres, is reportedly larger in women than in men. Science journalists often speculate that such neurological differences might explain why women outperform men on attention and social cognition tasks or why men outperform women on spatial reasoning and sensorimotor tasks.

In a 2010 article on CNN.com, scientist and writer Louann Brizendine reports that the amygdala, which alerts us to fear and danger, is larger in men while the mirror neuron system, which is involved in empathy, is larger in women. An even greater difference, she claims, is that men's "sexual pursuit area" is two and a half times larger than women's. (She doesn't say, at least in her CNN article, what or where the "sexual pursuit area" is.) Brizendine claims that the female brain is "driven to seek security and reliability in a potential mate before she has sex" whereas the male brain is "fueled to mate and mate again." She concludes that "we can't really blame a guy for being a guy."

News articles like Brizendine's are generally misleading and irresponsibly written. They often take gender differences in the brain as evidence of biological determinism, implying that the differences are innate and that men are just born with certain brain characteristics and women are born with others. The problem with this reasoning is that our brains are actually highly plastic. They develop throughout our lives in response to our environments, the social cues we receive, and our own behavior. Even if there are differences between adult male and female brains, those differences may not be innate. They may have developed as a result of socialization.

If men outperform women on spatial reasoning tasks, for example, it may not be because of genetics. We can improve our spatial reasoning abilities with practice and our improvements will be reflected in our brains. Men may simply practice more because they are socially conditioned to believe that they should be good at such tasks. The size of the corpus callosum is actually another example of a gender difference that does not seem to be innate. In her book, *Sexing the Body*, Anne Fausto-Sterling reports that there is no measurable difference in the size of the corpus callosum in young girls and boys (p. 131). A difference may develop later on as a result of the different ways girls and boys are encouraged to use their brains.

Though the view that gender is determined by sex has common-sense appeal, there is actually very little evidence for *any* hardwired biological differences between ladies and non-ladies. Not even anatomical differences can establish a clear-cut distinction. After all, there are people who are born with female reproductive organs who identify as men and there are people who are born with male reproductive organs who identify as women. There are also people who are born with some combination of male and female genitals who are typically assigned at birth to one sex or the other. (Some of them identify with sex they were assigned and some undergo sex change operations later in life. Fausto-Sterling provides a catalogue of such cases in Chapter 4 of her book.) Finally, there are people who do not identify strongly with either gender.

A biological determinist who insists upon a clear-cut distinction between men and women based on neurological or anatomical differences is unable to account for any transgendered people, people with unusual genitalia, or people who find themselves in the middle of the gender spectrum. So, if a given individual claims to not identify with his or her sex, a biological determinist would have to say that the individual is either disingenuous or mistaken. But surely we should take it seriously when an individual makes an assertion about *his or her own identity*. Surely nobody knows more about Jessa's identity than *Jessa herself*, not even Shoshanna.

Is "The Ladies" a Socially Constructed Category?

Given the problems with biological determinism, many philosophers have instead adopted the position that gender is a social construct. It may be useful for us to classify people as men or women, but there is no fact of the matter about who is a man and who is a woman, at least not independently of human attitudes and practices.

One of the earliest social constructionists was Simone de Beauvoir, who wrote in *The Second Sex* that gender is not innate but that "social discrimination produces in women moral and intellectual effects so profound that they appear to be caused by nature." More recently, an influential feminist philosopher named Elizabeth Spelman has advocated the social construction of gender. Spelman writes that "being a woman is neither the same thing as nor reducible to being [biologically] female. Women are what females of the human species become, or are supposed to become, through learning how to think, act, and live in certain ways" (*Inessential Woman*, p. 134).

There's a good deal of evidence that society treats male and female children differently, even from the moment that they're born. Mothers evidently treat female infants as though they are more delicate than baby boys. They give male infants more social reinforcement for moving their arms and legs around. Mothers touch male infants more and they speak more to female infants ("Baby X"). Though eleven-month-old babies exhibit no gender differences in motor abilities, studies show that mothers of eleven-month-old boys *overestimate* their children's performance on motor tasks and mothers of eleven-month-old girls *underestimate* their children's performance (Mondschein).

Girls itself is rife with examples of men and women receiving different social treatment, and we can often see the results of such treatment reflected in the development of the characters. Lena Dunham has suggested in interviews, for example, that Adam's character probably watches a lot of porn. He seems to have internalized the expectations and sexual preferences he has seen.

Shoshanna also seems to have internalized the social pressure to project an image that is "normal" for her gender. She feels pressure to lose her virginity to a man but to appear confident and self-possessed. It is important to her that Hannah and Elijah know that she "may be deflowered" but she is "not devalued." She proclaims: "I am Woman, hear me roar. You know what I mean?"

Social conditioning may also explain why Marnie is interested in Booth Jonathan and why she reacts with excitement rather than disgust when he tells her that he may scare her the first time they have sex because, as he puts it, "I'm a man and I know how to do things." Marnie is affected by social norms in at least two ways. First, she seems to have an explicit desire to conform to norms, of which she may be aware. Second, her other desires are infiltrated by social norms in more subtle ways. Social norms dictate that men should be dominant and women should be submissive, and Marnie seems to desire dominant men.

Like Marnie and Shoshanna, Jessa's desires have no doubt been affected by the norms of the culture around her. Unlike Marnie and Shoshanna, though, Jessa does not have an explicit desire to conform to those norms. She seems to rather enjoy defying them. She expresses interest in unexpected men—often men who are older or who are not conventionally attractive. Probably in a failed attempt to get a reaction, she tells Hannah that she wants to have children with "many different men of different races." She has sex with a young man in a bathroom as soon as she meets him.

Much of Jessa's sexual behavior contradicts the cultural norm for women. She may be acting purely on her desires, but sometimes her actions seemed designed to assert her autonomy or just to make people uncomfortable, like the young man in the bar. When he asks Jessa if what he's doing is "okay," Jessa tells him never to ask her that "ever again." She wants to think of herself as unaffected by social pressure. She wouldn't be having sex with him in the bathroom with him if it weren't "okay."

Who's Responsible for the Social Construction of Gender?

Though Jessa may like to think that she has not been affected by society's expectations of her as a woman, she did not grow up in a cave. Messages about the acceptable and unacceptable ways for her to behave come from everywhere—her family, her friends, strangers, and books—those messages would be impossible to ignore. Though she enjoys defying people's expectations of her, she will sometimes deliberately play into them as well.

Jessa ditches her usual harem pants and puts on a dress and lipstick before meeting an ex-boyfriend in the park. She flirts with many men, including the father of the young girls she babysits. Though she's seemingly not attracted to Jasper, her friend from rehab, she has sex with him when it seems that is all he wanted from her. In cases like these, Jessa seems resigned to the fact that everyone is playing a role that was prescribed to them. When the father she had been flirting with calls her a "tease," she bitterly replies: "I liked you better when you were being the good guy."

It's not always clear why Jessa rebels against stereotypes one day and gives in to them the next, but it's pretty clear that she's happier doing the former than the latter. She may feel it is a public service to cause anyone to question the norms we impose upon each gender. She does, after all, tell Hannah that she thinks posing for Playboy is "noble" because it can help young boys learn about sexuality. Quite plausibly, she thinks it is similarly noble to help older boys reconsider what they have already learned about sexuality.

In fact, some philosophers would agree that Jessa's rebellious behavior is noble insofar as it may cause a small shift in the way that society construes gender boundaries. As philosopher Sally Haslanger argues, the socially constructed meaning of gender terms are flexible rather than fixed. Because Haslanger understands the existing social meanings of gender terms as unjust, she recommends resisting the pressure to conform to gender norms. She would likely commend Jessa for having what Haslanger calls "an active political commitment to live one's life differently."

Jessa seems to be at her best when a bizarre desire strikes her and she pursues it. She revels in the befuddlement of her friends. But what about those of us whose desires are less bizarre? What about the Shoshannas and the Marnies in the world? If it's noble to pursue a desire that defies stereotypes, does that mean it's wrong to pursue a desire that conforms to stereotypes? If gender is a social construct, is each of us responsible for its construction?

Suppose, for example, that some men desire "sex from behind" because they have internalized the desire for women to be sex objects and women are more like sex objects when their faces are out of view. Does the fact that men's preferences are imposed by harmful social norms entail that acting upon those preferences is wrong? Is it wrong for a man to have sex from behind if that is what he wants? And what if Jessa wants to have sex from behind? What if, as she suggests to Shoshanna, she wants to "think about something else" or "feel like she has udders"? Is it wrong for her to pursue her strange desires because they perpetuate the objectification of women?

What about What Jessa Wants?

If we applaud Jessa for joyfully rebelling against the norm in order to redefine oppressive stereotypes, it seems to follow that behaving in a way that's typical for one's gender is wrong insofar as it perpetuates oppressive stereotypes. It seems wrong for Marnie to encourage Booth Jonathan, for Shoshanna to demand that a man take her on a traditional date, or for Adam to seek out the kind of sex he sees in pornography. From here, it wouldn't require a big leap in reasoning to come to the conclusion that seemingly innocuous expressions of traditional gender identity like wearing make-up, baking cupcakes, or putting on a dress are wrong as well.

It seems to me, however, that this line of reasoning must be misguided. *Listen, Ladies!* is abhorrent to Jessa precisely because of its implication that, regardless of what a woman wants, it's wrong for her to engage in certain behavior just in virtue of her gender. Uncontroversially, it would be wrong to tell a woman that she should behave a certain way in order to *conform* to social norms, and it seems to me that it is equally wrong to tell her that she should behave a certain way in order to *defy* social norms. Both are oppressive; both impinge upon her freedom.

Moreover, behaving in conformity with social norms need not always perpetuate those norms. For example, most of Adam's behavior towards Hannah, while it's often quite strange and is probably consistent with what Adam sees in his pornography, does not seem to me to be harming anyone or perpetuating the oppression of women. Hannah is autonomous and self-possessed and she willingly indulges Adam's fantasies. (Of course, Adam's behavior towards *Natalia*, on the other hand, does seem to me to be harmful, but the problem does not stem from the fact that his behavior is consistent with and might perpetuate stereotypes about men. The problem with Adam's behavior towards Natalia stems from the fact that Natalia does not want to be treated as a sexual object, so he harms her when he objectifies her.)

The best way to fight harmful societal expectations about gender roles cannot be for each individual to behave as a counterexample to stereotypes, even when doing so is unnatural or undesired for that individual. The best way to fight harmful societal expectations about gender roles is to try not to interpret individuals' behavior as necessarily representative of their gender. Granted, Jessa has been socialized a certain way in virtue of being perceived as a woman. Many of her desires are informed by the way that she has been socialized. But while she may be *one* of the ladies, she is right to deny that she is *the ladies*.

It would be wrong to interpret one person's behavior as representative of an entire gender or to insist that an individual has a moral responsibility to behave in any particular way in order to conform to or defy stereotypes. Provided that she isn't harming anyone, if Jessa wants to feel like she has udders, if she wants to have children with many different men of different races, and—for that matter—if she wants to wear dresses and go out on dates, she should pursue those desires, point blank.

17
Suffering for Want of Love

ZORIANNA ZURBA

The pilot episode of *Girls* begins with a nicely coiffed Hannah spending some quality time with her parents, Tad and Lureen at a white tablecloth kind of restaurant. Over dinner, Hannah's parents calmly announce that they "can't keep bankrolling" Hannah's "groovy lifestyle."

When Hannah protests and asks for at least two months to prepare herself, her father softens, but her infuriated mother scorns him: "You're being played by a major fucking player." Terrified by the news and losing her case, Hannah quickly downs her white wine and replies: "I could be a drug addict. Do you realize how lucky you are?"

While Hannah does not have a drug addiction, let alone a habit, she confounds her out-of-town parents by showing up at their hotel room the next night, high on an opium pod tea made by Ray. She hugs a stack of paper close to her chest announcing, "I don't want to freak you out, but I think that I may be the voice of my generation, or, at least, *a* voice, of *a* generation." She then shoves a pile of writing at each of them and demands they read it now. As her parents pore over the printed pages, Hannah passes out on the floor. All is not well in Hannah's world, and not just for Hannah, but for her whole generation.

A Voice, of a Generation

Hannah Horvath is a voice representing her generation. Which is to say that Hannah Horvath along with her alliterative allies Marnie Michaels, Jessa Johansson, and Shoshana Shapiro, and the motley crew of boys in *Girls* capture the ambivalences, ambitions, and the crises of a generation.

Girls doesn't shy away from showing the dirty, uncomfortable, or painful parts of life. Instead it revels in TMI (too much information). *Girls* reveals the prevalence of the lack of self-care, unhealthy eating habits, drug use, alcohol abuse, readiness to turn to New Age spirituality, and reliance on self-help books. Hannah is never quite on top of things but is determined to feel what she feels when she feels it. She is shown binge eating, slurping spaghetti as she fills her arms with leftovers from her parents' fridge; and struggles with an obsessive compulsive disorder.

Marnie repeatedly, aggressively shouts her mantras "I'm okay" and "I've got my shit together" as her life continues to unravel. Jessa indulges in drugs and alcohol. The extent to which drugs and alcohol have pervaded her life is made apparent by her two stints in rehab, and her nadir after Jasper's return.

Shoshana placates herself with celebrity culture, the power of positive thinking and popular modes of self-help: she smudges her apartment with burning sage, makes vision boards, quotes self-help books, and encourages Ray to think positively. Binge eating, out of tune mantras, drug abuse, and over-investing in positive psychology: these antidotes are to help cope with contemporary life, they are antidotes for a crisis.

The psychoanalyst and philosopher Julia Kristeva would agree with Dunham that her generation is experiencing a crisis. Where Kristeva's writing reflects the stories of her psychoanalytic patients, Lena Dunham has tuned in to the stories and experiences of her generation. Dunham expresses the crisis in the psyche of the Millennials. For Kristeva, this is a crisis that we all share.

Understanding the Crisis

Julia Kristeva is a philosopher on the margins, who, like Lena Dunham, is a provocateur. When Kristeva's works were first being translated and made available in North America in the 1970s, she was grouped along with Helene Cixous and Luce Irigaray as a Holy Trinity of French Feminism. However, Kristeva was born in Bulgaria, her mother tongue is Bulgarian, she emigrated to France to study, and throughout her career (as Schippers tells us) Kristeva frequently rejected being identified as a feminist.

In her job as a psychoanalyst, she is privy to the crises of her patients. After bearing witness to her patients' suffering, she wrote the book *New Maladies of the Soul* to shed light on her concerns. Kristeva's patients' stories mainly describe people who face difficulty or are unable to "form connections or bonds with others" (Schippers, p. 60). Trouble connecting with people and forming bonds is not something that is confined to these individuals, but is experienced on a collective level.

Hey, Girl

The show's title reclaims and recasts the word "girl," no longer pejorative or diminutive. A girl relishes her youth and explores all the options available to her before settling on who she wants to be: Hannah is ready to try anything so long as it's fodder for her writing; Marnie emphasizes her abilities as a singer after being fired from her job as an art gallery 'gallerina'; Jessa is free spirited with the intention to experience everything, end up looking fifty at thirty and get fat like Nico; and Shoshana pushes herself to divide her time between studying and partying before becoming a business woman.

A girl explores her body and her sexuality: Hannah surrenders to Joshua and takes on a reluctant role in Adam's fantasies, Marnie fools around with Booth Jonathan and later Ray; Jessa proves she is *'unsmoteable'* after having sex with an ex, and later gives marriage a shot; and Shoshana tries to be "the ladies" as prescribed by her book, *Listen, Ladies! A Tough-Love Approach to the Tough Game of Love*, despite her lingering feelings for a loser, Ray, and knows that "she may be deflowered, but she will not be devalued" ("It's About Time"). A girl believes in love and its power to transform her life. Girls, and specifically these girls, believe that there is someone, a love object, out there who will fulfill all of their needs, whose presence will make life easier and more wondrous.

The belief in the presence of an ideal love, for Julia Kristeva, is the belief of an adolescent. Like the use of the word 'girl', 'adolescent' isn't intended to imply immaturity or naivety. Neither does adolescence refer to a specific age or a marker of achievement. As Kristeva diagnoses, adolescence is the time when a person is overcome by an ideal, and made sick by acquiring this ideal (Kristeva, *This Incredible Need to Believe*). The adolescent malady is the adolescent belief: the belief in an ideal other. The special malady of the adolescent is not to be confused with the general crisis, which affects us all.

The adolescent's malady is her belief in an ideal, specifically in an ideal love that will satisfy her. As Kristeva says, "there is no such thing as an adolescent without the need to believe" (p. 16). The child exits childhood and transitions into adolescence as soon as she realizes that there is another ideal for her beyond the relationship with her parents. This new realization brings about a new kind of subject "who *believes in the existence of the erotic object*" (p. 14).

The adolescent not only believes that her ideal partner exists, but also that the partner will fulfill her needs and create a kind of paradise for her. The adolescent is certain of the existence of the ideal other; she has *faith* in their existence. The adolescent is guided in her faith that: "*There certainly can not not be an absolutely satisfying other*" (p. 16). Kristeva goes on to explain that "Since he believes that the other, surpassing the parental other, not only exists but that he/she gives him total satisfaction, the adolescent believes that the Great Other exists, which is bliss [*jouissance*] itself" (pp. 15–16). Simply believing in the presence of the other and the transformative powers of love provides the feeling of bliss. This bliss transforms us into adolescents; as Kristeva explains "All of us are adolescents when we are passionate about the absolute."

Belief and Nihilism

The contemporary crisis has rendered us all suffering for want of love (Kristeva, *Tales of Love*). The crisis is exacerbated for the adolescent who has faith in love. Their faith in love is expressed as a faith in finding a person, a love object, to fulfill them. Either an ideal love object is never found, or when a love object is found it doesn't live up to the expectations laid before them and falls short of being ideal. Adam is either too absent, too present or too weird; Charlie is annoyingly loving, then too casual; Ray doesn't like anything and has no passion; and Jessa won't be anchored by anyone who won't let her express herself.

Adolescent belief and nihilism cannot be viewed as separate. Kristeva explains it this way, "Since *it* [the ideal love object] *exists* (for the unconscious), but "he" or "she" lets me down (in reality), I hold this against "them" and I get back at them: vandalism follows. Or since it exists (in the unconscious), but 'he' or 'she' disappoints or fails me, I have only myself to blame and to take my disappointment out on: mutilations and self-destructive attitudes follow" (*This Incredible Need*, p. 16).

Kristeva has called this nihilism and self-destruction a "kamikaze syndrome," which reveals itself as depression, suicide, anorexia, drug use, and abandonment in popular culture's idealized forms. Where Kristeva points to self-harm including substance abuse and anorexia, *Girls* represents lack of self-care, emotional eating, substance abuse, engaging in demeaning sex, and obsessive behaviors.

Hannah: I'm Broken

Hannah's parents make frequent appearances and play a major role in her life. Kristeva explains that the adolescent seeks an ideal relation that is formulated with and against the parental relation. The parents are still idealized as a romantic couple and this idealization coincides with the wish not only to replicate the parental romance, but to improve it, to make it better. Hannah's ideal seems to include the stability of her parent's relationship, without their power imbalance. As a result, the same relationship that is idealized is also put down. By insulting and putting down the parental relationship, the adolescent distances herself from it. Once the adolescent has distanced herself from her parents, she tries to outdo the parental relationship with her relationship to her ideal love object. Hannah often shows her disapproval of Tad and Lureen's bickering banter by rolling her eyes and talking over them.

Girls begins with Hannah needing to steady herself after her parents pull the financial rug out from under her, a move that redefines their relationship. For Tad and Lureen, this push should bring Hannah further independence, yet for Hannah, the lack of financial security is devastating. While Hannah searches for an idealized object outside of the relationship with her parents, she idealizes the relationships with her friends in the meantime. Hannah holds her friends responsible for her well-being. Instead of fending for herself when her comfort is compromised, Hannah looks to Marnie to take care of her and pay for her share of the rent. In Kristevan terms, when her parents disappoint her, she turns to another idealized object to satisfy her needs.

Hannah often turns to the girls for attention, comfort, and reassurance. After Jessa has disappeared, Hannah calls her and leaves her an angry voicemail "You're forgetting about everyone who is fucking it up over here" ("Together"). Yet, despite Hannah's earlier reliance on Marnie and the others, once she moves in with Adam she tells him: "I'm not interested in anything they have to say. That's not the point of friendship" ("Females Only"). Hannah treated her friends like placeholders until Adam's arrival.

Hannah is persistent in her quest to have a relationship that satisfies her needs for what she understands to be real intimacy and care. Adam is selected as Hannah's idealized love object. The Hannah-Adam pairing began with Adam ignoring Hannah and never returning her texts; she confesses she sometimes feels like she imagined him ("Vagina Panic"). Yet Hannah desperately wanted to be with the absent actor, writer, and woodworker. Hannah romanticized Adam's quirks and behavior. She often awkwardly made excuses to stroll over to see him when she needed affection: after leaving her internship, after her attempt at blackmailing her boss backfired—and, not even her strangely penciled in eyebrows kept her away.

To convince herself that she has a role in Adam's life, Hannah consents to his perversions. Despite Hannah's intense feelings and their voracious intimacy, Adam complains, she "never asks him shit", and it was unclear if she wanted him to be her boyfriend ("Welcome to Bushwick aka The Crackcident"). When Hannah breaks it off with Adam, he records himself performing emotional songs about their break-up, and she worries that he is "not murder-y in a sexy way, but murder-y in a murder way". Adam then shows up at her place, and she calls the police on him, even though all she wanted was for him to stop texting her ("I Get Ideas"). Adam is either too weird, too absent, or too present and falls short of Hannah's expectations. The ideal love object has failed to fulfill its promise.

Disappointed, Hannah lashes out. As Kristeva explains, the very idealization that pushed the adolescent toward seeking satisfaction will send them into violence and frustration when their ideals are not met. "Because *the adolescent believes in the object relation, he suffers cruelly from its impossibility*" (p. 15); the bliss of belief becomes the devastation of dissatisfaction. This violence is either taken out against others, those who let us down, or ourselves, in the form of mutilation and self-destruction. While Hannah has emotional outbursts, blames and puts down others, more often she is shown engaging in self-destructive behaviors during moments of uncertainty and feeling as though her needs aren't met. Hannah engages in self-deprecating sex acts. She tells Joshua that she once asked someone to punch her in the chest and then ejaculate on that same spot. Hannah indulges in Adam's sexual role-play, agreeing to stand in for a junkie who gets sent home to her mommy and daddy covered in cum.

As Natalia warns an already experienced Hannah, "he'll fuck you like he never met you, and doesn't love his own mother" ("Ladies Only"). Without someone to watch over her and protect her from herself, Hannah's self-destruction worsens. When Hannah has difficulty writing her book, her editor David complains he doesn't see her "sexual failure pudgy face semen and sadness" ("On All Fours"). Hannah descends into isolation and begins to count compulsively. The options that Hannah faces are "take a pill or talk" (*New Maladies*, p. 30), of which she does both.

Adam returns to Hannah's life to rescue her. After a chance encounter when walking from the hospital following the q-tip accident, Hannah FaceTimes Adam to confess she isn't well. Adam recognizes Hannah's strange counting behavior as symptomatic of her obsessive compulsive disorder and heroically runs across Brooklyn with his iPhone in hand and Hannah on FaceTime, then bashes down her door to save her. Adam continues to care for her throughout her episodes of obsessive compulsion and ensures that she takes her meds, eats protein, and says a calming chant. They finally commit to each other, so they can, as Natalia says, enjoy their lives like the two feral children they are—wildly happy in their uncultured love. However heroic and romantic Adam's rescue may be, the idealized love object will continue to disappoint. The solution for Hannah's wanting of love will not be found in an individual. A source of renewal and healing for Hannah can be found in creativity, not Adam's love.

Writing from a vulnerable position and expressing terribly awkward life situations is central to Hannah's writing. Hannah tells Joshua that she just wants to be happy like everyone else, but has always pushed herself to take in every experience in order to tell others about it. This is a trait that Hannah recognizes in Adam's creative endeavors, such as the play he writes about being rejected by a girl, who uses a pink, feathered pen, in his class. Kristeva grimly pronounces how "an affirmation emerges: today's men and women—who are stress ridden and eager to achieve, to spend money, have fun, and die-dispense with the representation of their experience that we call psychic life" (p. 7).

Both Hannah and Adam use their dark experiences as fodder for their art: personal essays and short plays. They rethink, rework, rewrite and recast their experiences, transforming experience into an on-going project. The ability to be dynamic with your understanding of self is central to surviving uncertainty; Kristeva encourages "imagination as antidote to the crisis" (*Tales of Love*, p. 381). Accepting the individual's peculiarities and quirks "becomes essential elements, indispensable "characters" if you will, of a *work in progress*" (p. 381). To understand yourself as a work in progress is to be open to change, and to understand the self as always in flux. Still, Hannah is suffering for want of love.

Marnie: I May Not Seem Okay, but I Am Okay

After four years of being together, Marnie struggles with Charlie's smothering love and even sleeps in Hannah's room to avoid being with him. Her ideal object has disappointed her. She complains, "he's so busy respecting me that he looks right past me and my needs" ("Vagina Panic"). Marnie's "needs" don't include visiting Charlie at his own apartment, as she has no idea where he lives. What Marnie understands to be her needs are the assumptions and expectations she has as a result of her idealization. However, it is Charlie who breaks up with Marnie; he is upset after he and Ray read Hannah's diary and he finds out how the girls trash talk him. Marnie hasn't quite given up on Charlie; for her, this object still has promise. When they begin to spend time together again and become intimate, Marnie assumes that they've had "their experiences" and can now become old fogeys together. Marnie has no sense of Charlie's intentions and simply assumes that she knows *when* someone is her boyfriend—which is, of course, whenever she wants.

Marnie's frustration with her own situation extends to a lack of compassion for others, a trait that Kristeva observed in her patients. When the break-up inspires Charlie to create an app called Forbid, Marnie is upset by his success. Marnie is further upset by her own lack of success: "People who live their dreams are sad messes like Charlie, and the people who are left flailing behind are the people like me who have their shit together" ("It's Back"). And, in response to not being invited to pick up Jessa from rehab, she comments: "I didn't want to come. I just didn't want *anyone* to go" ("Truth or Dare"). Marnie seems to have an ideal that she is trying to live up to and punishes herself and everyone around her when they don't live up to it. Hannah is her usual target.

Marnie idealizes her relationship with Hannah, whom she understands to be her best friend, and is cruel to Hannah when she doesn't live up to Marnie's expectations. Marnie frequently complains of Hannah's unreliability and lack of attention since Hannah is busy "fucking that animal." Indeed, as Hannah complains, "the only thing you talk about are your issues with me" ("Beach House"). Marnie's frustration comes from her expectation that Hannah can simply drop whatever is going on in her life and attend to her needs. During a knock 'em out fight between Adam and his sister, Caroline, Marnie calls to have Hannah come over and see the kitten that she got from some guy who had a backpack full of them and is then upset because Hannah won't come over. When Marnie's healing dinner is sabotaged by the presence of boys, she snaps at Hannah "All you do is disappoint." When Hannah tells her to lower her expectations, Marnie retorts: "I can't lower them any further" ("Beach House"). Marnie's cruelty toward Hannah is a result of her own disappointment.

Marnie's growing boredom is the result of unsatisfied and unmatched idealization. When Marnie's life was still picture perfect with her creative and upwardly mobile job, handsome, loving boyfriend who is also in a band, and, eclectic Brooklyn apartment, her boredom was palpable.

As Kristeva explains, the very idealization that pushed the adolescent toward seeking satisfaction will send them into violence and frustration when their ideals are not met. Worse still, when the adolescent can't fully delve into other aspects of life: school, work, or hobby to counter balance or replace the loss of the ideal, it "leads inevitably to *depressiveness* in the guise of ordinary boredom: 'If I don't have Everything I'm bored' [capitalization hers]" (*This Incredible*, p. 17). This rings true for Marnie, who is continually dissatisfied and upset, and Jessa whose pretentious boredom is an honest reflection of her frustration in love, both parental and romantic.

Marnie's boredom worsened and became hostile as she took on a pretty-person job at Shoshanna's suggestion, found herself having casual sex with men she thought were her boyfriend, but weren't, and, had to move in with her mother. The more frightened Marnie grew, the scarier she acted. Shoshanna rightly observes of Marnie "You are tortured by self-doubt and fear" ("Beach House"). Her repeated positive affirmations, such as "I'm fine. I'm really good actually. I'm on a journey, and it is my journey" do not seem to be changing her outlook ("On All Fours").

Her anger, antagonism, and frustration mask her disappointment, loneliness, and sadness. She goes so far as to bluntly ask Ray, who she assumes loves to tell people what is wrong with them, to tell her what her problem is ("Only Child"). Ray is unapologetic in his description of her, and then adds the observation that the "deep dank toxic well of insecurity" is probably created by her absent father, and that allows her to be a sympathetic character" ("Only Child"). Ray recognizes in Marnie the frustration of idealized love lost in early life.

Unlike Hannah, whose parent's feature prominently in her life, Marnie's father is totally absent and she has an ambivalent relationship with her mother, Evie. Marnie is intent, through her adolescent's idealization of an object, to surpass her parent's relationship. Evie is annoyed by Marnie's inability to get over Charlie, and encourages her to do 'the work': self work, charity work, work out, work on whatever it takes to move on because she is "fucking sick of talking about him."

Marnie seeks her mother's consolation. Her mother should understand what it's like to lose the person you thought you would love for the rest of your life. Instead, her mother reminds her of her middle name, Marie, which carries a legacy of strength and independence. Refusing to acknowledge her mother's ability to transform her life and accept her suggestions, Marnie further shuts down her defenses, claiming, "I've already fixed every-thing." Marnie is stuck in her disappointment.

Marnie masks her Jersey shoreline origins and preferences for popular musical theatre with her participation in the art world and ability to replicate on trend outfits. She purchases a plastic dress to fit in as Booth's hostess, and irreverently dons a beanie to play down her beauty queen corkscrew curls when meeting Soojin. The influence of celebrity and popular culture on Marnie's values is less obvious, but still legible. For example, Marnie hosts a J. Crew/Martha Stewart/TED talk inspired beach house weekend complete with plans for dinner of duck and a juli-enned salad, and a healing session of burning notes with past woes in a fire. She even asks Ray "Which *Real Housewives* locale is most intriguing to you?"

The promises of love that are normalized by commercials and popular culture express another form of idealization, and reveal the extent to which Marnie is longing for love to support her. For Kristeva the idealization of popular culture and celebrity culture "are the visible secular face of the deep need to *believe* that nourishes adolescent culture" (p. 18). Marnie seeks for a love to sustain her, but does not find it in Charlie, her mother, or her friends.

It may be, that like the Edie Brickell song she apes, Marnie isn't aware of too many things. The cadence of her frustrated mantra "I'm okay" and her indignation indicate the need for renewal, despite her refusal. Marnie may not be prepared for change, or may not have reached her crisis point. Change comes, Kristeva explains, "when they have touched bottom, precisely, they are going to construct other possibilities for liv-ing, and so one cannot construct without destroying the old defenses" (Clark and Hully interview, p. 165). Indeed, the imperfection that Marnie refuses is an answer to her adoles-cent crisis.

Jessa: I Figured My Shit Out when I Was Five

Jessa's boredom, self-destructive drug use, and nihilism most clearly exemplify the adolescent psyche in crisis. Repeatedly, Kristeva emphasizes that the contemporary crisis has ren-dered us all suffering for want of love. In Jessa's case, this is worse still as the loving foundation of parental idealization has been missing from her early life. We eventually learn that Jessa's mother is ill and "can't go to the bathroom on her own" ("Ladies Only").

Jessa's absent father is far from the ideal: he has been in rehab twelve times and maintains his distance. When Jessa receives a text message of scrambled letters from her father, she understands it as a sign from the universe and decides to visit him. During the visit, Jessa struggles to find common ground with her father, who is currently living on in a farmhouse with his new-agey girlfriend, Petula. Jessa confronts him about his continual disappearances and demands that he finally recognize that she is the child, and that he is the father ("Video Games"). The relationships that should have provided Jessa with seemingly unconditional support, stranded her. As a result, Jessa's relationships are fraught with ambivalence.

The belonging, caring and shelter that the girls offer is a source of mixed emotions for Jessa. When the girls make her a welcome home dinner, she arrives late ("Pilot"), and typically comes and goes as she pleases. She strands Hannah at her father's country home in Poughkeepsie with only a note that says "see you around." And, then later lies to Hannah in order to be picked up after being kicked out of Sheltering Winds.

Jessa callously encourages Hannah by reminding her that her "book of shit" isn't going to "mean shit, and that's the first thing she needs to know" ("Boys"). Jessa loafs at Shoshanna's apartment watching episodes of *Forensic Files* all day ("Dead Inside"), and pushes the limits of Shoshanna's gracious hospitality by inviting Jasper over for cocaine-fuelled conversations. Jessa either uses her friends as stand-ins for an idealized object and then punishes them when they disappoint her, or punishes herself.

Most centrally, Jessa struggles with desiring men, and locating an object to desire. Unlike the other three girls, Jessa continually flits away from romance and love, and claims that dates are for lesbians ("Vagina Panic"). When the father of the girls she babysits, Jeff Lavoyt, becomes interested in her "face like Brigitte Bardot and ass like Rhianna," Jessa pretends to ignore his feelings, until he takes a sucker punch for her. His wife, Katherine, intervenes by explaining to Jessa that she distracts herself from becoming who she is supposed to be with "these kinds of situations" ("Welcome to Bushwick aka The Crackcident"). Accepting attention from unavailable men affords Jessa a way of experiencing affection with a built-in safeguard that prevent her from investing affection in them, and more importantly, prevent her from having any expectations which could lead to disappointment.

Later, in true bohemian fashion, Jessa, clad in an off the shoulder babydoll dress, has a surprise wedding to Thomas-John after their quick acquaintance a few nights earlier during which he serenaded Jessa and Marnie with his mash-ups and they excluded him from a make out session. When he comes to realize that Jessa, having completed only six weeks of college, having gone to rehab for heroin, and never having had a 'real job' really is the free spirit she claims to be, Thomas-John describes himself as unicorn and Jessa as a dumb hipster who is eating his hay ("It's a Shame about Ray"), and pays her to leave their marriage.

Indeed, it is Thomas-John who struggles with idealization, not Jessa. Jessa tells her father that she thought her husband's vows meant something, but she just takes everyone's shit because he never taught her anything else ("Video Games"). In this instance, Jessa most clearly recognizes the impact of her father's absence. Discouraged by her efforts toward cultivating intimacy, Jessa then sticks with her old habits, fending off men like Jasper at rehab who was "pants shittingly scared" she left before they could have sex, and swears off men ("Truth or Dare").

Jessa's self-destructive behaviors are a symptom of her adolescent crisis. Her father is unreliable; Thomas-John momentarily pretends to be free-spirited, but is really conservative; and her friends don't quite get it: Jessa is let down by the people around her. Jessa has already been to rehab for heroin, spends time at Sheltering Winds, and then sabotages her newly stable life to sniff cocaine with Jasper.

Jessa is a Kristevan kamikaze adolescent par excellence. Shoshana excuses Jessa's binge drinking and drug use as fun, and glamorizes Jessa's trip to rehab as a celebrity rite of passage, thus revealing the extent to which Shoshanna idealizes celebrity culture, her selected panacea for the crisis. At Sheltering Winds, Jessa mocks Dr. Sterns about her reasons for going to rehab: so her grannie will pay for her rent, a plane ticket, and buy her Uggs. Dr. Sterns tells Jessa that she has a skewed understanding of life, and fellow rehab patient, Jasper, advises Jessa to analyze her life through the "kaleidoscope of her own daddy issues" ("Ladies Only"). When confronted with the discovery that her friend Season had faked death in order to avoid spending time with her because she enables, she says, "I told you I needed help with cocaine, and you took me to an ayahuasca ceremony" ("Dead Inside").

Though Jessa claims to have figured her shit out when she was five," she still describes herself as living without a life vest. With nothing else to buoy her up, Jessa turns to drugs, which remove consciousness but "render belief in the absolute of orgasmic regression real in a hallucinatory kind of pleasure" (*This Incredible Need*, p. 18). A pleasure she continues to choose after working in a children's clothing shop proves to be unfulfilling.

The support that Jessa needs is to replenish the creative possibilities of understanding her potential during opportunities of change. During a group therapy session at Sheltering Winds, Jessa snidely remarks that she could easily cry and tell her life story, in fact "[She] is really good at it" ("Ladies Only"). She claims to have "figured out her shit when she was five years old": cocaine is really fun, and dangerous. Having retold her life story the same way, Jessa repeatedly closes herself to reconceptualizing her identity, to renewing herself. As Kristeva writes of the contemporary youth, the next step is to "Help them, then, to speak and write themselves in unstable, open, undecidable spaces" (*Tales of Love*, p. 380).

When Shoshanna intervenes and puts an end to Jasper's and Jessa's bender, it's Jasper who benefits. By reuniting Jasper with his daughter, Dottie, Dottie reminds Jasper of what "a beautiful person he can be" and he leaves with Dottie to start over. Jessa is left with a dismayed Shoshanna. Shoshanna tells Jessa that "She looks like a junkie," and in a moment of ultimate self-defeat Jessa responds, "I am a junkie."

Shoshanna: !!!!

Shoshanna's fast-talking, wildly gesticulating, emoji loving self-expression doesn't mask her nihilism, rather she exudes a strong faith in the "idealization of the *bourgeois couple*, as portrayed by TV soap opera cliché, or by *People* magazine-type glamorizing

the life of the couple" (*This Incredible*, p. 18). Shoshanna culti-
vates a confident and independent feminine identity, a pastiche
of recent single and strong urban women in popular culture
including the women of *Sex and the City*, whose poster adorns
her wall, and *Bridget Jones*, who is herself a pastiche.

Shoshanna dramatizes moments in everyday life through
hyperbole. Shoshanna's dramatization "takes the form of "soap
operas" that inevitably cater to the other side of the society of
performance and stress" (*New Maladies*, p. 29). For example,
Adam is "so dementedly helpful"; her friend "is going to freak"
when she sees her rustic souvenir; her "array of bandanas is
insane;" and, "I'm like the least virginy virgin ever."

Even though she's steeped in the rhetoric of popular culture,
Shoshanna negotiates her adolescent ideals by continually
attempting to improve herself and challenge herself to push
her boundaries—which are acts of creativity to produce her
self-identity. Shoshanna wanted a date with mood lighting, she
settled for tacos. Her dating expectations don't prevent her
from dating the anti-romantic, nihilist, and self-righteous Ray.
Ray isn't quite Shoshanna's ideal. Ray criticizes her use of air
quotes "Pantomime to express your emotions is a crutch. We've
talked about that" ("It's Back"), and disparages nearly all of her
preferences.

Shoshanna slowly comes to the realization that Ray doesn't
have a permanent address, typically lives out of his car, and
has been hiding his situation by staying with her. Still,
Shoshanna falls in love with him. But Ray's dark cloud of
gloom proved to be a tough challenge to her sunny disposition:

> "You hate everything. You hate the sound of children playing. You
> hate all of your living relatives. You hate people who wear sun-
> glasses, even during the day. You hate going to dinner, which you
> know I love. You hate colors. You hate pillows. You hate ribbons.
> You hate everything. Maybe I can deal with your black soul better
> when I'm older, I just can't handle it now." ("Together")

Unlike the adolescent who seeks their ideal, and is then dev-
astated when they disappoint, Shoshanna was willing to accept
Ray as he is, and Ray loved her for the "weirdo" that she is. Still,
Shoshanna breaks up with Ray, avoids him, and then dons a
trench coat and Jackie O glasses to stalk him. Ray's lingering

feelings for Shoshanna are evidenced in his inability to make small talk with her and his proclamation that "We shared true and stunning intimacy, and now we're nothing but strangers" ("Ladies Only").

The 'negative qualities' the two saw in each other became, the 'indispensable "characters' of their work in progress (*Tales of Love*, p. 380); they recognize the revision and rethinking, the creativity, that is necessary to continually write and live one's own life story. The dissolution of their relationship doesn't diminish their maturity. Despite Adam's assessment of the Shoshanna-Ray relationship as "just babies holding hands" ("Boys"), the mismatched twosome negotiated loving the other as they are, not as they wished they could be.

Hannah, Marnie, Jessa, and Shoshanna have taken up different methods of coping with both the larger crisis and their individual disappointments in love. To overcome the nihilism brought on by the disappointment of the ideal object, a new belief must take its place; that is to say, in the clearing made after the disenchantment with the ideal love object, emerges a wanting for a new love. As Kristeva says, "the shadow of the ideal had fallen over adolescent drive and crystallized into the need to believe" (*This Incredible*, p. 19). The girls suffer from want of love, and for Kristeva, their solution is in love.

For Julia Kristeva, following Sigmund Freud, our psyche is most functional when it is in love. When in love, the psyche is stable and resilient. In love, the psyche is an "open system" which is receptive to change and to exchange with others. In the process of idealization, the adolescent, as a lover, turns their beloved into an object, or as Kristeva declares "The lover is a narcissist with an object" (p. 33). The adolescent has invested her belief in the wrong thing because she has invested her belief in a thing to begin with. As Kelly Ives elucidates "Thanks to Freud, it's known that it is not so much the object of love that is really important as love itself, as it is experienced by the individual" (*Art, Love, Melancholy*, p. 117). It is the experience of love that renews the psyche, not the attainment of or attachment to an object.

The solution to the crisis is to offer psychic rebirth to the subject, "to give and give oneself a new time, another self, unforeseen bonds" through the experience of love (*This Incredible*, p. 25). The experience of love is received in what

Kristeva calls the incredible need to believe. For Kristeva, belief need not be religious: "Whether I belong to a religion, whether I be agnostic or atheist, when I say 'I believe,' I mean 'I hold as true'." Belief is an act of confidence "implying restitution in the form of divine favor granted to the faithful." Belief and the need to believe are incredible, which is to say, *unbelievable*.

Hannah describes an experience similar to that of the belief in love when she calls her parents from the train station in Poughkeepsie to thank them because she has always felt that she'd lived her life with the feeling of a safety net under her. Jessa's description of the feeling that she is swimming without a life vest is the result of her lack of belief. The willingness for personal growth and flexibility that Shoshanna welcomes is a part of this belief, the very same part that Marnie, in her refusal to acknowledge that everything is not okay, ignores.

The opposite of nihilism is not necessarily to find perfect meaning in life, nor is it to believe. Rather, it is to something more ambivalent, less grandiose, and more flexible. It is to be open to the question of believing in something, and to recognize in oneself the incredible need to believe. Taking notice of the adolescent experience of crisis and their need to believe offers insight into the larger cultural experience of crisis. The experience of the adolescent is like our own experience "that we take part in through our own eternal adolescence" so long as we need to believe in love.

18
Were We Educated for This?

DAVID LAROCCA

Lena Dunham didn't call her HBO series *Women*, or the ironic-cum-nostalgic *Golden Girls*, and not even the literarily inflected *Little Women*, but rather *Girls*, and so the title invites us to consider how the show's female protagonists are still being formed, still maturing, still not quite themselves. As Nathan Heller tells us in his *Vogue* article on the show, these "girls" and their male companions and counterparts are trying by their wits and talents to variously discover or establish their identities as adult persons in "middle-class postcollegiate life."

The fact that all these characters have chosen present-day Williamsburg, Brooklyn, or Manhattan, or New York City more generally, as the site of this experiment is evocative—since the "big city" is a place that is perennially characterized, especially in literature, movies, television, and popular culture, as a classical American location for self-discovery or self-fashioning.

The backstory of their education, especially of the four principal female leads, involves arriving in the city from a rural liberal arts college with a bachelor's degree in the arts and humanities. And so, what does the fictitious world of *Girls* tell us about its creator's inheritance of the liberal arts—about how girls are educated and what that education is for? Marnie yells a similar kind of question—with invective comments full of anger and frustration—to her boss as she quits her job at Ray's coffee shop, a job she believes is beneath not just her dignity but her education: "Do you know what kind of work I'm qualified to do out in the world?" ("Dead Inside").

When Hannah goes to work for *GQ* in the desperate wake of not being able to publish her memoir, she asks a rhetorical question in the same vein, with the same sense of clarity that she, for whatever reason, lives at a remove from her proper work: "Do you think that I think this is the best use of my literary voice and my myriad talents?" ("Free Snacks"). The presumptions nested in Marnie and Hannah's rhetorical questions make clear that the show is aware that these are worthy questions—perhaps ones it knows must be asked but doesn't quite know how to fully answer. Indeterminacy and ambiguity in knowing what to do are essential to the show's theme and its resonance.

We do know, however, that the show's chief writer and producer, Lena Dunham, grew up in Brooklyn, the daughter of two artists, graduated from Oberlin College—a school famous for its liberal arts tradition—with a degree in creative writing and that her education there informed the story dramatized in her first feature movies, *Creative Nonfiction* (2009) and *Tiny Furniture* (2010), and thereafter, several of the lead characters that populate *Girls*. But how precisely, or if at all, are the values and virtues of a liberal arts education learned at a place such as Oberlin, and its many equivalent institutions, translated—or not—into a fictional world that is often treated as an analogue of our own?

Author and Character

A first clue to replying to such a question comes in the fact that Lena Dunham not only stars in the show she writes, but that her character, Hannah Horvath, is understood—by Dunham—to be a sort of fictionalized doppelgänger. Like Charlie Kaufman who featured a character named Charlie Kaufman (played by Nicolas Cage) in his movie *Adaptation* (2002), and well before him, like Plato, who used fiction and fictitious characters (often based on historical people, such as Socrates and Gorgias) to explore his ideas, we find Dunham depicting Hannah's experiences as iterations or variations on Dunham's own experience as a young woman who graduated from a liberal arts college and wants to be a writer in New York.

Dunham herself acknowledges the relationship between herself and her "hapless alter ego," between real and fake worlds with a quick gesture of intimacy and interrelation: "the show is so personal—I have OCD, Hannah has OCD" (*Entertainment Weekly* interview, p. 40). And we know that Dunham's first book is a memoir—while Hannah works on her memoir to be published as an e-book, and as such, she emphasizes with regret, "It will never '*hit* the shelves'" ("Dead Inside").

Yet, as must be the case given Dunham's productivity and Hannah's apparent lack of it, we're encouraged to view them as related figures but also chastened by their differences. As Dunham's mother, the artist Laurie Simmons says of her daughter: "That character [Aura] couldn't write a script like *Tiny Furniture* and get the movie made," adding that when Lena lived at home after college, "I would go into her bedroom late at night, and she'd have fallen asleep amid a heap of cell phone, laptop, books, scripts, pencils, papers. She was in her bed covered with work" (Heller).

As Kaufman's critique of Hollywood storytelling takes place in a Hollywood movie with A-list actors, and as Plato's dialogues feature the star intellect, Socrates, who himself doesn't write a word, so we have in Dunham's creative project a show that is aware of itself as a show, standing in relation to a world it is meant to reflect and transform. And so Dunham is a liberal arts graduate in creative writing who, with her band of players in the city, aims to show what it's like for a liberal arts graduate in creative writing in the city.

There's a Thousand Yous, There's Only One of Me

What are the liberal arts for today? To a considerable extent, the long-standing and still-steadfastly held notion of liberal arts is the implied or assumed grandeur of an individual's identity—discovering it, developing it, defining it, defending it. One of the goals of such undergraduate education is self-exploration and self-expression. Meanwhile, cultures of technology are reinforcing and intensifying the self-centric nature of personal identity among young people—from Facebook pages to selfies, the latter now sanctioned by the *Oxford English Dictionary* as 2013's "word of the year" and another indication of the self-orientation of popular culture and its technologies for self-representation and self-reference.

Yet, as Andrew Delbanco has emphasized, college should help students "develop certain qualities of mind and heart requisite for reflective citizenship" (*College*, p. 3). One of Delbanco's distilled precepts for the undergraduate includes "A willingness to imagine experience from perspectives other than one's own." Being reflective, of course, may rightly involve the pursuit of self-knowledge, but it needn't devolve solely into a solipsistic project of *self*-reflection. Students are then asked to look *beyond* themselves—to develop empathy—as part and parcel of their individually designed and defined educational endeavor.

So, what is the liberal arts education, often undertaken in pastoral settings, meant to confer on its students, who upon graduation often relocate to large cities and trendy locations (Nashville, Austin, Portland)? And if that conferral was successful, of what relevance is it to a striving soul in the hustle and bustle of a congested urban context? Do you dutifully, earnestly train to be an independent writer or avant-garde artist and then end up being a secretary typing memos (Hannah) or a receptionist taking messages in an art gallery (Marnie)? Do you read lauded works of literature and perennially provocative philosophy in class only to feel a disjunction between the lessons of those works and your day-to-day life in the workaday world—that is, to find it hard to articulate your own ideas in writing or in the expression of artworks?

What's the meaning and status of the individual self in all of this—is it a knowing source from which to take dictation (one metaphor) or an empty vessel you aim to fill (a competing metaphor)? More than a cliché about creative writers and art students trying to "make it" in the big city—a phrase we find in Kayne West's "Stronger" (sung by Marnie in "On All Fours") and in the classic anthem "New York, New York,"—"if I can make it here, I'll make it anywhere"—*Girls* variously depicts, romanticizes, laments, skewers, and problematizes the nature and even the existence of the liberal-arts graduate in the early twenty-first-century American metropolis.

The inheritance of Sinatra's signature myth of how we "make it" (or not) is also echoed in "Empire State of Mind," where Alicia Keys belts the reassuring chorus "there's nothin' you can't do / Now you're in New York / These streets will make you feel brand new / Big lights will inspire you"—only to have her manic proclamation quickly chastened by Jay-Z's "City is a pity, half of y'all won't make it." And in *Girls* the terms and conditions of what it means to make it are perpetually under debate in some form or another—romantically, vocationally, emotionally, and intellectually.

A *Saturday Night Live* satire of *Girls*, featuring Tina Fey as a long suffering Albanian woman named Blerta, suggests that the characters on the show are out of touch with genuine pain, real trauma, and substantive problems. The characters seem to have quite shockingly failed to develop Delbanco's recommended trait of "reflective citizenship" along with a capacity to "imagine experience from perspectives other than one's own." Moreover, the fact that the short—presented as a mock coming attraction promotion for a future episode—features a *woman* among girls, creates something of an analogue to the age asymmetry that pervades, for example, the Platonic dialogues—where it is always men who instruct boys.

In the *SNL* send-up, an exasperated Marnie tells Hannah: "My ex-boyfriend is an Internet millionaire." Blerta overhears this from the other room and shares her experience in broken, accented English: "My ex-boyfriend is buried in shallow grave. On windy days the dirt covering him blows away and you can see skull." In a closing vignette, Hannah (Noël Wells) worries aloud—"I just don't know how anything is going to turn out"—so Blerta comforts her with an embrace and says with assurance: "It's okay, you are only fifteen." Hannah corrects her with injured pride: "No I'm not. I'm twenty-four." Blerta responds quizzically: "Twenty-four? What the fuck is wrong with you?"

The skit is very funny, and draws its humor from Blerta's desperate life and her incomprehension of the girls she's living with. From the popularity of the show—especially its critical success—audiences must be drawn to it not for its opacity but because it reflects something intelligible, something viewers can recognize in themselves or others. So like the *SNL* satire of *Girls*, *Girls* itself is taking seriously but also critiquing a pervasive predicament, or attitude, or style of life. And given the intergenerational characters—from Hannah's parents, literary editor, and afternoon lover, to Jessa's father, husband, and rehab friend—audiences will likely find points of resemblance and resonance. Parents spending huge sums of money on their child's education—or none. A daughter trying to do well by her parents' expectations, and failing to do just that.

These and related topics and issues suggest that *Girls* is an engaging and ongoing text for exploring a contemporary understanding of *paideia*—the classical Greek notion of culture, or education, or the process of becoming oneself (a whole and balanced individual) in the midst of a robust community of others—and its legacy in the modern university's exercise of the liberal arts. Are we, any longer, caught up in the hope of educating the young to realize their ideal humanity as citizens of the polis (one way of describing the Greek ambition), or has the self become sufficiently abstracted from its lived context that our focus turns to its expression (often in terms of creative work, or the persona that claims its authorship); its reference to itself (in moods of meta-critical ironic distancing); and its promotion (through various modes of display and digital mediation)?

To the extent that the present-day liberal arts preserves some of the ancient Greek notion of paideia, how does *Girls* portray the liberal arts as a pre-condition, condition, or context for the make-up of one's identity as a person and a professional—as an adult—that is, when girls become women? There are specific instances in the show when the characters engender these values and virtues—for example, Hannah defending her writing by saying "It's not a journal"; but the show itself, as it draws from the creator's contemporary experience and her contribution to contemporary culture, helps us think through the meaning of education and liberal arts—perhaps especially the role of the humanities in our lives, the training of artists, and thereafter the creation of art works.

Damn, They Don't Make 'Em Like This Anymore

What if there were a way of taking up the education of the young—both as the teachers of youth and as youth who seek instruction—that addressed them as individuals yet resisted the inculcation of individualism? Think of how Hannah becomes the unexpected mentor—a sort of emotional tutor—for her younger cousin, Rebecca (Sarah Steele), whose ambition for professional achievement is used as a prophylactic against undigested family trauma ("Flo"). For those who find Rebecca unsympathetic, perhaps it's worth considering how her self-understanding and self-valuation are distorted—in particular, focused too intently on her status as assessed by others and the institutions they run.

If Rebecca could see her medical training as part of a larger interaction between herself and her community—both of them in need of care—her painful complex of narcissism and shame might evolve into something like a sense of humble service to others in need—what medical doctors are mythically and practically promised to do. Hannah's uncharacteristically generous and patient attention to Rebecca reveals new empathic capacities in Hannah (a respite from her incessant self-involvement), and also makes evident the positive efficacy of mentors who do not stir and stoke another's resentment and fear, but guide her to a better view of the situation.

Turning to ancient Greek values, we find a complementary phenomenon in the notion of paideia—tersely defined as "education," or more fully construed as the art of aiming to create ideal, culturally and politically astute members of the polis. The term, along with the millennia-old debates over its precise meaning, emerged in a distinctive way in Plato, for example, in the *Protagoras*, where the question of education's *effect* is discussed—for instance, can virtue be taught?; in the *Gorgias*, where rhetoric's status as a "knack" is said to render it merely a superficial skill for gratification and pleasure, for persuading crowds and not the care and formation of the individual soul; and in the *Republic* where Socrates likens paideia to a process of becoming human.

We also find an engaging account of paideia from one of Gorgias's students, and one of Plato's chief rivals, Isocrates, who in his "Against the Sophists" and *Antidosis* lends helpful orientation to the meaning of the term and its potential relevance to an inquiry about the current status of the liberal arts, which after all drew its inspiration from ancient Greek modes of education. Werner Jaeger, who wrote the three-volume masterwork, *Paideia: The Ideals of Greek Culture*, referred to Isocrates—not Socrates—as "the father of 'humanistic culture'" (Volume III, p. 46). Jaeger contends that "since the Renaissance [Isocrates] has exercised a far greater influence on the educational methods of humanism than any other Greek or Roman teacher." Meanwhile, Jaeger cautions, "an understanding of the true

Greek paideia at once entails a criticism of modern academic humanism" (p. 47).

Have the liberal arts graduates portrayed in *Girls*—despite their pedigrees and credentials—benefited from ancient paideia or, as Jaeger suggests, would a robust engagement with the ancient Greek form of education undermine more contemporary notions of training individuals, who may or may not find fulfillment in a life shared with other people? Hannah's elation upon receiving an acceptance letter (in the wake of Rebecca's story, and Hannah's vocational struggles, the notion of "acceptance" here seems particularly painful—and telling), to graduate school invites a fresh consideration of the writer and the city ("Two Plane Rides"). Once again, it seems Hannah is drawn to a pastoral location to train in the liberal arts—now, perhaps, going even deeper into the Midwest than she did before.

What *does* a writer learn at Iowa? To study literature, to summon the spirit for writing it, to sort the craft of composition, to overcome craft as we have known it? Might those things be learned—learned better?—in an extracurricular life lived in New York City? These questions are familiar enough to have prompted a recent anthology of essays—*MFA vs NYC: The Two Cultures of American Fiction*—edited by novelist Chad Harbach. At a time when writers can, if only thinking technologically, transmit their work from any location on Earth, what would these realms—one in the academy (which has many locations), the other in the traditional, say, pre-Internet, capital of publishing (which was and still appears to be New York)—retain for the education and flourishing of writers? This is the sort of question Harbach's collection addresses, and it's also the kind we find serially at issue in *Girls* and in the journalistic and critical reception of the show.

As we're being entertained by Hannah's fraught decision making—whether to leave New York for Iowa, whether to agonistically engage "MFA vs. NYC" as an existential conflict—we are given a chance to wonder which life seems more appealing: one in which a young writer is accepted into the country's best graduate school for writing, or one in which that achievement is a fiction in a Golden Globe–winning series on HBO? Who knew that *Girls also* could be such a devastating "criticism of modern academic humanism"?

Though Plato and Isocrates offered, as Carlin Romano notes, "two visions of philosophy," they agreed that the constitution of the self cannot be understood as a project that takes place *within* the self, or that is generated *from* the self (*America*, p. 535). Rather, you must be other- and outer-directed. Hannah and Rebecca's relationship seems a meaningful clinic on this insight. And so the contemporary emphasis in liberal arts and creative writing on self-expression, self-reference, and self-promotion—that is, a habitual reference to the self as a *source*—all distort or distract from what might be considered the most crucial task of a liberal arts education, especially as derived from ancient Greek notions of paideia and their inheritance through the Renaissance and into our modern context: to address the work itself, with the aid and direction of your teacher or mentor—in a mood of wonder and receptivity, with an evolving and expanding sense of empathy for others, and with attunement to the moral edification made possible by the work.

Should we worry that Hannah's proposed educational training in Iowa will not likely help her dissolve habitual self-reference but, presumably, only exacerbate it further (for example, as authors become brands in need of endless self-promotion)? We may wonder about the difference between egos and ideas as we find them among ex-writers at the *GQ* roundtable meetings and those we discover among the most promising students around the seminar table in Iowa.

Girls reflects, and explores, the consequences of a culture that would decide that there are two fundamental options for the writer (if also, admittedly, caricatured and critiqued in the show): a life in "advertorial," and a life by way of an academically-trained, financially structured, institutionally-sanctioned path. (The third option, the most coveted—just being a writer and living from the proceeds that follow the work—no long seems viable for the vast majority of writers.)

At the core of Isocrates's paideia, according to Romano, is the "development of judgment"—not as a pronouncement of righteous condemnation, but in the philosophical sense as a capacity to measure, mediate, and modify ideas and beliefs based on experience. For this reason, among others, Romano recognizes Isocrates as "the father of what we now call 'liberal arts education,' the instilling in students of a flexible, critical spirit and a mastery of language" (p. 550).

One of the leitmotifs of *Girls* is the extent to which Adam Sackler is accepting of others—the way, to use the term under a different aspect, he lacks judgment. Many times, Adam's willingness to refrain from making or voicing judgments about others is regarded, by others, as an almost Christ-like attribute. Characters are in awe of his capacity to be without judgment— that is, without ever-expanding waves of stinging, acerbic irony and snark. But, importantly, it also seems he doesn't *form* judgments that he furtively withholds; he is not, that is to say, duplicitous or resentful. While this inflection of judgment is central to Adam's service as a counterpoint to Hannah's astringent, unceasing criticisms of others, this is *not* the sort of judgment Isocrates and other Greek philosophers have in mind. Their concern is with the judgment of value—what we find in matters of moral and aesthetic consideration—that defines our relationship to ideas and things in the world. And it's this kind of judgment that we hope to invest and evolve in our training of young people in the liberal arts.

While we *may* read to find a friend (someone we like or who is like us), and *may* write to express ourselves, a countermanding notion arises when we encounter people in books or on screen who are *different* from us—for it is in that difference and distance from ourselves that we catch a glimmer of our *common* humanity. In that moment of disorientation, of lostness, in our relationship to others—as the Greek experience of paideia presumed to be a merit of our conflicting and confounding intimacies with others—we also become both vulnerable and accountable to the conditions of the experience we share.

That's a good thing. And its opposite, as Hannah suffers it and describes it, is feeling "numb"—consumed by a sort of blasé indifference to whatever is happening outside herself, with or for others, or does not instantly relate to her perceived priorities, goals, and immediate desires ("Dead Inside").

Customary contemporary liberal arts training, broadly in the humanities and in the teaching of creative writing, with its focus on the evolution of the student's identity and her *opinions* about what she reads—and not necessarily on her development in contest with the wider world, including what she reads— encourages a student to read a work of literature or philosophy not for its own merits, to read it as Matthew Arnold once suggested, "as in itself it really is"—but rather for how the book relates to her own life, as if its creation were somehow addressed to her *personally*. Students are regularly encouraged, or perhaps willingly and gladly take the license, to read for immediate relevance, and if the work does *not* seem pertinent to their personal identities, experiences, and nascent aspirations, then the work may appear justifiably dismissed—a problem of the text, not its interpreter. If a reader doesn't see herself in the fiction, the fiction is deemed alienating or otherwise irrelevant.

The fact that paideia as lived and taught in ancient Greece was devoted strictly and solely to boys (*pais* is the Greek for "boy"), should not be lost on our discussion of the education of the young women in *Girls*. This shift in the scope of its application hardly means that paideia is a misplaced or misapplied term for our contemporary inquiry about the education of the young; rather, the historical context of paideia—as the education of boys by men—should be dwelled on, if only to consider the abiding *structural* attributes of having a knowing educational mentor (Gurley, pp. 351–377).

Do Anybody Make Real Shit Anymore?

One of the underlying assumptions shared by the girls in *Girls* revolves around the notion that you must achieve authentic experience—in fact, as Alex Williams emphasized in the *New York Times*, it's a show "that portrays a subculture obsessed with 'authenticity.'" The scare quotes give us a clue that the show is aware of this obsession and uses the term as part of its own self-explanation, as for example, when we hear Hannah chide her *GQ* colleagues by asking, in a caustic rhetorical question: "Am I seriously the only one of us who prides herself on being a truly authentic person?" ("I Saw You").

Sadly, what counts as authentic is often degrading, demoralizing, and sometimes simply illegal. At one point, Hannah says she took cocaine so she'd have something to write about, and that, with the presumed authority of first-hand experience (as if writing *fiction* required *nonfictional* substantiation), her writing would be taken more seriously. Marnie dated a famous artist, Booth Jonathan (Jorma Taccone), who was profoundly unkind to her (was he abusive?), but persisted with the relationship because she thought her association with him would be edifying (yet was her hope clouded by her vanity?). Hannah experienced sexual harassment in the workplace, but was told by her peers (in this case, all older women) to accept the mistreatment by her male boss, Rich Glatter.

What do these indignities amount to? Do they contribute to and reinforce the onward development of human excellence or do they further confound agents about how to live? Consider the show's awareness of the inter-relationship between meritocracy and mediocrity—that is, the way the former inspires a hope (even a presumed faith in the eventuality) of ever-upward achievement, while the latter suppresses or confirms your realized contributions; moreover, fame and popularity do not always register high values and bold talents; the truly gifted may remain obscured, or worse. (Here, the show's own fame and popularity add another moment of meta-critical self-awareness—is *Girls* as good as we think it is?) As Isocrates parses the phenomenon in *Antidosis*: "all knowledge yields itself up to us only after great effort on our part, and we are by no means all equally capable of working out in practice what we learn" (Norlin, p. 299). Or as the song goes, only very few awaken to find themselves "cream of the crop, and top of the heap."

Characters are recurrently presented with the paradox that excellence is the assumed goal of their efforts, struggles, sacrifices, and humiliations while the presence and imposition of equality (a city full of other equally welcome strivers in perpetual contest) counteracts their ambitions and over-valuations of personal worth. With greater numbers in contention, there are fewer slots of renown to fill, and more open spaces in which to inscribe defeats. This seems as evident in the boardroom as the bedroom, in public encounters and private relationships.

Reflecting a general logic of present-day American culture, each individual is said to be special and worthy, and yet that particularity and assigned value seems predicated on the notion that it is (also?) based on exceptional—*earned*—characteristics and the fruits of your labors. Hence Hannah's struggle to write something distinctive and Marnie's tenacious, self-imposed attempt to sing her way out of an anonymous, unproductive day-job.

In their pursuit of authentic or real experience, the characters all engage—or more often, are thwarted by—the city itself.

The imbalances of their personal life (either as atrophy or distension) are seemingly exacerbated by the high cost of living and a felt need for competitiveness with others. The city appears to stoke their vanity (and its underside, shame), since it itself is preoccupied with its premiere status among cities—the rhetoric of promotion routinely refers to it as the "Capital of the World"—and so anyone who *lives* there is presumed to partake, even unintentionally or unconsciously, in that grandness. And yet, your day-to-day reality often belies the presumed heights of the ideal global metropolis. In short, even as the city's idea of itself can bolster your own self-image, it can also erode it—hence the shame. Why is this? What makes the city so hard a place for an artist to live in and flourish? And is that harshness a criterion for the creation of great art based on authentic experience—or instead its opposite?

A recent anthology of twenty-eight essays, inspired in part by Joan Didion's essay about being a young woman who gave up on the city and moved to California, entitled *Goodbye to All That: Writers on Loving and Leaving New York*, is exclusively written by young women. In her day, decades ago, Didion "could afford to fall out of love with the city slowly," writes Alex Williams, "Not so for the would-be Didions of today. In their New York, the nice apartments with the bridge views tend to go to the underwriters of bond issues, not to the writers of essays for literary anthologies. The unaffordability of New York on a writer's budget is a theme running through several contemporary variations on the theme" ("The Long Goodbye," p. 15). And as the editor, Sari Botton, says: "more and more people are finding they can't afford to live in New York if they're in a creative field." The city, she concludes is "just not conducive to a creative life." As a result of the high prices, those trained in the liberal arts commonly find themselves living as a "bohemian-serf"—unmoored and at the mercy of a fickle market.

Success, as *Girls* shows, requires an ongoing process of selling yourself. The darker insinuations of the phrase are apt, at least as the show depicts these lives, since the girls often appear to suffer some form of humiliation or abuse in order to engage with others, or to even remain in the city (the earliest episodes of Season One revolve around Hannah's stress from relying on parental monetary support in order to pay her rent; and roommate shuffling in a bid to minimize rent is an ongoing theme of the series). Despite all, however, the belief that the experience is bona fide—and the expense justified—somehow trumps its variations of harshness, even brutality. Like the wider culture in which they live, the characters are prone to emphasize how things "literally" or "actually" happened—another way their language reflects their largely unarticulated anxiety and panicked skepticism that it didn't.

We can contrast the tones of darkness, sarcasm, snark, and irony found among the girls of *Girls* with the earnestness and joy of the titular character, Frances Halladay in the movie *Frances Ha* (2012). Frances, another graduate of a rural liberal arts college who moved to New York, feels the city as an environment for humble experiments, hobbies, and routines, not grand projects of the self—yet even in these modest actions she is thwarted and encumbered by others, and sometimes herself: at twenty-seven, she apologizes: "I'm sorry, I'm not a real person yet." Still, she takes up menial jobs with relative aplomb; she visits loving parents in California and there takes a welcome bike ride in the sun, showing no signs of regret or resentment; she moves in and out of apartments with roommates on good terms, with a good temper. In a bit of cross-fertilization, Adam Driver (who plays the character Adam Sackler in *Girls*), appears as a prospective mate, and then roommate, for Frances. Yet so thoroughly does Frances change the context of the city's frameworks and forces, that we don't feel any encumbrances from the world of *Girls*—even when one of the show's main characters shows up to court Frances.

I Know I Got to be Right Now / 'Cause I Can't Get Much Wronger

Because of the frank depiction of sex in *Girls*, one might expect that a turn to ancient Greek paideia would naturally link or lead to a consideration of *eros*. Yet, while eros is central to Platonic educational philosophy, the more relevant term for the present consideration of *Girls* is the *agon* and the agonistic—namely, a conscious embracing of conflict, competition, contest, and the moral and aesthetic lessons of limitation and constraint. Bonnie Honig, a political theorist and one of the principal advocates for the virtues of agonism, says that

to affirm the perpetuity of the contest is not to celebrate a world without points of stabilization; it is to affirm the reality of perpetual contest,
even within an ordered setting, and to identify the affirmative dimension of contestation. (Honig, p. 15)

Given that the inertia of habit and history is likely to propel
the onward braggadocio of New York's representatives, and the
expense and competitiveness of living there will abide for the
foreseeable future (perhaps becoming the main criterion that
justifies a resident's pride), it may be advisable to consider a
productive, even restorative, response to the infringements
imposed on the brave citizen. In the concept of the agonistic, we
find not a resolution of problems, but a faith in an endless creative conflict. And thus, following Kayne West's lyrics, we find
a need for *immanent* experiment ("I got to be right now"), but
also admit that we must allow for struggle and error ("'Cause I
can't get much wronger").

Perhaps one of the most promising aspects of the agonistic
is its pluralistic response to the conflicts that animate liberal-
ism. This feature is especially evident in politics, since its discourse distinctively preserves contest. Yet, as political theorist
Samuel Chambers has written in the context of another television show, *The West Wing*, "this agonistic element of discourse
must be rigorously distinguished from *ant*agonism." And the
same can be said for the speech that defines the characters in
Girls—as antagonists, they are also, as it were, agonists.

Agonism implies a deep respect and concern for the other; indeed,
the Greek *agon* refers most directly to an athletic contest oriented not
merely toward victory or defeat, but emphasizing the importance of
the struggle itself—a struggle that cannot exist without the opponent.
Victory through forfeit or default, or over an unworthy opponent,
comes up short compared to a defeat at the hands of a worthy opponent—a defeat that still brings honor. An agonistic discourse will
therefore be one marked not merely by conflict but, just as important,
by mutual admiration. ("Dialogue, Deliberation, and Discourse," p. 96)

In the kitchen scene at the end of "Beach House," when
Hannah, Marnie, Shoshanna, and Jessa renew the vigor and
clarity of their thoughts for (or about) one another, they
attempt to establish whether their contest is worthwhile, in

short, whether, the other is *worthy* of their conflict—their pain, their time.

Looking out from this scene of contest in the kitchen—where antagonists discern the parameters of their shared agonistic discourse, we glean how the contrast between *Girls* and *Frances Ha* remains fitting and fecund, since it's precisely in Frances's experience that trials are confounding (and yet mainly harmless), whereas in *Girls* they so often appear dehumanizing (and laced with a silent menace). On its own, but perhaps even more so when *Frances Ha* is placed beside *Girls*, the movie becomes a fairy tale of agonistic struggle—it even begins with *mock* fighting between Frances and her friend, Sophie (Mickey Sumner), as if to signal that the contests we are about to see are playful, unrehearsed, unselfconscious, and not harmful or calculated. But is Frances's experience a function of luck or her attitude? Is she savvy or delusional? And if Frances shares a liberal-arts education with the leading female characters in *Girls*, why does she seem to inhabit an attractive world—a world called New York City—that is nevertheless full of setbacks?

These philosophically oriented reflections on *Girls* remind us of the extent to which drama is based on conflict (something Aristotle noted in his *Poetics* two and a half thousand years ago), but also how contemporary drama on HBO and other television networks is especially dedicated to a kind of conflict that exposes characters' moral ambiguity, ambivalence, or even degeneracy. Viewers seem to prefer watching characters behave badly rather than nobly—from *The Sopranos* to *Deadwood*, *Mad Men* to *Breaking Bad*.

Someone being decent is not as funny or entertaining as someone being vain, mean, or jealous. "Critical artistic practices," as Chantal Mouffe has written, "do not aspire to lift a supposedly false consciousness so as to reveal the 'true reality'" (*Agonistics*, p. 93). Rather, *Girls*'s credentials as such a critical artistic practice reside precisely in its invitation, even demand, for us to dwell on its status as fiction. Only then—by looking at its world on its own terms—can we find what makes *Girls* what Mouffe calls a "truly subversive experience," for example in its frank depiction of the obviously provocative—nudity, body image, and sex—but also, more subtly, of gender roles, artistic practices, vocation, moral commitments, conversation, parenting, and friendship.

Meanwhile on network television, two sitcoms, which premiered the same week, *New Girl* (Fox, 2011–) and *2 Broke Girls* (CBS, 2011–), are, like *Girls*, ostensibly about "girls"—about twenty-something women trying to find their way in work and in relationships. Yet the tone and pacing of the network shows puts easy laughter (one-liners, put-downs, pratfalls, rude language, innuendo, and stereotypes) above nuanced explorations of the complicated inner lives of characters—the shows adhere closely to traditional television notions of joke set-up and punchline. In these cases, the shows are blithely complicit in proliferating the inherited forms of representation we are familiar with, and thus despite occasional shocks, they are hardly subversive: characters are, instead, in the service of the material, come what may, whereas in *Girls*, as in much of the programming on HBO and other paid-programming, the characters *are* the material. In this respect, *Girls* draws lessons from drama into its moments of comedy and satire, and for that reason also allows the space and time on screen to explore the issues that form the contexts, backstories, and aspirations of its characters.

Letter from a Known Woman

Perhaps *Girls* can be regarded as a kind of heuristic for considering the world we viewers live in—all of us, not just young women—and as a way of thinking further about the question "Whom, how, and why do we educate?" If *Girls* burnishes its realism—its "unvarnished naturalism"—with grit and grime, failure and misfortune, vanity and shame, self-aggrandizement and self-doubt, what are we to make of the world that gave rise to it—that is, our own? (Heller). These questions, in turn, direct us to the contestations that animate the education of humans and thus the making of humans. When a young person becomes a "real person," what kind of person does she want to be? And will her education—her paideia—be understood as the necessary condition for that agonistic achievement?

As if in reply to these questions, remarks by the novelist Claire Messud—that is, a writer of fiction—may orient us to the achievements of *Girls*, while also lending advice to the broad, diverse audience that assiduously and attentively watches the show either out of curiosity, or for a kind of companionship in a shared predicament. Messud helps us discern a sober, mature account of what kind of thing *Girls* is, and how we might profitably relate ourselves to it as a work of art. In this respect, Messud, is our mentor—our pedagogue.

Messud says "The more accurately one can illuminate a particular human experience, the better the work of art" ("An Unseemly Emotion"). In the radical specificity of a character, such as Dunham's Hannah and the figures who surround her, we are given a chance to consider the reality and truth of the fiction. As Messud emphasizes, the needs we seek from art "can only be addressed in the individual, not in the general." Thus, Dunham cannot satirize herself, as if offering us a caricature of her own qualities and foibles, but rather must commit to the individual existence of her fictitious creation, Hannah.

When Messud was in high school, she read Dostoyevsky, and "felt passionately about fictions that articulate anger, frustration, disappointment," and responded by saying "my God, fiction can do this? Fiction can say these unsayable things?" Later, in reading "Beckett or Camus or Philip Roth's *Sabbath's Theater* to Thomas Bernhard" she found authors who were "all articulating unseemly, unacceptable experiences and emotions, rage prominent among them."

As if cognizant of the spirit animating the agonistic, she adds "Because rage at life and rage for life are very closely linked. To be angry, you have to give a shit." And this we learn continually in the post-graduate world of *Girls*: the characters' anger is often as intense as it is empathetically applied—such as when Ray chastises Hannah that her response to her editor, David's death was full of self-regarding narcissism about the fate of her own book, that is, e-book: "Hannah, why don't you place just one crumb of basic human compassion on this fat-free muffin of sociopathic detachment? See how it tastes" ("Dead Inside").

Yet, in the wake of Ray's withering verbal lashing, in the tension between its justification and its truth, we can be reminded by Messud that as in *Girls*, so in literary fiction: "If you're reading to find friends, you're in deep trouble. We read to find life, in all its possibilities. The relevant question isn't 'is this a potential friend for me?' but 'is this character alive?'" Though Hannah's literary mentor, David, dies, it is the reality of Hannah's self-absorption that proves to be the truly vital feature of the event, and the reason we keep watching. As if meaningfully suited to the lessons of Greek paideia, a viewer's ambition should not be to judge the characters as possible friends, but to understand their contexts and conditions. We're watching *Hannah* struggle agonistically with her world—her ideas of herself, her ambitions, her talents, her friends, her parents, her mentors—to achieve her existence.

With Claire Messud's pedagogical intervention—we might say, the mentorship of an older female writer for a younger female writer (as is very much the case with Dunham's forty-something creative partner, Jenny Konner, "the queen of recognizing what a scene is missing," as Heller puts it)—we are in the position to describe how Lena Dunham, a graduate of a liberal arts creative writing program living in New York, has achieved a living character in the form of Hannah Horvath. As Konner confides: "Where it takes me twenty years to write about my twenties in a really honest way, . . . it takes [Dunham] twenty-four hours to, like, have gone on a bad date, experienced it, had pain about it, gone home, metabolized it, and turned it into art. It's the fastest system I've ever seen." Meanwhile, co-star Allison Williams refers to her boss affectionately and admiringly as an "aggregator of humanity" (Heller).

And thus as the character Charlie Kaufman struggled to write his screenplay, the screenwriter Charlie Kaufman created in *Adaptation* a masterful metafiction full of reality and consequence. Likewise, we find in Lena Dunham, as embodied in her creation, *Girls*, a power to express the "unseemly, unacceptable experiences and emotions" that undo her character, Hannah, "the confused, questing neophyte," but confirm Dunham as an artist of contemporary significance.

While Hannah may struggle to write, to love, to understand herself and her circumstances, it is in Dunham's television show that we find a proper object for considering the legacies of paideia, agonism, and the liberal arts.

19
Chinese Philosophy Looks at *Girls*

BOBBY CARLEO AND PAUL D'AMBROSIO

Hannah Horvath declares to her parents in the very first episode of *Girls*, "I have work, and then I have a dinner thing, and then I am busy trying to become who I am."

How can you try to become who you are? Contemporary American culture emphasizes individuality, and young Americans constantly find themselves told to "be yourself." TV insists on it just as much as teachers and grandparents, and the message seems to be getting stronger by the decade. It's an inspiring notion, but one that can leave us asking "Who am I?"

The American idea of finding or creating your own identity contrasts with Chinese tradition, which defines identity through people's roles in family and society. For instance, Confucianism demarcates specific relationships among people and insists they act properly according to their roles. For the characters of *Girls*, on the other hand, responsibility in interpersonal relationships is essentially non-existent, which helps the show to forefront one of its major themes: the struggle with identity.

Nothing plays a stronger role in *Girls* than how the characters see themselves. Rather than crises of responsibility, physical threat or love, we trace the failures of a group of young girls constantly battling problems created by their senses of identity. Within a cosmology of characters all of whom care primarily about themselves, we find the central romance of the show—Adam and Hannah. The couple presents strongly contrasting, extreme characters who deal with identity in very different ways.

Hannah fancies herself a "writer" and strives to live up to this romanticized notion, frequently allowing grandiose delusions based on this identity to control her despite little experience and success in writing. For her, the title of writer does not result from writing achievements; rather, it is an idealized vision of a lifestyle and perspective that leads to her writing a world-changing masterpiece and, most importantly, widespread acclaim.

Adam generally can't be bothered to define himself, apparently seeing little value in aligning his particularly spontaneous actions and emotions with a fixed label the way Hannah does.

Girls highlights three types of interaction with identity that we label "positive," "negative," and "non-identity." (No, these aren't standard philosophical terms; we just made them up.) "Positive identities" are defined by consistent striving towards ideals associated with certain names or titles, and this is how Hannah lives. "Negative identities" are the opposite and involve actively rejecting such labels, while "non-identity" means living without attachment to names—and Adam provides good examples of both.

Rectify Yo'self

Confucianism's emphasis on ordering relationships between individuals is marked by fixed understandings of roles and titles, establishing each person's position and its corresponding responsibilities. The subsequent importance of titles or names lead to heated discussions of the importance of labels being properly fulfilled by those who they were bestowed on. In fact, practically all of the major schools in classical Chinese thought, including Confucianism, Daoism (sometimes romanized as Taoism), Mohism, and Legalism, discuss the importance of matching names with real qualities and actual conduct.

The image of the "tally" (*fu*) is used in ancient Chinese thought to understand how name and actuality ought to fit together. As part of a contract or imperial order, an item would be carved of anything from wood to bone, metal or jade and then broken in half. Thereafter, the two parts together symbolized the authority of the contract or order, which required the words or concept (one half) to be carried out through actions (the other half). In the Confucian and Legalist traditions, praise or blame is only ever derived from a relational context in which a person's behavior (one part of the tally) is judged according to their role or position in society (that is, their "title" or "name," the other part of the tally).

In the *Analects*, in which Confucius's students recorded the master's words and deeds (similar to how the *Bible* relates stories of Jesus through his disciples), Confucius elaborates on this topic and calls for a "rectification of names." This means ensuring that names are aligned with corresponding realities so that people can be trusted and affairs successfully carried out. For Confucians, this is an ethical project as well as a political one, as they define moral conduct as correspondence between a person's actions and role-based title.

According to the master, "Rulers should rule, fathers should father, and sons should son" (*Analects* 2.13) (This, and all subsequent translations, are our own . . . but don't worry, we're trained professionals.) This means that people should live up to the requirements of their roles. For Confucian thinkers, personal moral cultivation is achieved through appropriating and modeling oneself on exemplars (either read in texts or experienced in real life).

In *Girls*, the concept of "writer" provides an identity, or role, that Hannah strives to fill. Her quest is similar to that championed in the Confucian tradition. Just as Confucians stress correspondence between titles and conduct, Hannah establishes her identity as a writer and then seeks to live her life accordingly. Unfortunately, she allows her image of herself as a writer to grow out of control, and with grave consequences.

Hannah's general failure to align her identity with her actual conduct becomes her character's central crisis and causes the majority of her difficulties over the first two and a half seasons. As an obvious danger of approaching life by assigning ourselves a name *before* filling the role accorded to it, Hannah's issue was unsurprisingly one of Confucian thinkers' most ardently discussed topics: the necessity of adequately performing our roles.

Hannah is able romanticize her image of herself because she lives "names first," which allows her to take her positive identification as a writer too far. She confuses her dream with reality and dislodges her identity from her actuality. This results in her image of herself as a writer not only becoming toweringly more important in her mind than the act of writing (her actual conduct), it also creates major problems in her relationships with others and eventually results in psychological breakdown.

Sheep Stealing and the Pudgy Face Slick with Semen and Sadness

Confucians identified and warned against Hannah's problem. In an often-misread passage from the *Analects*, Confucius is confronted with a governor who brags that a man in his village is so committed to being truthful that he reports his own father for stealing a sheep. Confucius warns that this is not necessarily the essence of proper conduct, and that sometimes lying in a moral way is more virtuous than telling the truth (13.18). The son's actions become unethical because he was identifying too strongly with being truthful, which leads him to ignore the practicalities of the situation in judging whether his actions are, in fact, moral.

Similarly, Hannah consistently fails both professionally and in interpersonal relationships because she identifies too closely with her vision of herself as a writer. Both her and the truth-telling son associate themselves with a particular title, which diminishes the significance they place on the actual effects of their behavior. Their failures arise from an unbalanced emphasis on names.

Throughout the series, Hannah's tight adhesion to her title blinds her in her actions and obfuscates and obstructs her goals. At first, her identification as a writer serves to facilitate her laziness. When her parents cut her off, she attempts to use her book as an excuse to wring an "investment" out of them. Her over-identification also disrupts her relationship with her friends. When her writing is responsible for Marnie's break up, Hannah's obsession with recognition as a writer completely impedes her ability to act as a friend. "If you had read the essay and it wasn't about you, do you think you would have liked it? Just as like a piece of writing?" she asks, in place of all sympathy. Her delusions even repeatedly disrupt her professional life, and after she tries to sue, seduce, and extort her boss, her final threat is to write an essay about him.

Her "names first" problem manifests in another dimension: her idea that worthwhile topics for her writing are limited to preset categories. This becomes pronounced at her (nemesis) classmate's publishing party when Hannah complains that her former classmate was blessed with a boyfriend who killed himself—a perfect topic to write about. Her e-book editor then reinforces such notions when he pigeonholes Hannah as a "pudgy face slick with semen and sadness," and the severity of her problem becomes more pronounced as we watch Hannah try to live up to this "ideal." In the end we find that by pre-emptively giving herself the title of "writer," Hannah has bestowed herself with a false success that has prevented her from actually succeeding at much of anything.

The Daoist tradition differs from the Confucian tradition in that rather than "rectifying" names with their actuality, it omits the importance of "names" altogether. In Daoism, humans are not asked to strive to fill predefined roles. Instead, Daoist texts see names as threats to a person's ability to behave productively. In the *Zhuangzi* (also romanized *Chuang-Tzu*), the second most famous ancient text on philosophical Daoism after the *Daodejing* (also romanized *Tao Te Ching*), we find a passage that explicitly warns about the delusional attitudes of people who value names too highly. It reads:

> If someone's understanding is effective for a certain job, or if their actions are useful in a particular village, or if their virtuosity is liked by a ruler, he or she may win acclaim in that country. Such people will view themselves the way that others see them, [as fitting a specific job or role]. But Song Rongzi laughs at this kind of person. Song would not be swayed even by the whole world's praise, nor would he be upset by the entire world's scorn. (*Zhuangzi* 1:3)

Song Rongzi provides an exemplary model that critiques people who value their titles too seriously. The text reminds us that people may wind up with a good job through luck alone, and that it would be mistaken to attribute this to actual skill (or virtuosity). The Daoist sage Song Rongzi does not concern himself with how others see him. He lives his life unattached to the names generated by his conduct. For Song, titles are superfluous, and he would rather focus on the specific actualities of his conduct than living up to, or identifying with, any particular role. The passage then continues:

> He fixed the distinction between the inner and outer, and distinguished the places of honor and disgrace. Nothing more can be done

than this. He did not worry himself over worldly matters, and remained poised—though he was not firmly planted. (1:3)

Song knows that names can be important for "outer" matters—that is, a person's social acceptance and identity—but he also knows that people's own self-definition should not be based on these names or the way others see them.

In this context, we find Hannah's devaluation of reality based on her "names first" attitude echoed in one of the central issues of both Confucian and Daoist philosophies. Both schools are aware that an emphasis on names can confuse people's perception of themselves and misguide behavior. For Confucius, this can result from over-identifying with a single moral term (such as telling the truth) and therefore fail to take into account our entire situation.

Daoists reject the value of titles entirely, warning that striving to fill a pre-established role may prevent a person from dealing with the realities of particular situations. The Confucian answer to Hannah's problem is the "rectification of names," which is a sincere engagement with titles through living up to the realities they stipulate. Such engagement never appears in the show, but the Daoist solution does, and is embodied by Hannah's lover Adam.

Dreams of a Life Without Names

Adam, in contrast to Hannah, embodies many characteristics of the Daoist sage as outlined in the *Daodejing* and *Zhuangzi*. These texts describe a type of person who is empty of any definitive ideas about right and wrong. They approach situations "empty" of predetermined notions about how things should be and deal with the particulars of the situation in the most efficacious way possible.

The *Daodejing* uses images like the unfilled vessel or valley (as opposed to mountains) to discuss how a sage should be empty. Non-sages are often full of ideas and therefore approach situations assuming that they know what needs to be done and how to do it. Sages are empty of such presuppositions and can thereby fill themselves with the particulars of whatever circumstance they are in. This is how sages are able to operate according to what Daoism calls non-interference, or more literally "doing non-doing." This concept describes acting according to the particular environments we find ourselves in. Daoist texts argue that many actions can be done with increased efficacy if a person empties their mind of fixed notions, including fixed identities. In fact, as representatives of what we call "non-identity," these sages have no continuous self at all. A famous story from the *Zhuangzi* presents this view perfectly:

> Once Zhuang Zhou dreamt of a butterfly, a lively butterfly, self-content and enjoying itself. It did not know Zhou. Suddenly Zhou woke up and was fully and completely Zhou. It cannot be known whether there was a Zhou that dreamt and became a butterfly or whether there was a butterfly that dreamt and became a Zhou in a dream. There must be a distinction between Zhou and the butterfly, this is called the transformation of things. (*Zhuangzi* 7:3)

Here Zhuang Zhou, the supposed author of the *Zhuangzi*, is said to transform from human to butterfly and then back again. We are told, however, that as a butterfly he is completely self-content and has all the ideas and emotions of the insect. When he is Zhuang Zhou again he is completely human, without any semblance of the butterfly.

Unlike many other parables in which people maintain their thoughts, emotions and memories—that is, their selves—during transformation, this Daoist tale underlines the distinction between Zhou and the butterfly, championing fluidity of identity. Although we do not find anything quite this fantastic in *Girls*, Adam likewise displays the ability to behave in complete accord with a variety of tasks unobstructed by adherence to a fixed identity.

Since Adam has no strong positive attachment to particular labels or titles, he is able to more fully involve himself in the tasks or hobbies he chooses. For example, Adam sees value in performing and woodworking without necessarily considering himself a performer or a woodworker, and without striving for praise or other external recognition. On stage he no longer identifies as a woodworker, and produces a moving monologue. While at home constructing things he is completely engaged with his work, and not thinking about performing for an audience. In bed, Adam is particularly fond of roleplaying, constantly attaching himself to all sorts of new "selves." Like

Zhuang Zhou and the butterfly, Adam forgets his other identities and becomes someone new.

This contrasts sharply with Hannah, who is so obsessed with "becoming who she is" through her prefabricated identity as a "writer" that it takes over essentially all her social interactions. Even the road trip to pick up Jessa in rehab disappoints Hannah when she finds nothing interesting to write about. At this moment, Adam's non-identity also poignantly expresses itself. He pulls the car over and literally wanders into the wild. Hannah decides to sit down and listen to music, returning to an activity that fits her image of herself while he rambles through the woods.

Adam maintains a clarity as well as a comfort with life that Hannah lacks. These stem from his Daoist-like emptiness, which allows him to act "without interfering" wherever he may find himself. He immediately pulls the car over and starts off into the woods to make his point to Hannah, namely that it's unnecessary and even unhelpful to conform to set notions like those that structure Hannah's view of the world. This scene forms a parallel with the earlier episode in which Jessa and Hannah pull over and Hannah proceeds to have sex with Jessa's stepbrother because she "thought that's what we were doing." Again, Hannah pre-emptively and mistakenly defines a situation and hurts others in the process. Adam walking off into the woods is the opposite of Hannah's sex in the bushes, and demonstrates explicitly his disregard for according his actions to defined categories (or "names").

Adam exhibits no instances of the type of "positive identification" that proves so destructive for Hannah. He does, however, identify in other ways, exhibiting "negative identification" in which he creates images or titles for himself that he strives to push away from and avoid. Despite having not had a drink since he was seventeen, Adam continues to turn to AA for support, pushing off his negative identification as an alcoholic as a way to keep psychologically stable.

Indeed, just as much as striving towards positive identification never succeeds and often fails miserably in the world of *Girls*—Hannah's writing, Marnie's singing and Jessa's marriage—casting off negative identities proves consistently successful. Soshanna's negative identification as a virgin leads her to Ray, who, in turn, revolts against his own negative identity as a loser and thereby grows. In the show, striving towards an ideal is doomed, but running away from fixed ideas or identities is healthy. Negative identification joins non-definition as successful methods of interacting with the world. Despite their foundational dissimilarity—one fundamentally admits the value of definition, the other fundamentally rejects it—the effects of both are similar. Negative identification repels us from undesirable characteristics, but does not proactively guide us in a particular direction the way positive identification does. This leaves us open to continue to "be ourselves" in either the contemporary American or Daoist understanding.

Kings, Sages, and Girls

The *Mencius*, named after the highly revered Confucian Mencius, comments, "Those who take the correspondence between name and actuality as primary act for others, those who take the correspondence between name and actuality as secondary act for themselves" (*Mencius* 6B26). According to the *Mencius*, positive identities can provide efficacious and productive models if names are properly matched with actuality. Fulfilling roles correctly guides people's behavior and benefits others by encouraging people to interact meaningfully with one another. This is why Confucius was so concerned with "rectifying names."

If a person's title appropriately corresponds to their behavior, the world becomes navigable and people enter into respectful and responsible relationships. When the link between names and actuality breaks down or becomes "secondary," however, people live in their own private worlds where their external image not only prevents others from knowing them, but actually hinders their own self-understanding.

The Daoist critique of this system calls for non-identity, or non-attachment to specific social roles and defined relationships. In this way Daoism is able to avoid some of the major problems Confucians worry about, but the Daoist solution is not perfect either. Shortly after the *Zhuangzi* was written, the third most celebrated Confucian philosopher, Xunzi, criticized the work as he saw that "Zhuangzi is limited by what is natural and does not know the human social world" (*Xunzi* 21.5). Even though this is not completely accurate, there is certainly a danger of misreading Daoism this way. Thus, even while Adam's carefree non-interference allows him to prevail for a while as a relatively enlightened and productive character, this relies on *Girls*'s fundamental absence of interpersonal responsibility. In the long run of post-twenties adult life, Hannah's "names first" mentality may prove successful after all.

Early in Season Three, Hannah gets a job writing at *GQ* magazine, where she shows fantastic potential to move up—and she is openly adverse to it. She immediately attempts to differentiate herself from her co-workers, saying, "No offense, but I'm like a writer writer, not like a corporate advertising, working-for-the-man writer." Her ideal of just what it means to be a "writer" is then confronted with the fact that her new co-workers are all previous virtuosos who have already succeeded as "writer writers." After considering quitting her job, she settles for writing "at night and on weekends," finally shocked closer to a realistic understanding of her label of "writer" and the real-world conduct it entails.

She then starts to, as Confucius put it, "rectify names" and embraces her new promising career, albeit with some anxiety. Adam is now the one who seems delusional. Unemployed, he only goes to acting auditions allegedly for the "challenge" of it. This claim serves as an anti-identity move against "having a job," and belies the practical importance of Adam finding a stable social role.

Towards the end of the third season Hannah and Adam are nicely situated in their familiar dynamic. After "trying to get fired" Hannah's "career" is over, and she receives an acceptance letter to do graduate work in writing. Meanwhile, Adam becomes seriously focused on his role in a Broadway play, where he seems to demonstrate excellent potential.

These two characters have matured closer to what the *Zhuangzi* calls being an "internal sage and external king." This essentially means being a Daoist in private and a Confucian in public. It does not, however, imply hypocrisy. In mainstream Chinese society as well as academia, this ideal is interpreted to mean that a person should not limit their identity to their social roles. People should sincerely behave according to names and titles while recognizing their creative potential to take on or even create new roles.

Girls thereby embraces the very same truths recognized by the founders of Chinese philosophy. It is only through an accurate understanding of the correspondence between name and reality that people can successfully live "names first" and develop productively towards their goals. Anti-identity or non-identity can be personal, but it should be coupled with recognition of the importance of titles in society.

References

Adorno, Theodor W. 2001. How to Look at Television. In Bernstein 2001.

———. 2009. On Popular Music. In Storey 2009.

Adorno, Theodor W., and Max Horkheimer. 1969. *The Dialectic of Enlightenment*. Herder and Herder.

Alford, C. Fred. 2004. Levinas and Political Theory. *Political Theory* 32:2.

Arendt, Hannah. 1979. Isak Dinesen, 1885–1962. Foreword to Dinesen 1979.

———. 1981. *The Life of the Mind*. Houghton Mifflin.

Arnold, Matthew. 1864. The Function of Criticism at the Present Time. *The National Review* (November).

Beauvoir, Simone de. 1949. *The Second Sex*. Penguin.

———. 2011. *The Second Sex*. Vintage.

Belliotti, Raymond. 2011. *What Is the Meaning of Human Life?* Rodopi.

Bernstein, J.M., ed. 2001. *The Culture Industry: Selected Essays on Mass Culture*. Routledge.

Bordo, Susan. 1998. Bringing Body to Theory. In Welton 1998.

Botton, Sari, ed. 2013. *Goodbye to All That: Writers on Loving and Leaving New York*. Seal.

Brizendine, Louann. 2010. Love, Sex, and the Male Brain. <http://www.cnn.com/2010/OPINION/03/23/brizendine.male.brain/>

Buckley, Caleb. 2007. Man Is Rescued by Stranger on Subway Tracks. *New York Times* (3rd January).

Butler, Judith. 1990. Performative Acts and Gender Constitution. In Case 1990.

————. 2004. *Undoing Gender*. New York: Routledge.

Camus, Albert. 1991. *The Myth of Sisyphus and Other Essays*. Random House.

Carlyle, Thomas. 1987. *Sartor Resartus*. Oxford University Press.

Carter, Michael. 2003. *Fashion Classics from Carlyle to Barthes*. Bloomsbury Academic.

Case, Sue-Ellen, ed. 1990. *Performing Feminisms: Feminist Critical Theory and Theatre*. Johns Hopkins University Press.

Caverero, Adriana. 2000. *Relating Narratives: Storytelling and Selfhood*. Routledge.

Chambers, Samuel A. 2001. Language and Agonistic Discourse in *The West Wing*. *C Theory* (November).

————. 2003. Dialogue, Deliberation, and Discourse: The Far-Reaching Politics of *The West Wing*. In Rollins and O'Connor 2003.

Clark, Suzanne, and Kathleen Hully. 1990. An Interview with Julia Kristeva: Cultural Strangeness and the Subject in Crisis. *Discourse* 13:1.

Confucius. 2008. *The Analects*. Oxford University Press.

Connick, Roxanne. 1973. Women Singers in Darfur, Sudan Republic. *Anthropos* 68:5–6.

Cottingham, John. 2003. *On the Meaning of Life*. Routledge.

Delbanco, Andrew. 2013. *College: What It Is, Was, and Should Be*. Princeton University Press.

Didion, Joan. 1968. *Slouching towards Bethlehem*. Farrar, Straus, and Giroux.

Dinesen, Isak. 1979. *Daguerrotypes and Other Essays*. University of Chicago Press.

Dworkin, Ronald. 2013. *Justice for Hedgehogs*. Belknap.

Fausto-Sterling, Anne. 2000. *Sexing the Body: Gender Politics and the Construction of Sexuality*. Basic Books.

Freud, Sigmund. 1995. *The Basic Writings of Sigmund Freud*. Modern Library.

Gendar, Alison, Larry McShane, and Geoff Gillette. 2009. Hero on the Hudson: Pilot of US Airways Flight 1549 Saved Every Passenger with Miracle Landing. *New York Daily News* (16th January).

Gross, Terry. 2012. Interview with Lena Dunham. Fresh Air Weekend (NPR, 12th May).

Gurley, Jennifer. 1999. Platonic *Paedeia*. *Philosophy and Literature* 23:2 (October).

Harbach, Chad. 2010. MFA vs NYC. *n+1* (Fall).

———. 2014. *MFA vs NYC: The Two Cultures of American Fiction.* Faber and Faber.

Haslanger, Sally. 2000. Gender and Race: (What) Are They? (What) Do We Want Them to Be? *Noûs* 34:48.

Heidegger, Martin. 1968. *What Is Called Thinking?* Harper and Row.

Heller, Nathan. 2014. Lena Dunham: The New Queen of Comedy's First *Vogue* Cover. *Vogue* (January 15th).

Honig, Bonnie. 1993. *Political Theory and the Displacement of Politics.* Cornell University Press.

Irigaray, Luce. 1993. *An Ethics of Sexual Difference.* Cornell University Press.

Irwin, William. 2000. Kramer and Kierkegaard: Stages on Life's Way. In William Irwin, ed., *Seinfeld and Philosophy: A Book about Everything and Nothing.* Open Court.

Ives, Kelly. 2010. *Julia Kristeva: Art, Love, Melancholy, Philosophy, Semiotics, and Psychoanalysis.* Crescent Moon.

Isocrates. 1929. *Isocrates: Volume II.* Loeb Classical Library. Harvard University Press.

Jaeger, Werner. 1944. *Paideia: The Ideals of Greek Culture.* Oxford University Press.

Kierkegaard, Søren. 1980. *The Concept of Anxiety.* Princeton University Press.

———. 2005. *Fear and Trembling.* Penguin.

Klemke, E.D., and Steven M. Cahn, eds. 2008. *The Meaning of Life: A Reader.* Oxford University Press.

Kristeva, Julia. 1987. *Tales of Love.* Columbia University Press.

———. 1995. *New Maladies of the Soul.* Columbia University Press.

———. 2009. *This Incredible Need to Believe.* Columbia University Press.

Lacan, Jacques. 2007. *Écrits: The First Complete Edition in English.* Norton.

Laozi. 2008. *Daodejing.* Oxford University Press.

Lindsay, Tony. 2007. *Darfur: A Cultural Handbook.* Defence Academy of the United Kingdom, Conflict Studies Research Centre.

Simmons, Bill. 2014. Interview with Lena Dunham. *Entertainment Weekly* (January 10th).

Matheson, Mark, ed. 2012. *The Tanner Lectures on Human Values.* University of Utah Press. <tannerlectures.utah.edu>.

Mencius. 2005. *Mencius.* Penguin.

Messud, Claire. 2013. An Unseemly Emotion. *Publishers Weekly* (29th April).

Moi, Toril. 1985. *Sexual Textual Politics*. Methuen.

Mondschein, E.R., K.E. Adolph, and C. Tamis-LeMonda. 2000. Gender Bias in Mothers' Expectations about Infant Crawling. *Journal of Experimental Child Psychology* 77.

Mouffe, Chantal. 2013. *Agonistics: Thinking the World Politically*. Verso.

Neiman, Susan. 2008. *Moral Clarity: A Guide for Grown-Up Idealists*. Houghton Mifflin Harcourt.

———. 2011. What It All Means. *New York Times* (20th January).

———. 2012. Victims and Heroes. In Matheson 2012.

Nietzsche, Friedrich. 2003. *The Genealogy of Morals*. Dover.

———. 2013. *The Anti-Christ*. SoHo.

Ortega y Gasset, Jose. 2001. *Toward a Philosophy of History*. University of Illinois Press.

Rawls, John. 1971. *A Theory of Justice*. Harvard University Press.

———. 1993. The Law of Peoples. In Shute and Hurley 1993.

———. 1999. *The Law of Peoples*. Harvard University Press.

———. 2001. *Justice as Fairness: A Restatement*. Harvard University Press.

Rivera, Ray. 2009. A Pilot Becomes a Hero Years in the Making. *New York Times* (16th January).

Robinson, Phoebe. 2012. Not One of Lena Dunham's 'Girls'. *Huffington Post* blog (19th April). <http://www.huffingtonpost.com/phoebe-robinson/not-one-of-lena-dunhams-g_b_1435664.html>.

Rollins, Peter C., and John E. O'Connor, eds. 2003. *The American Presidency as Television Drama*. Syracuse University Press.

Romano, Carlin. 2013. *America the Philosophical*. Vintage.

Russell, Bertrand. 2013. *The Conquest of Happiness*. Liveright.

Ruth, Sheila, ed. 1990. *Issues in Feminism: An Introduction to Women's Studies*. Second edition. Mayfield.

Sartre, Jean-Paul, 1957. *Being and Nothingness: An Essay on Phenomenological Ontology*. London: Methuen.

———. 2003. *Being and Nothingness: An Essay on Phenomenological Ontology*. London: Routledge.

———. 2007. *Nausea*. New Directions.

———. 2007. *Existentialism Is a Humanism*. Yale University Press.

Schippers, Brigit. 2011. *Julia Kristeva and Feminist Thought*. Edinburgh University Press.

Schumacher, E.F., and Peter N. Gillingham. 1980. *Good Work*. HarperCollins.

Scott, Catherine. 2012. *Girls* Is Not Diverse, Not Feminist, and Not Empowering. *The Independent* (24th October) <http://www.independent.co.uk/voices/comment/girls-is-not-diverse-not-feminist-and-not-empowering-8224704.html>.

Seavey, C., P. Katz, and S. Zalk. 1975. Baby X. *Sex Roles*. 1:2.

Shute, Stephen, and Susan Hurley, eds. 1993. *On Human Rights: The Oxford Amnesty Lectures 1993*. Basic Books.

Spelman, Elizabeth. 1988. *Inessential Woman*. Beacon Press.

Stevens, Angi Becker. 2013. Did *Girls* Romanticize a Rapist? *Ms. Magazine*, blog post (20th March).

Storey, John, ed. 2009. *Cultural Theory and Popular Culture*. Fifth edition. Harlow: Pearson Education.

Taylor, Richard. 1970. *Good and Evil*. New York: Macmillan.

Tolstoy, Leo. 2008. My Confession. In Klemke and Cahn 2008.

Welton, Donn, ed. 1998. *Body and Flesh: A Philosophical Reader*. Wiley-Blackwell.

Whipp, Glenn. 2013. Lena Dunham Analyzes Three Episodes of *Girls*. *Los Angeles Times* (6th June).

Wielenberg, Erik. 2005. *Value and Virtue in a Godless Universe*. Cambridge University Press.

Williams, Alex. 2013. The Long Goodbye. *New York Times* (24th November).

———. 2014. Riding the Wave of *Girls*. *New York Times* (19th March).

Wolf, Susan. 2012. *Meaning in Life and Why It Matters*. Princeton University Press.

Xunzi. 2014. *Xunzi: The Complete Text*. Princeton University Press.

Young, Iris. 1998. Throwing Like a Girl. In Welton 1998.

Zhuangzi. 2006. *Zhuangzi*. Pearson.

Žižek, Slavoj. 2013. *Demanding the Impossible*. Polity.

———. 2014. *The Most Sublime Hysteric: Hegel with Lacan*. Polity.

The Voices of Their Generations. Or at Least...

HAYLEY ADDIS is very definitely a girl, but is not particularly the voice of any generation. Nor would she wish to be, as it sounds like much more work than finishing her PhD in Wales (which is very nearly done, honest), telling local fairy stories, and exploring the philosophy of enchantment through aesthetics and continental philosophy. She does enjoy public speaking though, so perhaps there is hope yet.

TONI ADLEBERG has a master's degree in philosophy from Georgia State University. She writes about philosophy, science, and pop culture on a freelance basis. She's probably not the voice of her generation but who's to say that she isn't *a* voice of *a* generation?

CHELSI BARNARD ARCHIBALD has an MA in English from Weber State University. She writes television recaps for Socialite Life, a prominent celebrity gossip blog. Her nights consist of drinking craft beer, wearing thrift-store plaid, and listening to the most obscure bands on vinyl. Her days are full of hot yoga, organic coffee dates in locally owned book shops, and biking around town while taking nostalgic snapshots with her vintage 35mm camera.

JOEL AVERY lives in Brooklyn and is finishing a Master of Divinity degree at Yale. He writes mainly about radical theology and movies. Like Hannah, he's still figuring out ethics, one mistake at a time.

KIMBERLY BLESSING is professor of philosophy at SUNY Buffalo State. She teaches courses in modern philosophy, existentialism, philosophy of religion, and the meaning of life, and edited *Movies and the Meaning of Life: Philosophers Take on Hollywood* (2005). She enjoys working with young women in the philosophy program who are, thankfully, very unlike the characters on *Girls*. She thinks her co-author, and former student, Sam is going to rock the world of philosophy. You go "girl"!

BOBBY CARLEO is a research assistant at the Chinese University of Hong Kong and experienced translator of Chinese academic philosophy as well as movies and television. Exhausted by the deeply introspective nature of his work, he's thinking about shifting to food writing. Bobby prefers the light floral hints of Confucian sage over the deep, earthly tones of its Daoist counterpart.

RACHEL CROSSLEY is currently studying for a master's degree in philosophy at the University of St Andrews and writing her dissertation on human rights. When she's not worrying about deadlines, she can be found desperately maintaining her caffeine levels, drinking cocktails with her two cats, and making questionable life decisions (yes, even more questionable than the decision to study philosophy).

PAUL D'AMBROSIO received his PhD in philosophy from the National University of Ireland in 2012. He then took a position as a post-doctoral researcher at East China Normal University in Shanghai, mainly to avoid having to get a "real" job. However, he still has to work quite a bit, he teaches philosophy at Merrimack College (in the US) in the summer, and during the school year teaches courses in Chinese philosophy for the Masters programs at both East China Normal University and Fudan University. He has published a dozen articles and book chapters in Confucian and Daoist philosophies, but the one in this volume is the only one he finds interesting (and you should believe this because these bios are written in the third person).

KENN FISHER has a Bachelor of Arts degree in Philosophy and Political Science from the University of Toronto. This has made him qualified to work at a coffee shop, a children's clothing store, or as a babysitter. Somehow, he has gotten work in movie and television production in Toronto. He has previously contributed to *The Wire and Philosophy* (2013) and *Jurassic Park and Philosophy* (2014). The fact that he sees a lot of himself in the *Girls* characters has made him reconsider many life decisions.

DAVID J. FROST, PhD, is an independent scholar who writes on popular culture and philosophy and on the ethical implications of contemporary empirical psychology, such as what the science of how the brain works says about how to live a better life. He believes these topics are universally interesting, but he does not think he is the voice of his generation or any generation. His website is davidjfrost.com. He had his shit figured out by the time he was thirty-five.

RICHARD GREENE is a professor of philosophy at Weber State University. He's also served as Executive Chair of the Intercollegiate Ethics Bowl. He's co-edited a number of books on pop culture and philosophy including *The Sopranos and Philosophy* (2004), *Quentin Tarantino and Philosophy* (2007), *Dexter and Philosophy* (2011)*,* and *Boardwalk Empire and Philosophy* (2013). Richard would like to believe that we are all a little Hannah, a little Jessa, a little Marnie, and a little Shoshanna, but if he's being honest with himself, he's mostly Ray.

ANNA KESZEG is a lecturer in the Department of Communication, Public Relations and Advertising at Babe -Bolyai University, Cluj-Napoca, Romania. When trying to act like Hannah Horvath during her classes, it's always a clash of cultures with her Transylvanian students. She travels a lot to find other *Girls*-fanatics while protecting weirdos and adventurous women in her hometown.

CHRISTOPHER KETCHAM is neither hopeful nor hapless, but a doctor of philosophy: PhD. Nor is it true that he is haunted or hounded. Yet it is a fact that he is both harried and hurried. And he hopes that your Hannah has more ambition than Horvath. Be humble and not hollow his motto be. So he leaves you with that for he's off to hunt down another haunch on which to chew. And his haunts are in Pennsylvania where he hews tales of both the hopeful and the hapless such as the two who have found themselves in blessed Blandland.

DAVID LAROCCA is Visiting Scholar in the Department of English at Cornell University and Lecturer in value theory and film in the Department of Philosophy at the State University of New York College at Cortland. He's the author of *Emerson's English Traits and the Natural History of Metaphor* and editor of *The Philosophy of Charlie Kaufman* and *The Philosophy of War Films*. A former resident of Manhattan, he made brief visits to Brooklyn where he drank fair trade single origin cold brew pour-over coffee served with cream derived from regionally sourced grass-fed cows or imbibed raw micronutrient-rich unfiltered organic cleansing juice made using a nine-ton hydraulic press with non-GMO vegetables grown on local rooftop gardens, while talking with creative writers and critics who have work published or forthcoming in *The New Yorker*, *Cabinet*, or *n+1* and have or will seek an MFA or a Ph.D. but are currently exploring possibilities and just remaining open. At no point during his conversations were drinks consumed ironically.

JAMES EDWIN MAHON is Professor of Philosophy and head of the Department of Philosophy at Washington and Lee University. He has contributed to *Psych and Philosophy* (2013), *The Good Wife and Philosophy* (2013), and *The Devil and Philosophy* (2014). He divides his time between Lexington, Virginia, and Brooklyn, where he eats frozen yoghurt and keeps hoping to run into Lena Dunham.

TRIP MCCROSSIN teaches in the Philosophy Department at Rutgers University, where he works on, among other things, the nature, history, and legacy of the Enlightenment. His chapter in this book is part of a broader effort to view literary and other forms of popular culture through the lens of Susan Neiman's understanding of the same. Sometimes, on the first day of classes, he thinks to himself, "I'm very moved . . . people finding each other . . . taking shelter . . . I'm very moved."

RACHEL ROBISON-GREENE is a PhD candidate in philosophy at UMass Amherst. She is co-editor of *The Golden Compass and Philosophy* (2009), *Dexter and Philosophy* (2011), and *Boardwalk Empire and Philosophy* (2013). She has contributed chapters to *Quentin Tarantino and Philosophy* (2007), *The Legend of Zelda and Philosophy* (2008), *Zombies, Vampires, and Philosophy* (2010), and *The Walking Dead and Philosophy* (2012). Rachel thinks that co-editing *Girls and Philosophy* is the best use of her literary voice and her myriad of talents.

ROBERTO SIRVENT is Associate Professor of Political and Social Ethics at Hope International University. He has published essays on theology, political philosophy, and David Foster Wallace. While Roberto isn't sure whether he has a bigger crush on Marnie or New York, he's pretty sure both would drive him absolutely crazy.

MARIE VAN LOON is completing her Research Masters in Philosophy at the University of Amsterdam. Marie has been exploring with fear and anxiety a great number of topics from existentialism and responsibility to the question of non-existent objects. After a long day of struggling with infinite possibilities, or deeply reflecting on the great questions of life, Marie enjoys following the adventures of her fictional *Girls* friends, Hannah, Jessa, Shoshanna and Marnie.

NICOLE KIMES WALKER is a writer living in Brooklyn. She mostly writes for children, so it was a nice change for her to write about sex, drugs, and Hannah's "groovy lifestyle."

SAMANTHA WEZOWICZ is a graduate of the philosophy program at SUNY Buffalo State, where she earned the 2014 Outstanding Philosophy Student Award. She also completed a minor in Women and Gender Studies, and was one of the founding members of WIP: Women in Philosophy, which is a support group and academic club for women in the philosophy program. Sam is pursuing a PhD in philosophy at Temple University in Philadelphia, where she enjoys courses in Kant, Aesthetics, and Continental Philosophy. She's pretty sure she taught her prof, and co-author, a thing or two about *Girls* and girls.

ANDY WIBLE is an instructor of philosophy at Muskegon Community College in Michigan. He humbly teaches and writes on business ethics, biomedical ethics, the philosophy of sport, and LGBTQ issues, even though his true calling is writing about his own amazing talents, accomplishments, and friends. He enjoyed writing this awesome bio.

ZORIANNA ZURBA is currently completing a PhD in Communication and Culture at the program jointly held between Ryerson and York Universities in Toronto, Canada. Zorianna's dissertation examines cinephilia and love through the prism of Woody Allen's movies. Zorianna longs to live in Brooklyn, and sip lattes at Cafe Grumpy or Ray's. In her spare time Zorianna enjoys quilting and sewing, but would rather borrow clothes from Jessa's closet than make her own.

Index

Mosby, Ted, 45
Mother Teresa, 49
Mouffe, Chantal,
Agonistics (book), 214
Mount Olympus, 41
Mr. Roger's Neighborhood (television series), 59
Murder on the Orient Express (book and movie), 37, 41

Narcissus, 51
Nashville, 202
Natalia, 33, 122, 124, 180, 187
The National Business Ethics Survey, 135
natural law theory, 142
Navy, United States, 35
Nazi Party (National Socialist German Workers' Party), 142
Neiman, Susan, 35
Netflix, 40
New Girl (television series), 215
New Jersey, 34, 191
"New York, New York" (song), 202
New York City, 17, 34, 39, 44–45, 76, 79, 85, 144, 165, 199–200, 206, 211, 213–14
New York Daily News (newspaper), 34
New York Review of Books (magazine), 9
New York Times, 209
Nico, 53, 183
Nietzsche, Friedrich, 54, 56, 109–110, 112, 114
The Genealogy of Morals (book), 111
North America, 182

O'Dowd, Chris, 203
Oberlin College, 54, 62, 135, 200
Oedipus, 37
Ohio University, 136
"On All Fours" (episode), 95, 101, 187, 190
"One Man's Trash" (episode), 144, 157
"Only Child" (episode), 190
Ortega y Gasset, Jose, 87
Oxford English Dictionary, 201
Oz, 41

paideia, 204–05, 207–09, 212, 215, 217
Paris, 149
Park Slope District, 143
Petula, 192
Pew Report, 135
Pew Research Study, 136
"Pilot" (episode), 3, 8, 181, 192
Planet of the Apes (movie), 37, 42
Plato, 200–01, 207
Gorgias, 205
The Republic (dialogue), 205
Platonic dialogues, 203
Playboy (magazine), 178
Ploshansky, Ray, 9, 31, 41, 43, 77, 80, 89–92, 107, 119–120, 124, 126–27, 132, 139, 161, 181, 184, 188, 190–191, 199, 216, 226–27
relationship with Marnie, 45,77, 81, 159
relationship with Shoshanna, 45, 97, 122, 132, 159, 161, 183, 195–96, 226
Portland, 202
Pompeii (movie), 42–43
Pope John Paul II,
Mutual Attraction Differs from Lust (lecture), 121
Poughkeepsie, 192, 197
Pound, Ezra, 148
Pressler-Goings, David, 216
PS 235, Brooklyn, 41
Psycho (movie), 37

racism, 20
Rawls, John,
　The Law of Peoples, 146–151
The Real World (television
　series), 59
Rebecca, 204–207
"The Return," (episode), 158
Rhianna, 192
Richards, Mary, 40
Robinson, Phoebe, 17, 23–24
Rogien, Jen, 169
Romano, Carlin,
　America the Philosophical
　(book), 207–08
Romeo and Juliet (play), 42–43
Rongzi, Song, 223–24
Rousseau, Jean-Jacques,
　169–170
Roth, Philip,
　Sabbath's Theater (book), 216
Russell, Bertrand, 123

Sackler, Adam, 20, 29, 31–33,
　36, 39, 41, 43, 45, 55, 75, 77,
　78, 80, 95, 102–03, 104, 107,
　112, 119, 126–27, 148, 157,
　168, 170–71, 180, 184, 189,
　195–96, 208, 224–26, 228
　actor, 38, 51, 186, 188, 212
　alcoholic, 79, 124
　hero, 27–36
　relationship with Hannah, 19,
　　27–28, 30–34, 42, 44–45, 51,
　　77, 102–03, 114, 118,
　　121–22, 144, 155, 161, 171,
　　180, 186, 219–220, 224
　sexual proclivities, 16, 19, 39,
　　158, 177, 179–180, 183, 187
Sackler, Carolyn, 189
Sahara Desert, 144
San Francisco Giants, 39
Sartre, Jean-Paul, 64–66, 69,
　86–87, 89, 96, 99, 101
　Being and Nothingness (book),
　　87, 90

Existentialism Is a Humanism
　(book), 58, 87
　No Exit (play), 89
Saturday Night Live (television
　series), 203
Scherbatsky, Robin, 45
Schifrin, Tally, 123
Schippers, Brigit,
　*Julia Kristeva and Feminist
　Thought* (book), 183
Schumacher, E.F.,
　Good Work (book), 132–33
Scolari, Peter, 203
Scott, Catherine, 16
　"*Girls* Is Not Diverse, Not
　　Feminist, and Not
　　Empowering," 12–13
Seinfeld (television series), 41,
　166, 168–69
Seinfeld, Jerry (character), 6,
　41, 166–68
Seven Deadly Sins, 117–18
Sex and the City (television
　series), 7–8, 85, 97, 163–65,
　168, 195
Shapiro, Shoshanna (character),
　16, 38–40, 44, 49, 51–52, 54,
　62, 64, 78, 80, 88, 96–97, 99,
　102, 107–111, 113, 119,
　124–27, 164–65, 167,
　169–170, 173–74, 176–77,
　179, 181–83, 190, 192–95,
　197, 213
　relationship with Ray, 45, 97,
　　122, 132, 159, 161, 183,
　　195–196, 226
Shakespeare and Company, 148
Shaw, George Bernard,
　Major Barbara (play), 38, 40
"She Did" (episode), 144, 155
Sheltering Winds, 193–94
"The Shoes," (*Seinfeld* episode),
　168
Showden, Carisa, 36n
Simmel, Georg, 163–64
Simmons, Laurie, 201